"A fitting tribute both to Leland Ryken as a superb teacher and to the importance of the liberal arts in the life of the Christian mind and soul. Few will fail to benefit from its expanded and enriched vision of the life of faith."

Alister McGrath, Professor of Theology, Ministry, and Education, King's College, London

"This fine volume honors a marvelously gifted evangelical scholar-teacher. But it is itself a significant contribution to the cause that Leland Ryken has served so well, offering much wisdom on what it takes to sustain and nurture a life of the mind that will promote the goals of Christ's kingdom."

Richard J. Mouw, President and Professor of Christian Philosophy; Fuller Theological Seminary

"*Liberal Arts for the Christian Life,* written as a collection of reflections on the liberal arts by colleagues of Leland Ryken, certainly captures clearly the range, the richness, and the complexity of the connections between a liberal arts education and the Christian life. Even more compelling is the way the book represents the incarnational nature of a liberal arts education—a single professor embodying a vision of learning that entices thousands of students over several generations to follow in his footsteps, not by becoming more like him but by becoming more fully the unique individuals that God created them to be. This book is a 'must read' for Christian liberal arts educators and their students!"

Shirley A. Mullen, President, Houghton College

"Clement of Alexandria, one of the earliest proponents of Christian liberal arts education, observed that excellence in such educational attainment was widely regarded in the second century as evidence that a person was a Christian. The authors of this volume likewise affirm that liberal learning centered in Christ ought to be the trademark of Christians in any walk of life today. In a fitting tribute to the life work of Leland Ryken, they have created a lively and accessible introduction to the advantages of such an education for a young Christian who wishes to grow in maturity and wisdom."

David Lyle Jeffrey, Distinguished Professor of Literature and the Humanities, Baylor University

"All who love the life of the mind, who care about the education of our youth, or who are devoted to the intellectual and spiritual vibrancy of our churches will relish this diverse collection of essays by premier Christian scholars and academic leaders. *Liberal Arts for the Christian Life* is both a fitting tribute to an extraordinary Christian college professor and a most welcome collection of thoughtful excursions into the enduring purposes of the liberal arts in the Christian college curriculum."

Darryl Tippens, Provost, Pepperdine University

D0176565

"This volume provides a rich collection of wisdom concerning Christian liberal arts education. Students will find in it valuable guidelines for reflecting on how to get the most out of their education. It is an apt tribute to a scholar who has dedicated his career to imparting such wisdom, and this book should be provided to help carry on such work into the future."

> **George M. Marsden,** Francis A. McAnaney Professor of History Emeritus, University of Notre Dame; author, *The Outrageous Idea of Christian Scholarship*

"The beneficial impact of Leland Ryken's contributions to God's kingdom extends far beyond the campus of Wheaton College. The scholarly work of faculty from across Christian higher education has been influenced in professional development workshops led by Dr. Ryken including 'The Bible as Literature,' 'The Bible in Literature,' and other topics related to his own research and writing. With dignity, warmth, and great dedication, Dr. Ryken has invested himself in the intellectual and spiritual development of others. This *festschrift* represents a collective and heartfelt 'thank you' from the authors and on behalf of so many others!"

> **Karen A. Longman,** Professor and Program Director, Department of Doctoral Higher Education, Azuza Pacific University

"This celebration of the liberal arts through the eyes of Christian faith pays a fitting tribute to Dr. Leland Ryken's many contributions to this great conversation. May students and future colleagues reap the blessings of the seeds sown in this text for many more generations."

> **Michael Le Roy,** President-elect, Calvin College

"Higher education is undergoing an awakening, and in *Liberal Arts for the Christian Life* we have a clarion call to the liberal arts through dedicated Christian learning. Leland Ryken—a teacher of English and a scholar of Milton—has spent his life asking students to think about the purpose of education, careers, and lives; in this volume he is celebrated by his colleagues who, in turn, are asking these questions of their own students. Whether Christian or not, educators will want to read this book, asking students to read in it, too—that is, if they want them to consider what the liberal arts are for."

> **J. Scott Lee,** Executive Director, Association for Core Texts and Courses, Liberal Arts Institute at Saint Mary's College of California

LIBERAL ARTS FOR THE CHRISTIAN LIFE

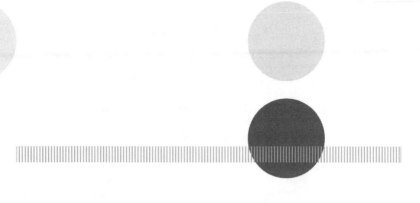

LIBERAL ARTS

FOR THE

CHRISTIAN LIFE

EDITED BY JEFFRY C. DAVIS
AND PHILIP G. RYKEN

::: CROSSWAY

WHEATON, ILLINOIS

To Leland Ryken
Professor of English Literature
Champion of the Liberal Arts

*The end then of learning is to repair the ruins of our
first parents by regaining to know God aright,
and out of that knowledge to love him,
to imitate him, to be like him.*

—John Milton, *Of Education*

CONTENTS

PREFACE

Like a lot of students graduating from high school, he wasn't entirely sure what he wanted to do with his life. He had done very well in his studies, graduating at the top of his class. Active in sports and other extracurricular activities, he enjoyed spending time with his friends. And he was actively involved in worship and fellowship at his local church, even if sometimes he chafed under its legalism. Possibly he would become a high school teacher, but he felt unsure about what God was calling him to do.

One thing was certain: he didn't want to do what his father did and work the family farm in Central Iowa. Not that he minded hard work, but somehow he knew that the struggles of living off the land were not for him. Maybe he should go to college, he thought, but times were tight; frankly, he wasn't sure how he would pay for his education.

Family members remember differently what happened next. His older sister was away from home at the time, but she heard that he went to the local factory to apply for a job. His mother wasn't too keen on the factory idea, however, because manual labor was the reason her parents had forced her to drop out of school after the eighth grade, so that she could help out at home. As far as she was concerned, her son was too gifted to miss out on the kind of education she had always dreamed of getting. So she let her son apply at the factory on one condition: he had to ask if they offered any college scholarships.

It didn't take long for the foreman at the factory to realize that the teenager who had come in to apply for a job really belonged in college. Soon it was all arranged: the young man would attend the local Christian liberal arts college in the fall, partly on a scholarship the factory sponsored for a local student, and partly from money he earned by leasing and then farming land owned by a mining company.

What happened to him at college was life changing. His high school English teacher had challenged him to read *Paradise Lost* the summer before his freshman year, but he found Milton's epic poem difficult to comprehend. Yet by the time he had completed four years of liberal arts education, he was launched on a trajectory that would lead him to become a Milton scholar. Through his readings in theology, he came to a settled conviction that the Bible is the very Word of God and that the gospel of Jesus Christ is absolutely true. He found a growing passion for reading literature. More broadly, he developed a love for the life of the mind—for thinking about everything from a Christian point of view. And when he was asked to cover high school classes for his old English teacher, his calling as a teacher became strongly confirmed.

The man I have been describing—Leland Ryken—is nearing the end of a long and distinguished career as a professor of English literature. He grew up in and around Pella, Iowa, and attended Central College on a scholarship from the Rolscreen Factory, which produces Pella Windows and Doors. After studying with the noted Milton scholar Kester Svendsen at the University of Oregon, and earning his doctorate there, Ryken was offered a position on the faculty of Wheaton College, where he has taught since 1968.

This book has been written by some of Professor Ryken's many colleagues from Wheaton College as a way of honoring his service as a teacher, scholar, mentor, and friend. Published to coincide with his seventieth birthday in May of 2012, it focuses on a subject close to his heart: Christian liberal arts education.

As editors, Jeffry Davis and I are deeply grateful to many people: to the scholars who contributed their essays to this volume; to Marilee Melvin for her labors in assembling the manuscript; to Kailey Cole and Drew Melby for their research, corrections, and insights as perceptive student readers; to the editorial staff at Crossway for seeing this project through from beginning to end; and to Ruth Davis and Lisa Ryken—our spouses—remarkable women who use their background in the liberal arts to serve the body of Christ, to love their friends and neighbors, and to make a home for their families.

In academia it is customary to honor an eminent professor with a *festschrift*—a volume of scholarly essays written by learned colleagues. What makes this book different, however, is that it is primarily for college undergraduates. Rather than writing for other academics, the authors have chosen to honor Professor Ryken by producing a book especially for students. This is fitting because Dr. Ryken has served students for more than forty years through his brilliant teaching, faithful mentoring, and voluminous publishing.

We begin with an address entitled "The Student's Calling," which Professor Ryken first delivered at a chapel service in the fall of 1984. I was there when he delivered the address and remember the occasion well—not only because it was the second day of my freshman year and the speaker was my father, but also because it helped me understand why God had called me to be a liberal arts student.

"The Student's Calling" has been reprinted often, and thousands of incoming freshmen have read it as part of their preparation for college. Its defining principles are valuable for anyone studying the liberal arts and sciences in Christian community and desiring to love God with mind, heart, soul, and strength.

The essays that follow expand on "The Student's Calling" by exploring its themes and showing their implications for the Christian life. Whether you are getting ready for college or studying on a Christian or secular campus, we hope this book will inspire you to make the most of your college education and to dedicate your mind to the service of Jesus Christ.

—Philip G. Ryken
President
Wheaton College

THE STUDENT'S CALLING

Leland Ryken

"Education is not a preparation for life—it *is* life." So claims a headline in one college's promotional brochure.

College was once a time of preparation in which young adults could search for truth, broaden their intellectual and cultural horizons in multiple directions, and decide what vocation best suited their talents. Today many of you are pressured to regulate your college years around the job you think you have the best chance of landing upon graduation. In the process, you may be tempted to turn your back on the very subjects that interest you most, which may be the areas where your greatest potential contributions to church and to society lie.

Today's college students are caught in an identity crisis. Your instincts as learners pull you in one direction, while voices of activism and preoccupation with landing a job pull you in other directions. It was once an axiom that education was a preparation for something in the future. Today young people are made to feel guilty about being in a preparation phase.

The time has come to revive an idea that once seemed natural: the student's life as a Christian calling. By *calling* I mean vocation—the occupation of being a student. It is an idea that you students and your parents need to hear.

When we begin to describe the ingredients of the student's life as a calling, we quickly start to formulate a theory of education as well. Some methods of education measure up to the description of that calling, while others do not. This should not surprise us, for, as T. S. Eliot once noted, "we must derive our theory of education from our philosophy of life. The problem turns out to be a religious problem."[1]

---

[1] T. S. Eliot, "Modern Education and the Classics," in *Essays Ancient and Modern* (New York: Harcourt, Brace, 1946), 169.

WHAT IS EDUCATION FOR?

In one important way, a Christian student's calling is the same as it is for a Christian in *any* situation of life. Its central focus is the individual's relationship to God. Loving and serving God should be the foundation for everything else that you do at college. It is a requirement, not an elective.

When the Puritans founded Harvard College just six years after arriving in Massachusetts, one of the rules at the new college was this: "Let every student be plainly instructed, and earnestly pressed to consider well, [that] the main end of his life and studies is, to know God and Jesus Christ . . . and therefore to lay Christ in the bottom, as the only foundation of all sound knowledge and learning."[2] When Thomas Shepard's son entered the college, Shephard wrote to his son, "Remember the end of your life, which is coming back again to God, and fellowship with him."[3]

And in the noblest of all educational treatises, John Milton's *Of Education*, Milton gave this definition of Christian education: "The end then of learning is to repair the ruins of our first parents by regaining to know God aright, and out of that knowledge to love him, to imitate him, to be like him."[4] Contrary to trends in our own century, Milton here defines education in terms of its end or goal. There may be many ways to achieve a Christian education, but in the meantime we must not lose sight of what it is *for*. What it is for is to produce Christian growth.

Albert Einstein once remarked that we live in a day of perfect means and confused goals. When we obscure the goals of education, we trivialize it. It is no wonder that students today so easily reduce education to completing the required number of courses and obtaining a degree (but often not an education). Too often our vision is limited—in that most irritating of all student clichés—to getting a requirement "out of the way."

Our whole milieu has conditioned you to conceive of your education in measurable quantities, with grades and jobs upon graduation topping

---

[2]*New England's First Fruits* (New York: Joseph Sabin, 1865), 26.
[3]Shepard to his son, 1672, in *Transactions: 1892/94*, The Colonial Society of Massachusetts, vol. 14 (Boston: Cambridge University Press, 1913), 192.
[4]John Milton, "Of Education," in *Complete Poems and Major Prose*, ed. Merritt Y. Hughes (Indianapolis: Hackett, 2003), 631.

the list. But to conceive of the student's calling in Christian terms—to view it (as Milton did) as a process of redemption and sanctification—is to substitute an entirely different agenda of concerns. Here the crucial question is not how many requirements you meet or even how much you know, but rather what kind of person you are in the "process of becoming" during your college years.

The nurture of your soul is finally a more important part of your calling than obtaining marketable skills. I said at the outset that my description of the Christian student's calling would be at the same time a theory of education. Education governed by a goal of Christian maturity certainly implies Christian education, however it might be achieved.

You who are new to college may think that in a Christian atmosphere the spiritual aspect of your calling will automatically take care of itself. This is not true. It has sadly become a regular part of my life to hear about former students who two, five, or ten years after graduation have repudiated the Christian faith. The casualties include people who, as they sat in my office or accompanied me to England or greeted me at church, were the last people in the world I would have expected to drift away from the faith.

So consider the matter well: there is ultimately *one* indispensable thing during your education. Be diligent "in season and out of season" to make your calling as a Christian believer sure. Do not close the chapter on this formative era of your life having neglected your spiritual health.

ALL OF LIFE IS GOD'S

A second cornerstone of the Christian student's calling is the premise that all of life is God's. There is no division of life into sacred and secular. For a Christian, *all* of life is sacred.

What goes on in chapel is not more glorifying to God than what goes on in the classroom. What goes on in the classroom is not more important to God than what goes on in the dorm room or the dining hall. We have no basis for viewing some academic courses as sacred and others as secular. Nor are some academic majors holier than others. God calls Christians to make his will prevail in every area of life.

As a variation on that theme, we should be convinced that all truth is God's truth. In the New Testament, Paul several times quotes with approval from pagan Greek poets whom he apparently knew by heart. In his commentary on one of these passages, John Calvin wrote, "For since all truth is of God, if any ungodly man has said anything true, we should not reject it, for it also has come from God."[5] Thomas Shepard wrote to his son at college, "Remember that not only heavenly and spiritual and supernatural knowledge descends from God, but also all natural and human learning and abilities; and therefore pray much, not only for the one but also for the other."[6]

The integration of every academic discipline with the Christian faith is an essential part of the Christian student's calling. It is the distinguishing feature of Christian education. A college is not Christian simply by virtue of having chapel services. By the same token, a weekly meeting with a Christian student group on a university campus is not the same as an education in which the very curriculum is structured to help us view human knowledge from a Christian perspective.

LIBERAL ARTS EDUCATION

It is an easy step—I would say an inevitable step—from the idea that all of life is God's to the idea of a liberal arts education. What is a liberal arts education? I recall sitting as a freshman in a history course where that question was directed to one of the "lesser lights" in the class. His reply was, "Isn't that where you know a little about everything but not much about anything?" The definition was seriously intended, but it nearly sent the professor laughing hysterically out of the room.

Liberal arts education is comprehensive education. Martin Luther wrote to the councilmen at Germany, "If I had children and could manage it, I would have them study not only languages and history, but also singing and music together with the whole of mathematics. . . . The ancient Greeks trained their children in these disciplines. . . . They grew up to be people of wondrous ability, subsequently fit for everything."[7]

"Fit for everything": that has always been the goal of liberal arts

---

[5]John Calvin, *Calvin's New Testament Commentaries: 2 Corinthians and Timothy, Titus and Philemon*, ed. David W. Torrance and Thomas F. Torrance, trans. T. A. Smail, vol. 10 (Grand Rapids, MI: Eerdmans, 1996), 364.

[6]Shepard, *Transactions*, 196–97.

[7]Martin Luther, "To the Councilmen of All Cities in Germany That They Establish and Maintain Christian Schools," in *Selected Writings of Martin Luther*, ed. Theodore G. Tappert (Philadelphia: Fortress Press, 1967), 61–62.

education, as distinct from vocational training in a specific field. Milton's definition is even more famous. He defined "a complete and generous education" as one that "fits a man to perform . . . all the offices, both private and public, of peace and war."[8] The heart of Milton's definition is that a complete education frees a person to perform "all the offices" of life. A liberal education prepares people to do well in all that they might be called to do in life.

May I add that such an education is possible only as you realize that all education is ultimately *self*-education. Education is learning, and someone else cannot learn for you. The most perfect educational climate in the world will not make you an educated person. Moreover, an adequate education does not stop after one's college years. To be generously educated is to have acquired the lifelong habit of self-education.

What are the "private and public" roles that Milton had in view when he defined liberal education? Education in our day is obsessed with a single public role, getting a job, which is increasingly defined in terms of one's income. But the public roles that a person fills cover much more than that. They include being a good church member, a good board member or committee member, and a positive contributor to the community. One of the criteria that I apply to people's education is whether they can teach a good Sunday school lesson.

And what are the private roles of life for which an education should prepare you? They include being a good friend or colleague, and a good spouse or parent. And they include the most private world of all—the inner world of the mind and imagination. One of the best tests of whether people are liberally educated is what they do with their free time.

LET'S BE PRACTICAL

The liberal arts education I have described is not necessarily more Christian than other types of education, but it is more practical. More practical? Surely we all know that liberal arts education is impractical in today's specialized world. But do we? In a rapidly changing world, how can anyone know what he or she will be doing five or ten or twenty years from now?

---

[8]Milton, "Of Education," 632.

Several years ago I spoke at a conference at which I had dinner with a couple who had graduated several years earlier. During their college years, she had gone on a summer missions program, and he had been a research intern overseas. Both had come back from those experiences painfully aware of the human needs that exist right now. However, their ministry activism was followed by a time of intellectual lethargy in which they regarded their academic courses as misspent time.

Two years later both could speak with regret about the wasted time that their attitude had produced in the long run. She was a resident director in a dorm on a university campus, holding weekly meetings with Christian students who were trying to relate their studies to their Christian faith. The liberal arts courses that she had once regarded as impractical were now exactly what she most needed. Her fiancé was trying to make up for what he had neglected in college by taking a year of science courses at a university near home, trying to raise his MCAT scores so he could get into medical school.

Let me encourage you to believe that your liberal arts education is a foundation that is worthy of your best effort. There is much to commend the wisdom and practicality of T. S. Eliot's theory that "no one can become really educated without having pursued some study in which he took no interest—for it is a part of education to *learn to interest ourselves* in subjects for which we have no aptitude."[9]

THE LEGITIMACY OF PREPARATION

I urge you to view your time of preparation as a calling in its own right. We live at a time when education is regarded in such a utilitarian way that its legitimacy finally depends on its being a ticket to a job. In recent years I have seen pathetic examples of parents putting so much pressure on students to know exactly what job they expect to enter upon graduation that the students could not possibly avoid feeling guilty about taking time for an education.

Parents and advisors to young people need to stop making students feel guilty about being in a period of preparation. When God calls people

---

[9]T. S. Eliot, "Modern Education and the Classics," 178.

to a task, he also calls them to a time of preparation. This preparation time, moreover, is as important as the performance of the task.

What should we say about the hours it takes to prepare for a sermon or Sunday school class or lecture or term paper or ball game or recital? Is this time and effort somehow ignoble? Does God turn his head the other way when a person prepares? Jesus did not begin his earthly ministry until the age of thirty, living until that time as an obscure carpenter in an out-of-the-way village. We might protest: Think of all the people he could have preached to and healed between the ages of twenty and thirty.

Moses spent forty years of his life being educated in the court of Pharaoh, receiving the best education his day afforded. Then he spent forty years in Midian, from a human point of view rotting away in exile, but actually being prepared for wilderness survival, the skill he needed to lead the Israelites from Egypt to the Promised Land. According to Galatians 1:17, Paul, upon his conversion, did not at once become an evangelist. Instead, he spent three years in Arabia and Damascus being instructed in the gospel.

Learning, in whatever form, *is* the student's calling. It is the arena within which you display good stewardship or lack of it. Several years ago I entered my office to find the following letter that had been slipped under my door:

> I do not know where to begin, except I am preparing for the next test. I tried reading late into three successive evenings and found myself moving in and out of consciousness. I fell behind early after the first exam. This year I am heavily involved in the community. I am trying to wean myself from college life (not studying). College is just a transition period (a period of preparation). This term I have four reading courses, 20–30 hours in a ministry, a job, and meetings almost every night, and two speaking engagements a week.

What was this person's problem? An inadequate view of the student's calling. And where did he get it? From his pastor, his family, some of his fellow students, and a general atmosphere that denigrates the idea of intellectual preparation for one's eventual vocation in life.

During your college years, being a student is your vocation. That occupation involves more than studying, but studying is by definition its major ingredient. Why not look up the word *student* in the dictionary?

YOUR FUTURE AT COLLEGE

A number of recent surveys have shown that the majority of today's college students are primarily concerned with getting out of school and finding a lucrative job. Students will do almost anything for a good grade, but zeal for learning is currently at a low ebb. The quality of your education is *your* choice to make.

In a sermon entitled "Learning in War-Time," C. S. Lewis compared the Christian student's calling to the soldier's life. The Christian church, he said, cannot survive without Christian students taking time for an education. "To be ignorant and simple," Lewis said, "would be to throw down our weapons, and to betray our uneducated brethren who have, under God, no defense but us against the intellectual attacks of the heathen. Good philosophy must exist, if for no other reason, because bad philosophy needs to be answered."[10]

John Calvin said that God's calling is the sense of duty that God gives us to enable us to reject what is superfluous. In Calvin's terms, a calling is a sentry that spares us from distractions to our main task.[11] There is much that would divert you from getting a high-quality education, but your *calling* as a Christian student is something that you can protect.

Your college years are uniquely wonderful. Few other experiences in life will have the same once-only quality of your college education or provide you the same luxury of opportunity to expand your intellectual and spiritual awareness. So, I prayerfully urge you to make the most of your valuable time at college.

---

[10]C. S. Lewis, "Learning in War-Time," in *The Weight of Glory and Other Addresses* (New York: HarperCollins, 2001), 58.
[11]John Calvin, *Institutes of the Christian Religion*, ed. John T. McNeill, trans. Ford Lewis Battles (Philadelphia: Westminster Press, 1960), 3.10.6.

INTRODUCTION

"If you don't know where you are going, you will wind up somewhere else." So remarked the great American baseball player and amateur philosopher Yogi Berra, famous for his sage quips. It may seem like an oddly stated proverb, but his point has profundity: without a purposeful destination in mind, you may arrive at a place in life that you never wished to be. To put it another way, the path you follow leads to a particular location, whether you know it or not.

This truth holds special significance with regard to education. Paradoxically, without an end to education—what the ancient liberal arts teachers called a *telos*, which motivates your passions and directs your disciplined behavior—true learning cannot really even begin. Without the intentional investment of your will, along with the imaginative consideration of where education might lead you, and the reasonable expectation of how it might change you, the forces of the dominant culture—subtle but powerful—will surely take you where you may not intend to go, influencing your thoughts and actions. Your view of what a college education is for, and where it should lead, will shape how you think, learn, and act—both in and out of the classroom—over the four years of your undergraduate experience.

Tragically, far too many graduates from high school enter college without much thought about the ultimate goal of their education. Three approaches to college seem all too common. Some apply to college simply because their friends are going and "it's the next thing to do" on the checklist of life. Yet they may have never really asked themselves why it matters—or if it does matter. Likewise, others feel the strong influence of parents to "study something marketable," getting a degree in a field that is practical in order to land a secure job. Yet they may never have really wondered what sort of education is best for all of life, apart from the forty-hour work week, and what kind of learning best prepares you for an ever-changing world. Even worse, many perceive college as a playground, "a time to party and have fun" that involves participation in all sorts of new experiences, many of which have little, if anything, to do with learning or living well. Yet despite all the tuition paid, the classes unattended, and the learning opportunities lost, they may never have truly considered the personal cost of such a wanton lifestyle, which passes for "an education." In the final analysis, all three of these approaches prove to be deficient.

Sad though it may be, too many students enroll in college without even engaging their minds in connection to what really matters: they go through the motions without the meaning; they strive to pursue a dream that they themselves have not actually dreamed; they pursue destructive pleasures while ignoring purposeful passions. To put it bluntly, "they are clueless in academe," though it is not entirely their fault.[1] Far too many teachers fail to offer a compelling vision for learning that captures students' imagination, one that elevates their human spirit. In the absence of such a vision for education, too many college students do what they do not by design but by default. And since they often do not know where they are going, in the words of Yogi Berra, they end up "somewhere else."

Presenting a meaningful alternative, this guidebook offers some fresh perspectives for a new direction—liberal arts learning from a biblical perspective. Especially intended for *disciples* (followers of a teacher and a school of thought) who believe that Jesus Christ has called them to Christian liberal arts study, such readers will be challenged with reasons for learning that are bigger and more consequential than the status quo or job security or fun and games. Because "liberal arts" learning is distinct from the pursuit of a specialized degree at a state university, or career training at a pre-professional school, or even preparation for the ministry at a Bible college, it requires a thoughtful orientation. This guidebook will provide just that—a clear starting point and route toward a meaningful way of learning, one that has been traveled by thinking Christians for centuries.

The working premise of this collection of essays, all written by Christ followers who believe in the importance of purposeful living, is that you cannot truly experience a liberal arts education without a

---

[1]Gerald Graff, *Clueless in Academe: How Schooling Obscures the Life of the Mind* (New Haven: Yale University Press, 2003).

concerted effort to do learning differently. In its purest form, Christian liberal arts education requires the learner to affirm certain basic pursuits: growth, depth, and compassion. The development of the whole person for all of life, not just for a job; the deepening of faith in God through intellectual testing, not merely attaining answers; and the commitment to using knowledge and skill to build the church and serve the world, not simply to satisfy the self: these represent some of the core distinctives of Christian liberal arts learning.

The following chapters may best be appreciated as a thoughtful conversation among faithful advocates of the liberal arts way of teaching and learning. Approaching the topic not from a single, monochromatic point of view but from a dynamic, polychromatic variety of perspectives, this book is intended to provoke good conversation as well. In fact, according to Robert M. Hutchins, a great conversation best describes liberal arts learning.[2] The following chapters reflect the multiple voices, varied disciplines, and theological diversity of the contributors. United in the importance of liberal education and the centrality of Christ, the authors of these chapters represent the splendid array of thinking Christian scholars. Likewise, this book is not offered as the final word on Christian liberal arts; rather, it is presented as an extension of the many strong scholarly views that have already come before. Ideally, reading and discussing this book should foster a form of liberal learning itself.

Although there is a sequential order to this book—moving from historical conceptions of liberal arts, to theological considerations, to practical habits, to divisional areas of study, and finally to ultimate ends—there is no single way to use the book. Readers can follow the natural organization that builds section by section or dip into select chapters based on topical interest. As a resource, this book works both ways. Our aim, regardless of your approach, is for you to come away from this collection of essays with a new enthusiasm (from the Greek *en theos*—to be inspired within by God) for doing college differently. Our goal is your transformation into the fullness of the person that Christ intends you to be.

To that end, we offer you our sincere blessings.

---

[2]Robert M. Hutchins, *The Great Conversation: The Substance of a Liberal Arts Education* (Chicago: Encyclopedia Britannica, 1952).

TERMINOLOGY AND BACKGROUND

The nineteenth-century educator and Oxford theologian John Henry Newman, describing the duty of the serious Christian liberal arts student, penned the following words in his famous book *The Idea of a University*: "If he would do honour to the highest of subjects, he must make himself its scholar, must humbly follow the thoughts given him, and must aim at the glory, not of his own gift, but of the Great Giver."[1] Newman argued that because God created the universe and all things that we study, therefore we should understand all subjects from a distinctly theological perspective. To ignore biblical truth, from Newman's perspective, is to reduce education to mere job preparation, and the student becomes nothing more than a small cog in a huge economic wheel. "Education," he explained, "is a higher word; it implies an action upon our mental nature, and the formation of a character."[2]

Newman believed in liberal arts learning from an informed biblical perspective, and, as we shall see, throughout the history of the church many great Christian thinkers and leaders pursued a liberal arts education with a theological grounding. But what does the term *Christian liberal arts* mean, and how should students think about it as a distinct approach to higher learning?

First, consider the word *Christian*. As a noun it refers to someone who takes seriously the teachings of Jesus Christ and follows them, as found in the Gospels; and as an adjective, it means an approach that demonstrates consistency with Christian teachings, often promoting a biblical worldview. Keep in mind that there are many Christian perspectives and ways of thinking about biblical truth, from Roman Catholic to Protestant (with its varied denominational views), especially in relation to learning. Christian education takes the basic tenets of the historic, orthodox church seriously.

Second, consider the word *liberal*. In a similar manner, this word

---

[1] John Henry Newman, *The Idea of a University* (New Haven: Yale University Press, 1996), 64–65.
[2] Ibid., 85.

can be understood in two ways. As a noun it refers to someone who is politically or theologically progressive; such a one may be a member of "the liberal party." Because this contemporary definition predominates our thinking, it gives many people the wrong idea when it is used for other purposes. However, etymologically speaking, the word possesses a noble significance. A better way to think about this word, *liberal*, particularly in relation to education, is as an adjective meaning "suitable for a free person." Implicit in the term *liberal arts* is the goal of making students more free. What kind of freedom? Well, first and foremost, spiritual freedom. Christian teachers take seriously the claims of the Gospels and the other books of the New Testament as the fulfillment to the law of the Old Testament. "If the Son sets you free, you will be free indeed" (John 8:36). Christian liberal learning builds upon biblical views of bondage (sin) and salvation (freedom), and promotes ways of thinking and living that enable students to realize God's purpose for their lives, and, in response, to offer their lives freely back to God in his service.

Third, think about the word *arts*. Like the word *liberal*, many people have a limited conception of the term, defining it almost exclusively in a contemporary manner, such as "the visual or musical or dramatic arts." This narrow understanding proves to be insufficient for liberal arts students. As the ancient Greeks and Romans understood them, the arts represented subjects of study, what we now call "disciplines," that directed human capacities according to particular procedures of thinking and behaving toward beneficial ends. For example, by becoming learned in the use of grammar, logic, and rhetoric (the *trivium*), students could avoid being manipulated by the crafty speeches of unsavory leaders. Such disciplines of study gave students options that they did not have prior to the development of their knowledge or skill acquisition. In this historic sense, an "art" is a way of knowing or doing something that leads to a whole set of options previously unavailable. Today, whether through the study of physics or philosophy, music or mathematics, students can become enlightened by new ways of knowing and thinking that open up options on the path of life. Such options should increase our sense of gratitude to God and our awareness of the need for giving back: "Much will be required from everyone to whom much has been given" (Luke 12:48 ISV).

As believers in gospel freedom, early Christian educators took the ancient liberal arts instructional methods of the Greeks and Romans and used them for kingdom purposes—to develop God-given gifts for service to Christ and neighbor. Thus, the Christian liberal arts college or university continues in the tradition of faithful learning that emphasizes study as a form of worship, affirming the Creator as the source of all things that are possibly known and recognizing his immanence in all that we examine, all that we know, and all that we do.

Christian liberal arts learning, rightly understood and done, sees God at the center of everything. The educational term offers a bold enterprise for Christian teachers and students, one that affirms the importance of being created in the image of God but also finds freedom in our need of God's grace and guidance. By appreciating the rich heritage of the liberal arts tradition, before and after its adoption by the church, students can come to recognize their place in the history of ideas and the legacy of learning that many have contributed to over the centuries. Christian liberal arts learning depends upon the past but is not constrained by it. Advocates of Christian liberal arts wisely find insight from the past, but they must also innovate to make the disciplines of freedom relevant for today.

CHAPTER ONE

THE COUNTERCULTURAL QUEST OF CHRISTIAN LIBERAL ARTS

Jeffry C. Davis

I shall be telling this with a sigh
Somewhere ages and ages hence:
Two roads diverged in a wood,
and I—I took the one less traveled by,
And that has made all the difference.
—ROBERT FROST, "THE ROAD NOT TAKEN"

Trust in the LORD with all your heart,
    and do not lean on your own understanding.
In all your ways acknowledge him,
    and he will make straight your paths.
Be not wise in your own eyes;
    fear the LORD, and turn away from evil.
It will be healing to your flesh
    and refreshment to your bones.
—PROVERBS 3:5–8

Choosing a college or university represents a momentous fork in the road of life. Every fall, hundreds of thousands of students pack up their belongings and leave home, heading off on a journey to learn something that they hope will enable them to live better. They say goodbye to familiar faces—their parents, their siblings, their friends, and their pets—often amid long hugs and many tears, expressing a mix of sadness and excitement.

    This rite of passage—the pursuit of an undergraduate degree—may perhaps best be understood as an archetypal event, a quest for something worthwhile, requiring deliberate choices and actions. Although many go

31

on this quest, no two travelers experience the same journey. Each passage proves to be unique, with powerful influences and effects that will last a lifetime.

Of the myriads who attend a college or a university, some intentionally pursue an unusual undergraduate experience, one in which they learn how to integrate an understanding of the Bible with all other texts, a belief in divine revelation with scholarly investigation, and a knowledge of orthodox theology with other disciplines of study. These students seek the wisdom of liberal arts for the Christian life.

A DIFFERENT KIND OF EDUCATIONAL VISION

Of all the options available in higher education, the road to a liberal arts institution epitomizes the one "less traveled." Of the more than four thousand colleges and universities in the United States, secular and religious, the vast majority provide a pre-professional or specialized sort of education, reflecting the pervasive values and goals of the dominant culture.[1] Clearly, a liberal arts diploma lacks the popularity of other more specialized degrees deemed by many to be trendy, lucrative, and respectable. Students who want that sort of a sheepskin may be disappointed at a liberal arts school.[2] However, at a Christian liberal arts college or university, the goal remains even more distinctive: gospel-infused instruction, by professors who genuinely *profess* Christ as central to a proper understanding of their subjects, and the formation of your whole being for the complete journey of life, which signifies their greatest concern.

Students in my courses often find the Christian liberal arts perspective surprising, if not perplexing, when I present it to them. Most American college students, including Christians, choose a college or university, and eventually a major, with the intent of establishing a career—a ticket to the good life. This approach reflects the predominant "commonsense" view of college, namely, that an education gives you earning power. And why shouldn't students think this way? Politicians talk about the benefits of advanced schooling almost strictly in terms of

---

[1]EducationUSA, June 5, 2011 (http://www.educationusa.info/pages/students/search.php). See also David W. Breneman, *Liberal Arts Colleges: Thriving, Surviving or Endangered?* (Washington, DC: Brookings Institution, 1994).
[2]*Sheepskin* is a slang term for an academic diploma, originally made of the tanned leather from sheep.

creating job opportunities and making a more skilled workforce. Parents often express the importance of choosing a practical major, one that readily answers the question, "So what are you going to do with *that* when you graduate?" At times, even secondary teachers pressure students to perform well in order to move up the ladder of success, using the fear of bad grades as an extrinsic motivator. Pragmatic attitudes about learning abound, especially in the land of the American Dream, where many feel that they must attend school in order to become successful.

In effect, for most students, a college education has become an expensive set of instructions on how to move to a higher socio-economic plane, a form of self-reliance that supposedly guarantees a comfortable, carefree life. Ironically, this "normal" view of college comes at a price, especially for Christians. Pursuing the perfect life can become idolatrous when we try to control the outcome. "Our eyes are not on God. At heart we are practicing Pelagians,"[3] warns Brennan Manning. "We believe that we can pull ourselves up by our bootstraps."[4] Yet, Christ offers a very different orientation for the disciple who genuinely desires college to be a liberating season of life—radical dependence. In Matthew 6, and in other places throughout the Gospels, he bids his followers to faithfully look upward and then step forward: give what you have freely and discreetly to the poor, ask God for daily bread and forgiveness of debts, resist the temptation to lay up treasures on earth, and be anxious for nothing you truly need. Jesus places his disciples right at the crossroads, forcing a deliberate choice between two contrasting destinations, one toward God and the other toward Mammon. These roads cannot be traveled simultaneously. Christ becomes emphatic about this concern: "You cannot serve God and money" (Matt. 6:24).

In *Paradise Lost*, the great Christian poet John Milton portrays Mammon as the demon god of earthly treasure, who weighs people down by making them want more material things, and who spreads a particularly perverse way of thinking contrary to God's way: "Rather seek Our own good from ourselves."[5] The demon whispers fear into

---

[3]Pelagius, a fifth-century teacher, pushed a heretical view of living that minimized the effects of Adam's fall on humanity, thus diminishing belief in the pervading nature of sin and the need for Christ's costly grace in all aspects of life.

[4]Brennan Manning, *The Ragamuffin Gospel* (Sisters, OR: Multnomah, 2000), 19.

[5]John Milton, *Paradise Lost* (New York: Norton, 1993), 39.

the ears of Christian students: "You have to make your own way in the world, on your own terms, or you will never survive." When it comes to choices regarding college and life, far too many Christians heed Mammon's false eloquence rather than obey Christ's life-giving command: "But seek first the kingdom of God and his righteousness, and all these things will be added to you" (Matt. 6:33). Christ wants us to travel by faith. "Get rid of the boots," he urges. "Slip on some sandals, and follow me." Rightly understood, the pursuit of Christ is the supreme liberal art—the fundamental discipline that sets us free.

The ancient Hebrews urge us toward unique wisdom (*hokmah*) when it comes to traveling by God's directing power. As T. A. Perry notes, "one has to have a *derek*, meaning both a way with things and also a proper path or road to follow. There is nothing more dear to the wisdom tradition than this notion, heavily weighted in the direction of right and wrong."[6] The Hebrews carried low-tech oil lamps close to their bodies, casting just enough light to illuminate the path ahead for the next few steps—nothing more. They could readily say with the psalmist, "Your word is a lamp to my feet and a light to my path" (Ps. 119:105). Obviously, they did not possess the technology of flashlights with alkaline batteries and Kryptonite bulbs, able to produce a powerful bright-white beam a hundred feet ahead. In contrast to the ancient Hebrews, we twenty-first-century Americans like our trip gadgets—Mapquest, GPS, and Google Earth—so that we can scan every square inch before we take a single step, anticipating every bump in the road ahead. We don't want any surprises.

Needless to say, when we hear the phrase "God has a wonderful plan for your life," something gets lost in translation. We think it is our job to figure out "the plan" and then manage things thereafter. But we overlook the best part of the phrase: *wonder*. Reveling in the wonder of the created universe, we should realize, with wise King David, that we cannot know everything, especially the mind of God: "When I look at your heavens, the work of your fingers, the moon and the stars, which you have set in place, what is man that you are mindful of him?" (Ps. 8:3–4). Creation should strike us with slack-jawed awe and dazzle us to

---

[6]T. A. Perry, *God's Twilight Zone—Wisdom in the Hebrew Bible* (Grand Rapids, MI: Baker Academic, 2008), 172.

quieting reverence. The pursuit of knowledge should start with wonder and curiosity, not the motive of controlling our destiny. Because a liberal arts education represents a quest for truth rather than an information download, it moves us toward the unknown every bit as much as the known. Truth is big. It emanates from God. And we never possess it; it possesses us. Biblical wisdom corrects our hubris and frees us from the illusion of control. Relying on the light of his revealed Word and guided by the input of fellow travelers, Christian students become empowered to boldly choose the road less traveled, one that can be boot-loose and wonder-full.

LIVING IN THE TENSION BETWEEN ATHENS AND JERUSALEM

With an expanded vision of wonder, how, then, do we explore the academic disciplines—such as philosophy, psychology, biology, and art—in a manner that is integrated with biblical wisdom—its values, and its view of the cosmos? Serious Christians who pursue the liberal arts should have a compelling answer to this question, first for themselves, and then for others. For despite a liberal arts institution's strong affirmation of orthodox Christianity, some may still raise their eyebrows, and their voices, at the idea of integrating the two realms: secular knowledge and biblical belief. They ask, "Why would you want to study at a liberal arts college that is Christian, anyway?"

This question actually has legitimacy and importance. It represents an old debate among early believers. During the late second century, Tertullian, a prominent leader of the church, put forth a challenging series of similar questions:

> What indeed has Athens to do with Jerusalem? What concord is there between the Academy and the Church? What between heretics and Christians? Our instruction comes from "the porch of Solomon," who had himself taught that "the Lord should be sought in simplicity of heart." Away with all attempts to produce a mottled Christianity of Stoic, Platonic, and dialectic composition![7]

In essence, Tertullian asked, "How can a student of the liberal arts, one

---

[7]Tertullian, "Latin Christianity: Its Founder, Tertullian," Christian Classics Ethereal Library (http://www.ccel.org/ccel/schaff/anf03.v.iii.vii.html).

who examines the world and its ways (symbolically represented by pagan Athens), be a disciple of Jesus Christ, one who pursues spiritual reality and its practices (signified by the holy city of Jerusalem)?" For Tertullian, the contrast between the two activities could not be denied or dismissed. He saw an inherent contradiction between the wisdom of pagan philosophers, as demonstrated in the writings of Plato or Zeno, versus the wisdom of God, as exhibited in the sacred books of Proverbs and Ecclesiastes. Therefore, since Athens and Jerusalem did not seem compatible, Tertullian cautioned Christians about roaming the streets of *both* cities.

For Tertullian, the power of the liberal arts, the curriculum that formed the minds of pagan thinkers, ought to be taken seriously, because it has the potential to corrupt a Christian's faith in the gospel, which he argued must remain pure, without the blemish of harmful influences. Christians who experience God's grace in the breaking of their bondage to sin participate in the redemption of Christ through his death on the cross, his resurrection, and his indwelling Spirit. But the enlargement of their capacities toward greater personal and social liberties has serious risks; namely, it can lead Christians to possess a greater confidence in themselves and their own abilities rather than in their Creator and his sovereignty. Thus Tertullian wanted them to carefully examine the inherent tension of pursuing both freedoms together.

This tension between the ways of Athens and those of Jerusalem remains as a vital consideration for any serious Christian who has decided to pursue a liberal arts education. In fact, a regular acknowledgment of the allure of Athens (secular knowledge) can prove to be peculiarly beneficial, prompting the student to deliberately exercise faith back toward Jerusalem (biblical wisdom). This dialectic serves to strengthen the Christian mind, not weaken it, allowing for what Milton described as the antidote to a "cloistered virtue" or a sheltered faith: the regular testing of one's beliefs by what is contrary, strengthening them through the rigorous challenge that comes from oppositional worldviews and even the contemplation of evil.[8]

---

[8]See Milton's *Areopagetica* and *Paradise Lost* as examples of this kind of oppositional engagement.

UNDERSTANDING THE BASICS OF THE ANCIENT LIBERAL ARTS

A thoughtful understanding and defense of Christian liberal arts learning requires a basic knowledge of its pagan precursor. The *enkyklios paideia* of ancient Athens (a "complete cycle of education"—the same basis for the English word *encyclopedia*, with its comprehensive survey of knowledge) shaped students with powerful results, developing them into the kinds of human beings who could become effective leaders in all areas of society. During the fifth century BCE, the great Athenian teacher Isocrates, in his *Panegyricus*, one of the earliest works to describe the benefits of liberal learning, asserted that students who received this kind of education would possess not only "power in their own cities but . . . honor in other states."[9] Similarly, during the fourth century BCE, Aristotle proposed that this noble form of learning—expressly for the free citizens (*eleutheroi*) of a democracy[10]—was the perfect preparation for the exercise of virtue (*areté*: excellence) in realms of intellectual thought and moral action.

Within this distinctly pre-Christian program of education, students labored to learn specific classical disciplines known as "arts." First they acquired skill in the "three core studies," called the *trivium*: grammar (the way language works), dialectic (the logical development of sound thinking), and rhetoric (the means to persuade others). Then students explored "the four ways," called the *quadrivium*: arithmetic (the knowledge of quantity), geometry (the measurements of the earth), music (the art of the Muses), and astronomy (the examination of the stars). Together, these seven studies became what the Roman orator and statesman Cicero first described as the *artes liberales*, a term relatively understood in the first century BCE as "the academic disciplines for freedom."[11]

The arts proved to be freeing or liberal (a word that comes from the Latin *liber,* meaning "free person") because they quite literally disciplined students toward new habits of thinking and behaving that were enriching. (Coincidentally, *liber* is also the word for "book.") The *liberal*

---

[9]Isocrates, *Panegyricus*, trans. J. A. Freese (http://classicpersuasion.org/pw/isocrates/pwisoc4.htm).
[10]Mogens Herman Hansen, "Democratic Freedom and the Concept of Freedom in Plato and Aristotle," *Greek, Roman, and Byzantine Studies* 1 (2010): 1–27.
[11]Cicero, *De Oratore*, 3.7.26.

arts ideal encouraged an important connection between a student's freedom to study (few people enjoyed that luxury) and the means to sustain and inform that freedom, explicitly through a disciplined regimen using worthwhile books from many disciplines. For this reason Quintilian, the influential advocate for liberal learning during the first century CE, argued that "we should read none but the best authors, who are least likely to betray our trust."[12]

Ancient liberal arts learning, then, depended upon reading a diverse selection of core texts with the aim of critical engagement and evaluative judgment. Properly conceived, reading provided students with the means to dialog with dead authors—the great thinkers of the past. With every book read, liberal arts students took the opportunity to interact with one another in spirited conversation, making sense of the contents, offering possible interpretations, and debating their significance. In this context, the skills of precise speech and careful listening naturally came into play. And on regular occasion, students crafted their own written ideas to present to peers in class. Historically, a liberal arts education offered students a complete orientation to the known world and the cultivation of the skills needed to flourish in it, including the critical literacy skills that made human beings distinct from the animals—reading, writing, speaking, and listening. The end, or ideal objective, was to shape good people who would regularly exercise freedom in society and responsibly serve the common good.

THE EMERGENCE OF CHRISTIAN LIBERAL ARTS

Ironically, Tertullian himself was the recipient of a liberal arts education, and some recent scholars suggest that he would not have been the great theologian of the Trinity that he became were it not for his classical studies. Fluent in Greek and Latin, he read widely in a variety of subjects, such as history, literature, law, medicine, philosophy, and rhetoric, engaging ideas with the fierce conviction that every thought must be surrendered to Christ. As Robert D. Sider observes, "His conversion to Christianity brought to him a radically new vision of the world, while his pagan education provided him with the tools to express that vision with

---

[12]Quintilian, *Institutio oratoria*, 10.1.20.

almost unparalleled power."[13] Contrary to popular opinion, Tertullian was not an anti-intellectual Christian but a rational thinker who gained clarity of thought by facing ideas contrary to his faith.[14] In other words, Tertullian demonstrated his vast knowledge of Athens and its emphasis on human reason to show the comparative superiority of Jerusalem and its insistence upon supernatural faith.

Christians of Tertullian's day had good reasons to question the benefits of the classical way of life, including its educational goals and methods. He himself, prior to his conversion, marveled at the steady courage of Christians who faced unspeakable horrors at the hands of their educated and supposedly "civilized" Roman torturers; it was the witness of these martyrs that profoundly moved him toward faith in Jesus Christ. Tertullian knew that "the Faith which had built the catacombs and sustained the tortures of the arena had its roots in experiences of which its persecutors were necessarily ignorant."[15]

Over time, pagan converts (who could not easily forget or let go of their liberal arts educational past) gradually entered and influenced the church. After the Roman Emperor Constantine adopted Christianity in the fourth century, the values of the church gradually merged with the Hellenized culture of the Mediterranean basin. Classical education eventually became converted and baptized, if not fully sanctified. Whereas in the pagan past students sought the liberal arts with the goal of personal enrichment for civic participation, in the Christianized West students recognized the importance of a new version of liberal arts, one with the goal of preparation to think deeply about God and to serve his church. As Christian educators asked new questions about liberal arts learning and strove to reconceptualize it, they adapted the ancient methods and ideals to achieve aims that were distinctly biblical. In the midst of urgent educational needs to shape the members of a growing church, Christian leaders made a calculated compromise between the ways of Athens and those of Jerusalem.[16] They realized, as Tertullian once argued, that

---

[13]Robert D. Sider, *A Christian and Pagan in the Roman Empire: The Witness of Tertullian* (Washington, DC: Catholic University of America Press, 2001), 182.

[14]Eric Osborn, *Tertullian, First Theologian of the West* (Cambridge, UK: Cambridge University Press, 1997).

[15]R. R. Bolgar, *The Classical Heritage and Its Beneficiaries* (Cambridge, UK: Cambridge University Press, 1974), 46.

[16]For an excellent overview of the development of Christian higher education, see Arthur F. Holmes, *Building the Christian Academy* (Grand Rapids, MI: Eerdmans, 2001).

"Christians are made, not born."[17] The church appropriated liberal arts instructional methods for its own purpose of making Christians.

LIBERAL ARTS FOR THE CHRISTIAN LIFE

Tertullian's famous challenge deserves to be pondered regularly by students who attend a Christian liberal arts college or university and by the teachers who teach them. The questions he raised defy easy answers, requiring sustained reflection about issues that aim toward the heart— one's abiding commitments for living.

Regrettably, few institutions offer students "higher learning" that integrates Christian spiritual truths with secular studies. The original meaning of the term "university" (from the Latin *universitas*, emphasizing "the whole," as in "the connected universe") no longer characterizes most undergraduate institutions that use the title, given their lack of curricular coherence (many courses, few connections) and disciplinary specialization (narrow focus, little breadth). However, for the Christian who decides to pursue a liberal arts education, this unique college or university experience becomes an education for all of life, and for all of one's being, in service to the church and the world. Christian liberal learning, at its best, teaches students that God is the unifying source of all knowledge, all skill, all wisdom—"every good gift" (James 1:17). In this light, a Christian education itself should be seen as a vehicle of grace, a divine provision, a means by which the student gains clarification of a calling (*vocare*: to call) from God, and in so doing, lives the abundant life with uncommon purpose, grounded in Christ's love.

Ponder, for a moment, a simple argument for why this sort of education makes sense. Every week contains 168 hours. According to the United States Bureau of Labor Statistics, the average worker spends 8.7 hours each day on job-related activities, five days a week, for a total of 43.5 hours; and then that same adult sleeps 7.7 hours each night, seven nights a week, for a total of 53.9 hours.[18] In other words, the total number of hours for working and sleeping each week comes to 97.4 hours. So then, what about the remaining 70.6 hours a week? How should your

---

[17]Sider, *A Christian and Pagan in the Roman Empire*, 38.
[18]"American Time Use Survey," United States Department of Labor, Bureau of Labor Statistics, June 5, 2011 (http://www.bls.gov/tus/charts/).

college education prepare you for what this part of your life entails? Most people fail to ever consider this piece of the pie chart, which denotes the largest amount of conscious hours in a person's existence.

Regarding the importance of gaining a bigger, more comprehensive understanding of learning, professor of philosophy Arthur Holmes explains how liberal arts learning prepares students for *all* of life:

> A liberal education is not job training, although it will of course have career outcomes. It is not just broad learning across various arts and sciences. Nor is it just an introduction to the heritage of our past: great events, great people, great ideas. Education helps shape people, cultivating abilities that last throughout life and transfer to a myriad of tasks.[19]

From a liberal arts perspective, then, especially one informed by biblical values, college should prepare you to be a good neighbor, a loyal friend, a devoted spouse, a committed church member, a loving parent, a responsible citizen, and, of greatest importance, a faithful disciple of Jesus Christ. It is an education that develops your God-given traits and capacities as a person, preparing you to serve effectively in a number of life roles. Wherever you go, there *you* will be. The person you become in college—not just the knowledge you carry in your head—will matter. That is why Christian liberal arts prepares the whole person, for all of life—nothing less.

To illustrate this unconventional approach to higher learning, consider this concluding example of a life well lived by a person dedicated to liberal arts learning—my good friend Quinn. After choosing to attend a Christian liberal arts college in the Midwest, he decided to major in what he loved—biblical studies. Quinn had no particular desire to "go into the ministry" or "enter the mission field." He simply enjoyed the Word of God and wanted to become more knowledgeable and effective in reading and interpreting it. Besides enrolling in Bible courses, Quinn was required to take a lot of general education courses, too. To his surprise, he appreciated many of them. They broadened his horizons, affording him the chance to think critically about topics he never considered before, all taught by dedicated Christian professors, from a biblical

---

[19]Arthur F. Holmes, *Shaping Character: Moral Education in the Christian College* (Grand Rapids, MI: Eerdmans, 1991), 4.

standpoint. Visual art, music, natural sciences, and the humanities: they all challenged his understanding of the world, pushing him to grow in ways he would not have chosen on his own. In particular, he really came to value the social sciences, and especially psychology, because of its examination of personhood.

Upon finishing his undergraduate degree, he applied to another Christian liberal arts institution for graduate work in clinical psychology, and during that time we happened to live together as roommates. Often, after I arrived home from my nine-to-five job, we would dialogue and explore important questions together. "What does it mean to be human?" "How should we come to understand and integrate our emotions into everyday life?" "Why do we interact with others the way that we do?" "What are healthy versus unhealthy behaviors, and where do they come from, relative to our development?" The root of the word *question* says it all—*quest*—a search, a pursuit, a journey. Quinn asked all the big questions, and he read many provocative books (several of which he placed on my desk for me to read). The books we read challenged our thinking and forced us to consider new ways of living.[20] Quinn willingly tested his faith with the truth he encountered, even when it challenged his presuppositions. During the time that we lived together, we spent countless hours talking about our families, our friendships, our aspirations, and our God. And through our conversations, I learned an incredible amount about living a rich, reflective life, so much so that when Quinn finished his graduate degree, I felt as though I was graduating with a degree in clinical psychology, too. Outside of my own formal education, I never learned so much. My roommate gave me a liberating gift.[21]

So where did Quinn end up, after all that time, effort, and money in the pursuit of two degrees from two different liberal arts institutions? Today he delivers mail for the United States Postal Service in a major metropolitan city. That has been his career for over twenty years now. He would be the first to say that mail delivery does not represent his calling, nor would he say that his education went to waste. To the contrary,

---

[20]Of the many books we read, *The Dangers of Growing Up in a Christian Home*, by Donald Sloat, was one of Quinn's favorites, addressing issues that many Christian families encounter.
[21]Most college students affirm that of all influences that affect their lives, their peers are most significant.

Quinn uses what he learned every week during the 70.6 hours that he spends in relationship with important people in his life, especially his best friend—his wife—and his two boys. Quinn's calling requires that he serve the people whom God brings across—and onto—his path each day, and he does that better because of his Christian liberal arts education. As he walks with a bag of mail, traveling his daily route, making deliveries, he maintains his physical fitness (aerobic exercise without a gym), and he keeps his mind engaged (listening to audio books and sermons). And in his free time, he actively participates in the life of his church, attends his kids' sporting events and dramas, takes care of his aged parents, and finds creative fulfillment as an amateur inventor.

A rugged Renaissance thinker on the road through all seasons, Quinn certainly is not the typical liberal arts graduate. In truth, there is no typical Christian liberal arts graduate. Whether a corporate executive or a church pastor, a heart surgeon or a school teacher, each graduate travels a distinct path, fulfilling a unique calling from Christ, which may or may not reflect a career. Yet, one thing remains characteristic of the Christian committed to a liberal arts orientation, which Quinn's life reflects: after graduation, there is a serious contemplation of the word *commencement*, and its meaning is taken literally. As a Christian dedicated to the liberal arts, Quinn, like many other lifelong learners, began a quest for wisdom, "and that has made all the difference."

CHAPTER TWO

LIBERAL EDUCATION AND BOOK LEARNING

Lisa Richmond

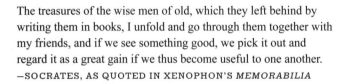

The treasures of the wise men of old, which they left behind by
writing them in books, I unfold and go through them together with
my friends, and if we see something good, we pick it out and
regard it as a great gain if we thus become useful to one another.
—SOCRATES, AS QUOTED IN XENOPHON'S *MEMORABILIA*

"How can I [understand], except some man should guide me?"
And he desired Philip that he would come up and sit with him.
—ACTS 8:31 (KJV)

Liberal education began with the ancient Greeks.[1] It was the education
for boys who were not slaves and whose families were wealthy enough
that they did not need to apprentice their sons to a trade. Thus liberal education was the education of an elite, for those who would become citizens
of the society they inhabited, debate laws and actions in the assembly,
lead their society in peace and in war, and become the arbiters of aesthetic values. Liberal education was an education in culture. These boys
were given the incomparable gifts of time and freedom from financial
pressure that enabled them while they were young to study for the sheer
pleasure and excellence of doing so, and for the cultivation of intellect,
taste, and virtue. The root meaning of the Greek word σχολή (*scholē*),
from which the English word *school* derives, in fact is "rest" or "leisure."
Leisure is the freedom that makes this kind of education liberal.

THE EDUCATION OF THE CITIZEN

By this reckoning, every Christian student, male or female, who attends
a liberal arts college today is kin to these young men of ancient Greece.

---

[1]Part of this section was first written in collaboration with members of the General Education Exploratory
Committee at Wheaton College, 2010–2011.

God has blessed you with the leisure that financial resources make possible, the leisure necessary to undertake four years of study for its own inherent rewards, not especially to train for employment—and this is true even though almost all of you, unlike your ancient counterparts, go on to pursue a paid occupation of one sort or another. For this difference we praise God, since the freedom of some in ancient Greece was dependent upon the slavery of others. We note also that early Christians developed a positive theology of work that was at odds with the Greek heritage: while Aristotle remarked that wage-earning and all arts associated with such work were incompatible with virtue,[2] the apostle Paul, for example, drew a favorable analogy between scriptural study and skilled manual labor (2 Tim. 2:15). And while Aristotle warned that one should apply oneself to study only up to a point, because excessive zeal produces an abject mind, the Jewish heritage endowed Christians with such models of all-consuming studiousness as that expressed in Psalm 119.

To these Greeks, the aim of liberal education was the formation of the moral "gentleman," the καλοκαγαθός (kalokagathos: he who is fine and good). This valuation continued far into the Christian era, for until the Protestant Reformation, a theology of lay vocations or sanctification in ordinary economic life was not seriously explored. The aim of education as fundamentally an education in culture was overcome decisively only in the twentieth century, when the various forms of scientific, technical, and managerial power, and the kinds of education that produced these, became too influential to ignore. Yet education as culture is viewed still today as a highly desirable complement or addition to education as technical mastery. Some obscure sense of things still prompts the opinion shapers of contemporary American society to consider it preferable for medical doctors, for example, to study serious works of history or literature before entering upon their professional training.

Thus liberal education was undertaken "for one's own sake, or the sake of one's friends, or with a view to virtue"[3] and sought the fulfillment of the citizen who had the legal right and economic leisure to participate in self-government. In the democracy of ancient Athens,

---

[2]Aristotle, *Politics* 1337b. Note: this form of citation to the works of Aristotle and Plato enables the reader to locate the cited passage in any scholarly edition of these works.
[3]Ibid.

citizenship was restricted to a very few. Does this political meaning of liberal education have relevance for us today in our age of mass democracies? The most thoughtful advocates of liberal education in the twentieth century asserted its contemporary relevance precisely on this basis. In the transition from aristocracies, in which "the best" ruled, to democracies, in which "the people" ruled, the intention was that all persons would increase in virtue and that democracy would become a "universal aristocracy."[4] With the passage of time, however, this noble goal has become increasingly discredited. Democracy, it would seem, tends to produce a mass society that is unable and unwilling to participate wisely in self-government, and an elite, ruling for its own ends, that reinforces these conditions. Against this fate stands liberal education, whose advocates assert,

> Liberal education is the counterpoison to mass culture, to the corroding effects of mass culture, to its inherent tendency to produce nothing but "specialists without spirit or vision and voluptuaries without heart." Liberal education is the ladder by which we try to ascend from mass democracy to democracy as originally meant. Liberal education is the necessary endeavor to found an aristocracy within democratic mass society.[5]

THE EDUCATION OF THE SKEPTIC

There were other Greek thinkers, however, who held to a different purpose. These men, most notably Plato, believed that liberal education ought to aim at the cultivation not of gentlemanship but of reason. Liberal education by this reckoning is primarily concerned not with the fulfillment of citizens engaged in self-governing political institutions but with the transcending of error and ignorance that leads to inner freedom.[6] Plato most famously expressed this aim in his myth of the cave, in which one leaves behind the bondage of mere opinion and emerges

---

[4]Leo Strauss, "What Is Liberal Education?," in *Liberalism Ancient and Modern* (New York: Basic Books, 1968), 4.
[5]Ibid., 5. The phrase "specialists without spirit or vision and voluptuaries without heart" is from Max Weber. See Weber, *The Protestant Ethic and the Spirit of Capitalism*, trans. Talcott Parsons (New York: Scribner, 1958), 182.
[6]These two conceptions of liberal education and their history are examined in Bruce A. Kimball's *Orators and Philosophers: A History of the Idea of Liberal Education* (New York: College Board, 1995).

into the light of actual knowledge.[7] The cave apparently includes the ordinary political and legal institutions of one's society.

The most outstanding exemplar of this form of liberal learning was Socrates. With unique tenacity, Socrates sought to examine the beliefs and traditions of his society, to sift them, to find out what was well-founded and what was not. Socrates did not speak much about what he knew. His emphasis instead was on the difficulties of knowing, and he claimed to know only that he did not know. The classic Socratic claim has been not wisdom but philosophy, understood as the skeptical quest for wisdom. In respect of this claim, the Delphic Oracle declared that there was "none wiser" than Socrates.[8] Socrates was not especially a moral gentleman in his way of life; Aristotle even used him as an example of vice, for his deficient truthfulness.[9]

Socrates's favorite questions began with the phrase *what is*. "What is justice?" he would ask; "What is virtue?" Many of his dialogues as recorded by Plato address a question of this kind. In one dialogue, for example, Socrates meets a young man named Euthyphro, who is initiating legal proceedings against his own father. Euthyphro claims that his father has committed an unjust action and that piety requires him to be denounced in the courts. This assertion greatly interests Socrates because he himself has recently been charged with impiety. He therefore asks Euthyphro, "What is piety? Surely you must know, if you are willing to prosecute even your father on the strength of your understanding. Please tell me what piety is, so that I too may know."

Euthyphro begins his response confidently, even condescendingly, yet under Socrates's relentless questions he offers one inadequate answer after another until finally declaring that piety is activity that honors the gods by, among other things, strengthening family life. But clearly if this definition is true, then Euthyphro's course of action in the name of piety is impious in the extreme, for he is acting against his own father. Unwilling to admit this, Euthyphro runs away, claiming that he is late for an appointment. Plato's message in part is that when one can

---

[7]Plato, *Republic* 514a–519b.

[8]Plato, *Apology* 20e–21e.

[9]Aristotle, *Nicomachean Ethics* 1127b. According to Aristotle, Socrates's ironic self-deprecation does not exemplify the "mean condition" (virtue) of truthfulness that lies between boastfulness and its opposite.

recognize oneself in that foolish and dangerous young man, one's actual education can begin.

Holy Scripture tells us that the beginning of wisdom is found in the fear of the Lord (Ps. 111:10)—not in the awareness of one's own ignorance or in the confidence of one's own reason, no matter how valuable such awareness and confidence also are to the believer. This is the fundamental difference between liberal learning in the pure Socratic mold and liberal learning as framed and practiced by Christian believers. Pure Socratic-style liberal education is the effort to replace opinions about the nature of things with knowledge of their nature, through reliance upon human reason alone. Christian liberal education is the effort to replace opinions with knowledge through reasoning that operates in love and obedience to divinely revealed truths—and one such truth is that human reason is disordered by sin. Christian thought thus requires both "submission and use of reason."[10]

Pure Socratic-style liberal education may easily be criticized for elevating questions over answers, even for asserting that the answers are unknowable or nonexistent.[11] Christians hold in faith not only the possibility of final answers and the final unity of knowledge but also the promise that all the treasures of wisdom and knowledge are hidden in Christ (Col. 2:3). This can give the believing student a humility and a confidence that are truly precious and transformative intellectual and spiritual goods.

BOOK LEARNING

We know of Socrates and can learn from his teachings only because his students Plato and Xenophon recorded his life and teachings in written form. Socrates himself wrote nothing. He believed that education occurs best through dialectic, through disciplined conversation between teacher and student, and to this form of teaching he devoted himself. Socrates did not oppose the writing and reading of books—see the epigraph to this chapter—but he believed that dialectic was the superior activity. In

---

[10]Blaise Pascal, *pensée* 167 (Lafuma numbering). See Pascal, *Pensées*, trans. A. J. Krailsheimer (New York: Penguin, 1966).

[11]I criticize this aspect of secular programs of liberal education not a priori as a Christian believer but because in my experience these programs are rarely willing also to address the full outworkings of their counsel of despair.

the *Phaedrus*, he pointed to a serious difficulty that can attend an education mediated solely or primarily through books:

> Writing, you know, Phaedrus, has this strange quality about it, which makes it really like painting: the painter's products stand before us quite as though they were alive; but if you question them, they maintain a solemn silence. So, too, with written words: you might think they spoke as though they made sense, but if you ask them anything about what they are saying, if you wish an explanation, they go on telling you the same thing, over and over forever.[12]

Students therefore often find themselves in the position of the Ethiopian eunuch who sat puzzling over the prophecy of Isaiah. "Understandest thou what thou readest?" Philip asked him, and he replied, "How can I, except some man should guide me?" (Acts 8:30–31 KJV). How precious it is to sit under a real teacher's discourse "that can defend itself," as Socrates phrased it, the "living, animate discourse of a man who really knows."[13]

Euthyphro could not defend his discourse. Further, Euthyphro exemplifies the second serious problem with an education that relies on book learning only. Separated from the discipline that is gained through dialectic, book learning can reinforce the very lack of self-knowledge that liberal education seeks to overcome—and it can do this all the more insidiously when it cloaks itself in the guise of learnedness. Socrates told of a conversation between the Egyptian king Thamus and the god Thoth, the inventor of writing. Thoth praised his invention, but the king replied,

> Thanks to [books], your pupils will be widely read without benefit of a teacher's instruction; in consequence they'll entertain the delusion that they have wide knowledge, while they are, in fact, for the most part incapable of real judgment. They will also be difficult to get on with since they will have become wise merely in their own conceits, not genuinely so.[14]

Against such defective education Socrates proposed in a beautiful metaphor the teacher as a sower acting upon the fertile soil of the

---

[12]Plato, *Phaedrus* 275d.
[13]Ibid., 276a.
[14]Ibid., 275b.

student's mind. (In this way, we come full circle to liberal education understood as a means of *culture*, the cultivating of the mind.) Such education leads to "discourse that is inscribed with genuine knowledge in the soul of the learner": "Far more noble and splendid [than the writing of books] is the serious pursuit of the dialectician, who finds a congenial soul and then proceeds with true knowledge to plant and sow in it words that are able to help themselves and help him who planted them."[15]

The centrality of teaching to liberal education was emphasized in the controversy aroused by the publication of Allan Bloom's *The Closing of the American Mind*.[16] Bloom was a formidable proponent of undergraduate studies in which important books were carefully studied, but his driving concern was that teachers in the humanities and social sciences were failing to communicate to students the richness of understanding that is possible and that should be their heritage as citizens of Western civilization. Bloom held that the promotion of a superficial knowingness about important books would not suffice to maintain the tradition of serious liberal education.

And yet one of Bloom's own teachers noted that as beautiful and fertile as the best teacher-student relationship may be, there will always be many more serious students than there will be wise teachers available. Truly wise teachers, he remarked, are extremely rare.[17] Socrates was one such teacher, and as noted earlier we can learn from his teachings only because they were recorded in books. Thus many advocates of liberal education conceive of books, the "great books" in particular, as the very greatest teachers to whom any student may have access. The careful study of such books (preferably still within a community of learning) can be viewed in this light as itself a kind of dialectic. The works of Plato, Dante, Descartes, and the other great thinkers of our civilization can be read as forming an ongoing conversation with one another. An education in great books can then become a listening in on this conversation. It can even be, absurdly but quite truly, a participation of one's own puny mind in this conversation of the very great minds.

---

[15]Ibid., 276e.
[16]Allan Bloom, *The Closing of the American Mind: How Higher Education Has Failed Democracy and Impoverished the Souls of Today's Students* (New York: Simon & Schuster, 1987).
[17]Strauss, "What Is Liberal Education?," 3.

While the great-books form of liberal education emerged in the West, it may of course be applied and is being applied to the foundational works of other civilizations. But there is an important sense in which an understanding of these Western books in particular is urgent and necessary for all people, regardless of their cultural origins. Modern technological science, now holding utter decisiveness over vast areas of human life, even over the nature of human life itself, is fundamentally a Western development. Why did it arise in the West? Was that emergence a mere fortuity, or were Western conceptions in some way necessary? To understand this and other defining influences of contemporary life, whether that life is lived in the United States or Lesotho or Japan, we must understand the civilization out of which they arose. Even the most resolute opponent of the West cannot function without this understanding. To some extent the West can be studied by examining Western institutions and practices—the usual ground of historians, sociologists, and anthropologists. But the gradual construction of the West occurred as a result of the thoughts spoken in the great books, and the study of these books provides a deeper and richer means of understanding why the West occurred or unfolded as it did.

Understanding and reflection lay the foundation for action. For several centuries, social activism has been a distinctive feature of evangelical Christian faith. Yet we know that naïve activism may be ineffectual and even damaging. Before he began his public ministry, the apostle Paul spent three years in Arabia and Damascus, presumably undergoing some form of self-preparation (Gal. 1:5–18). One's years of undergraduate study may be viewed in a similar light. If these years are lived as an unrepeatable and therefore precious time of preparation, focused in prayerful study and serious conversation about the most important things, a grounding can emerge from which to serve our troubled world with a deeper understanding. "Brethren, be not children in understanding; . . . in malice be ye children, but in understanding be men" (1 Cor. 14:20 KJV).

CHAPTER THREE

EVANGELICALS, COLLEGES, AND AMERICAN NATION BUILDING

Edith Blumhofer

At the West, society is yet to be formed. There in the process of being united into a great empire are minds of astonishing energy and hearts of fire that need to be taught and guided and restrained. . . . Never was the need of education so pressing; never was its power for good so full of promise. . . . It is not enough to send tracts, Sunday schools, and even preachers. . . . There must be the expenditure of tens of thousands, it may be millions of money in founding religious colleges and seminaries which shall be strong enough in intellect and other resources to do for Western society what the Jesuits did for Europe in the sixteenth century.

—NOAH PORTER, *THE EDUCATIONAL SYSTEMS OF THE PURITANS AND JESUITS COMPARED*

That the soul be without knowledge,
　　it is not good.
—PROVERBS 19:2 (KJV)

In the mid-nineteenth century, literate American Protestants could hardly escape the recognition that their leaders believed that the steady westward march of the American population presented a strategic challenge of the first magnitude. At stake was nothing less than the soul of the nation. For civilization to triumph over rampant individualism, for the nation to realize its God-given destiny, Protestants in the eastern United States heard often that they had to take responsibility for Christianizing the frontier.

In the idiom of the times, the case for action often took the form of a "Plea for the West," and such "pleas" placed Christian liberal arts education at the heart of a nineteenth-century Protestant vision for the nation. "Pleas for the West" were both spoken and published, and as fundraising sermons, they organized arguments around biblical texts. Presbyterian Albert Barnes headed his "Plea in Behalf of Western Colleges" (1846) with the verse from Proverbs quoted above. Lyman Beecher's "Plea for the West" (1835) took as its text Isaiah 66:8 (KJV): "Who hath heard such a thing? Who hath seen such things?"—words Beecher used to convey astonishment at the scope of gospel opportunity American expansion presented—while Episcopal bishop and educator Philander Chase placed the Golden Rule on the title page of his own "Plea for the West" (1827), which he subtitled, "A Plea for Learning and Religion in Ohio." These Bible verses highlight different aspects of a single theme: the West presented unprecedented opportunity, demanded unselfish sacrifice, and required the founding of Christian colleges to perpetuate Protestant religion and democratic institutions.

Christian liberal arts colleges had a prominent place in the Protestant vision for nation building: they drew on classical models, recalled Puritan convictions, and easily merged political and religious objectives. In the first half of the nineteenth century, educators considered the combination of democracy, Protestant beliefs, and Christian learning invincible: they dared to believe the expanding United States would be a Protestant nation and a blessing to the world. Within a century, profound cultural shifts eroded such confidence and prompted productive reflection on the purpose and value of Christian liberal arts learning on its own terms.

HOPE RISING

Our story properly begins in the early nineteenth century, though its roots stretch back to colonial beginnings and beyond to Europe's universities. As a young nation faced its future, Americans eager to invest their lives in the nation's destiny heeded calls to action delivered from pulpits up and down the East Coast. On Thursday, September 29, 1825, for example, two graduates of Andover Seminary stood face-to-face on the platform of Boston's historic Old South Church. The elder of the two, the Rev. Elias Cornelius, had just passed his thirtieth birthday but was already a celebrated preacher with uncommon zeal for evangelism and education. He delivered an ordination charge to John Ellis, a recent volunteer for home missionary work in Illinois.[1] Cornelius solemnly challenged Ellis to establish "an institution of higher learning" that would "bless the West for all time."

The challenge reflected the growing consensus among evangelical Protestants in the Northeast that the welfare of the nation depended on the progress of religion and education on the expanding frontier. A promotional circular for the American Education Society stated it this way: "Do you tremble lest the rising hopes of our common country should yet be dashed by the prevalence of vice and irreligion? Give your prayers and your influence to an object [the American Education Society] which alone can establish, in the temple of our independence, the pillar of virtue."[2] The American Education Society (1826) directed some of the energy unleashed by revivals that swept the young nation between 1800 and 1840. Like other voluntary associations, it gave national scope to formidable tasks too ambitious for local or regional societies to accomplish alone. The American Home Missionary Society (1826), dedicated to "the religious benefit of a great and growing nation," coordinated a vision for national uplift that had previously been managed separately by state Congregational associations.[3] Such national associations testified that forward-looking Protestants in the Early Republic believed wholeheartedly that vigorous, united, and persevering Christian effort would accomplish the goal of a Christian America. Religion and education would plant civilization, the gospel, and democracy in the West, assuring the future of the distinctive American mix of liberty and justice for all.

To be sure, the conviction that education informed by religion—and religion informed by education—produced citizens equipped to lead and influence the culture already figured prominently in the founding of the nine colleges chartered in the colonial era. The oldest, Harvard College (1636), existed first to provide the Massachusetts Bay Colony with learned ministers, although from the start its supporters imagined graduates equipped by college studies to glorify God in all walks of life.

[1]George Thomas Chapman, *Sketches of the Alumni of Dartmouth College* (Cambridge, MA: Riverside Press, 1867), 209.
[2]Elias Cornelius, *Memoirs of the Rev. Elias Cornelius*, ed. B. B. Edwards (New York: Saxton & Miles, 1842), 204.
[3]"Introductory Remarks," *The Home Missionary* 1 (May 1, 1828): 1.

New England's First Fruits (1643) connected the early settlers' resolve to "advance learning and perpetuate it to posterity" to their dread of "leav[ing] an illiterate ministry to the churches when our present ministers shall lie in the dust."[4] The learning and piety of early Harvard students, one observer remarked in 1642, "do fill our hearts with comfort and raise them up to more expectation, of the Lord's goodness for hereafter, for the good of posterity and the churches of Christ Jesus."[5] The school's animating idea at least until the Revolutionary War, Harvard historian Samuel Eliot Morison observed, was to attain "a more perfect knowledge of God by the discipline of the mind."[6] For New England Puritans, then, learning and piety went hand-in-hand. Other colonial college charters concurred in the long tradition of Western Christian affirmation of the affinity between faith and learning.

Together, the first American institutions of higher learning modeled a new concept that quickly became the American custom: the college as a degree-granting entity unattached to a university. After independence, colleges multiplied rapidly, and most had a decidedly Protestant cast. When Williams College obtained its charter in 1792, it was already the second college in Massachusetts, the sixth in New England, and the twenty-first in the nation. A solid body of American Protestants clearly believed that faith and learning promoted the American way of life with its democratic ideals, rugged individualism, and keen sense of destiny. Most colonial-era colleges had firm ties to local churches, denominations, or religious associations, and that trend continued in the Early Republic. Students attended daily chapel and Sunday services; leaders made the integration of academic and religious pursuits intentional. When intellectual fashions challenged faith, college leaders were likely to address the imbalance—as at turn-of-the-century Yale when President Timothy Dwight (1752–1817) set out to reverse student religious indifference with a four-year sermon series on revealed religion.

The citizens of the Early Republic who made Christian colleges part of their strategy for the West came of age during the revivals collectively

---

[4]*New England's First Fruits* (New York: Joseph Sabin, 1865), 23.
[5]Ibid., 32.
[6]Samuel Eliot Morison, *The Founding of Harvard College* (Cambridge, MA: Harvard University Press, 1998), 251.

known as the Second Great Awakening. In New England, revivals at Yale College and Williams College revitalized religious convictions about nation and destiny, as well as about private faith. Scattered intermittent revivals occurred in the original states, as well as on the frontier, while the nation began its steady march westward. Democracy and the separation of church and state were untested experiments; the West invited settlement; the world needed the gospel. From America's campuses, college men rose up to meet these challenges, energized by ideals that had public as well as private implications. The famous Haystack Prayer Meeting (1806) at Williams College—so named because a rainstorm forced participants in a missionary prayer meeting to take shelter under a haystack—became enshrined in Protestant memory as the source of the American foreign missionary movement. College men also committed themselves to making America a Christian nation, as well as to saving the regions beyond.

The early nineteenth century was arguably a turning point in the story of American Christian liberal arts education. Earlier endeavors provided relevant precedents, but in the Early Republic, assumptions about their utility for shaping public discourse, community values, and private faith gave Christian colleges new visibility. Modern Christian colleges arose out of a vigorous vision for Christian education that was tied to hopes for the nation and was most striking in the North during the Early Republic. This vision rested on an evolving myth of New England as source of the God-inspired American Way.

In the heady days of the Early Republic, when all things seemed possible in a new democratic culture, then, evangelical Christians (the vast majority of the population) promoted Christian colleges as a means to an end: shaping moral citizens, planting democracy on the frontier, and assuring the realization of God's purpose for the United States— purposes they rooted firmly in the New England heritage.

Christian colleges East and West came to be identified with the agendas for social reform that thrived in the wake of the era's revivals: women's collegiate education; education for African Americans; abolition; temperance. Amherst College opened in 1821 to train "indigent young men of piety and talents for the Christian ministry." In 1826, Amherst graduated its first African American student, Edward Jones, who became a distinguished missionary educator in Sierra Leone. Chemist, educator, and evangelical Mary Lyon established Mount Holyoke in South Hadley, Massachusetts, in 1837 to provide rigorous academic training for women. Moravian, Presbyterian, and nonsectarian schools outside New England offered education rooted in similar assumptions. The organization of denominations that followed the end of the Revolutionary War fueled enthusiasm for denominational institutions. The West, however, preoccupied articulate Protestants of all denominations who focused on America's future. Amid the bustle and excitement that accompanied national expansion, Christian colleges participated in the crucial task of forging vast territories and scattered, diverse peoples into a nation.

Perhaps the best-known apology for this strategic use of Christian colleges took the form of the sensational sermon called "A Plea for the West," delivered in 1834 by one of the nation's most prominent preachers, the Rev. Lyman Beecher. Alarmed by rapid population shifts and—like many of his contemporaries—by the first surges of Roman Catholic growth, Beecher implored Northeastern Protestants to support Christian (understood as Protestant) education on the frontier. "The religious and political destiny of our nation is to be decided in the West," Beecher thundered from East Coast pulpits. "The conflict which is to decide the destiny of the West will be a conflict of institutions for the education of her sons, for purposes of superstition or evangelical light; of despotism or liberty."[7] The looming crisis demanded schools, colleges, seminaries, pastors, and churches—permanent institutions in the West, where the inevitable clash with irreligion, Catholicism, and lawlessness would play out.

The West presented enormous diversity: it had no "unified public sentiment" binding it to the older states. Pressing need demanded prompt response from people who lived where the joint blessings of faith and learning were "most eminently enjoyed."[8] Beecher urged New Englanders to resettle in the West and bring their influence to bear on the prairies. But he also called for the establishing of "permanent powerful literary and moral institutions which, like the great orbs of attraction and light, shall

---

[7]Lyman Beecher, *A Plea for the West* (Cincinnati: Truman & Smith, 1835), 11–12.
[8]Ibid., 17.

send forth at once their power and their illumination, and without them all else will be inconstant and ephemeral." Leaders for the West should be educated in the West; the "great work" of planting Christian colleges was the only way to assure national prosperity, East and West, and to fulfill the nation's calling as a beacon of liberty to the world.

Beecher imagined schools that manifested "habits of intellectual culture which spring up in alliance with evangelical institutions." They could not be legislated into being: they would result only from the embrace of a patriotic and Christian calling, and they would prosper alongside local churches. Beecher took it for granted that faithful gospel preaching would naturally yield "schools, academies, libraries, colleges, and all the apparatus for the perpetuity of republican institutions."[9] The alarmist anti-Catholic diatribe that punctuated Beecher's *Plea for the West* lent force to his call for immediate action. Beecher's was only one of many voices summoning citizens to act for the national good. His contemporary Albert Barnes summarized the distinguishing features of a "Protestant seminary of learning": "instruction in the arts and sciences" and "extended and diligent cultivation of Greek and Roman classical learning . . . arranged with a view that the heart shall be pervaded with the most thorough religious principles drawn directly from the Bible."[10] At every level, Americans were exploring what it meant to be a nation, to have a national literature, national music, and a national language, to pay taxes and to build national roads. Evangelical Protestants, especially those in the Reformed tradition, built on that discussion to make their case for integrating the nation by planting Christian colleges in the West, binding it in a common commitment to Puritan values.

Remarks like Beecher's and Barnes's renewed the case for efforts that were already well underway. The mandates of the American Bible Society (1816), the American Tract Society (1824), the American Sunday School Union (1825), and other voluntary associations committed them to participate in civilizing the West. Denominations moved West with the population, and Western circumstances birthed new denominations. In the mix, Congregationalists and Presbyterians, acting together at first under a Plan of Union devised for the West in 1801, were poised to lead.

---

[9]Ibid., 23.
[10]Albert Barnes, *Plea on Behalf of Western Colleges* (Philadelphia: William Sloanaker, 1846), 3.

A regard for a particular version of the New England Puritan heritage, strengthened in December 1820 by festivities marking the two hundredth anniversary of the landing of the Pilgrims, shaped their purpose. At the celebrations, Daniel Webster gave a memorable oration detailing the distinctive legacy the Pilgrim Fathers bequeathed to the nation. The timing was auspicious. The new nation was searching for a national story, and Webster found it in the events of 1620, "the great event with which [our] history commenced."[11] He led the nation in "homage for our Pilgrim Fathers; sympathy in their sufferings, veneration for their piety; and attachment to those principles of civil and religious liberty" they established. In Massachusetts, Webster enthused, "Christianity, and civilization, and letters made their first lodgment in a vast extent of country." He invited the nation to see fortitude, dignity, decisiveness, piety, thoughtfulness, and "high religious faith, full of confidence and anticipation," in the little Mayflower band.

Webster summoned his compatriots to transmit faithfully "this great inheritance unimpaired," so that "in our estimate of public principles and private virtue, in our veneration of religion and piety, in our devotion to civil and religious liberty, in our regard for whatever advances human knowledge or improves human happiness, we are not altogether unworthy of our origin."[12] Webster challenged Americans to be imbued with the Pilgrims' spirit, to survive and thrive by persistence, hard work, moral sturdiness, and democratic ideals. His summary of Pilgrim traits described rugged souls who acted on principle, took their cues from the Bible, devoted themselves to the common good, survived against the odds, and prospered in a wilderness. In Webster's words, these characteristics became the heartbeat of a national ideal. They defined the essential American character and were at once enviable, attainable, and essential for the common good if America was to fulfill its divine destiny. This rendering of the American story gave pride of place to a version of the Puritan past made less formidable by reducing strict Calvinism to "religion and piety."

---

[11]Daniel Webster, *A Discourse Delivered at Plymouth, Dec 22, 1820. In Commemoration of the First Settlement of New-England* (Boston: Wells & Lilly, 1821), 5–6.
[12]Ibid., 10–11.

HOPE REALIZED

In 1833, concern for the spiritual state of the West led a Presbyterian minister to establish Oberlin College, one of the most influential schools of the era. Its mission was to prepare "teachers and other Christian leaders for the boundless most desolate fields in the West." Twenty-nine men and fifteen women composed the first class at Oberlin Collegiate Institute. Oberlin's first two presidents, Asa Mahan and Charles Finney, were clergymen, authors, abolitionists, social reformers, and college professors active in the contemporary revivals that fashioned an evangelical consensus about the common good. Donors in the Northeast sustained Oberlin through its early financial difficulties and made it a model for the upstart schools that followed.

Similar endeavors prospered elsewhere at about the same time. Knox College, in Galesburg, Illinois, opened its doors in 1837. Founded the previous January in Upstate New York by subscribers to a plan to establish literary institutions in the West, the town and college owed their existence to the leadership of the Presbyterian clergyman George W. Gale.[13] The academic course at Knox was to be "liberal and thorough," with the Bible in its original tongues "a class book" and one faculty member designated as "pastor to the students."[14] At Knox College, Jonathan Blanchard, son of Vermont, Middlebury College alumnus, and student of Lyman Beecher's at Lane Seminary in Cincinnati, began the career in Christian education that led him in 1860 to the presidency of another Christian institution: Wheaton College.

The heirs of the Puritans integrated Christian education into a comprehensive worldview, and their networks not only facilitated a steady stream of East Coast support for Western colleges but also helped integrate East and West. Other denominations, meanwhile—most of them more bureaucratic than Congregationalist—established colleges specifically to serve their members, supply their pulpits, and train leaders to Christianize the West. Methodists were especially active in the West. Mount Union College in Ohio (1846), Iowa Wesleyan (1842), and Illinois Wesleyan (1850) are a few of a host of enduring results. Illinois

---

[13]John W. Bailey, *Knox College: A Review* (Chicago: Press & Tribune Printing Office, 1860), 1.
[14]Ibid., 10–11.

Wesleyan's 1851 brochure expressed the intentions of such upstart Methodist colleges when it described that school as "an institution of learning which shall shed brightness on all the land around and send down floods of light and blessedness upon generations yet to come." Even brand-new denominations—such as The Wesleyan Connection, established as the result of a Methodist schism in 1843—thought immediately of the potential of Christian higher education for their identity and the nation's good. In 1853 they launched the collegiate institute that in 1860 was transferred to Illinois Congregationalists and became Wheaton College.

Many new Protestant colleges survived only briefly and never thrived; others (like Wheaton College) changed hands in order to prosper; some were intentionally denominational and, as immigration accelerated, others were both denominational and ethnic. For example, Swedish Lutherans established Gustavus Adolphus and Augustana Colleges in 1862, and Norwegians started St. Olaf in 1874. In fact, Christian colleges proliferated until critics suspected that they glutted the market: founding Christian colleges, some opined, was as much about denominational empires as about a commitment to liberal arts education.

HOPE REVISED

By the end of the century, the myth of the West had changed several times, and "West" conveyed a variety of ideas. The frontier was gone, and in the American imagination, the West no longer figured as either a promised land or a wild, lawless expanse. Economic incorporation had proceeded alongside political incorporation, and the idealistic rhetoric of pre–Civil War Protestants seemed increasingly out of touch with reality.

After the Civil War, at least three specific challenges accompanied profound alterations in national mood and forced Christian liberal arts colleges to rethink identity: modern theological scholarship, arguments by prominent educators for curriculum revision, and the promise of financial security at the expense of confessional commitments. Debates about the authority of Scripture or the exclusivity of Christianity questioned the assumptions behind Christian liberal arts education; schools that affirmed the claims of modern science and theology showed a willingness to replace the time-honored certainties undergirded by Scottish

Common Sense Realism with new ways of perceiving reality. Inductive reasoning lost favor; words such as *evolution, progress*, and *immanence* anchored a radically different pursuit of truth that enlivened a decidedly modern conversation about traditional Christian affirmations. In 1872, when Harvard president Charles Eliot introduced an elective system, he set aside the prescribed course of study common in American colleges since 1636.[15] Although Harvard retained a core curriculum in the humanities, opponents bristled that curricular changes amounted to a rejection of the forms of education historically associated with Christian learning. Prescribed courses assumed that a common system of truth constituted a basis for professional studies. Newer approaches featured education as a search for truth rather than as the communication of truth. Critics lamented that modern education removed from the curriculum the subjects that "produced the modern democratic state."[16]

Andrew Carnegie's decision to create a foundation to benefit education gave college trustees another incentive to face the implications of change over time for their institutions. Carnegie hired Henry Pritchett, a respected scientist and president of the Massachusetts Institute of Technology, to administer the new Carnegie Foundation for the Advancement of Teaching (established 1906) and its academic pension funds. Pritchett developed grant guidelines that restricted Carnegie money to colleges dedicated to education without reference to religion.[17] Denominational colleges could expect no Carnegie funds, nor could any schools that failed to demonstrate their commitment to education regardless of auspices. The Carnegie Foundation and, from 1913, the Rockefeller Foundation, gave grants only if schools met certain conditions, and the conditions often either excluded sectarian and independent Christian liberal arts colleges or mandated basic changes in their boards of trustees, their funding sources, and their curricula. Foundations' grant guidelines promoted nonsectarianism, worked against redundancy, and encouraged consolidation of struggling schools. After considerable soul

[15]Jon H. Roberts and James Turner, *The Sacred and the Secular University* (Princeton, NJ: Princeton University Press, 2000), 61–84.

[16]Walter Lippman summarized objections in "Education versus Western Civilization," *The American Scholar* 10 (Spring 1941): 184–93.

[17]John Brubacher, *Higher Education in Transition: A History of American Colleges and Universities, 1636–1976* (New York: Harper & Row, 1976), 362; Christopher J. Lucas, *American Higher Education: A History* (New York: St. Martin's Press, 1994), 189.

searching, many colleges established decades earlier in order to promote specifically Christian liberal arts education (Vanderbilt University, for example) recast their identity, either acknowledging changes that were already underway or deciding to face the future with different priorities.

These changes were part of a broad cultural transition. The specific conditions that shaped a burst of enthusiasm for Christian colleges had passed. More liberal Protestant theological assumptions that emerged in the early twentieth century contrasted sharply with those that commonly shaped Christian college identity in the nineteenth century, and curricular developments along with the rise of modern universities complicated an identity crisis.

But despite defections and realignments, Christian colleges did not disappear, and new Christian colleges arose in response to new circumstances. The national fervor that sustained Christian colleges in the Early Republic vanished. Evangelical colleges formed after 1875 tended not to share the millennial cultural hopes that buoyed early Christian educators. The Christian colleges established in the first flush of confidence about education and democracy, learning and faith, and nation and millennium inevitably changed along with the Protestant establishment. The need to rethink identity and mission proved salutary in the long run for institutions that resisted new trends: it promoted a clearer understanding of the purpose of Christian liberal arts education on its own terms, apart from Manifest Destiny, economic incentives, and directions in modern education, although it also diminished the sense of common purpose that once informally connected Protestant-founded schools. Changes in the twentieth century set the stage for negotiating the limits and possibilities of the Christian college in modern America.

For much of the nineteenth century, Christian liberal arts colleges and associated evangelical churches loomed large in Protestant hopes for a Christian America. In the next century, the concept of Protestant liberal arts colleges existed on the periphery rather than at the center. In the late twentieth century, new public awareness of evangelicals brought Christian liberal arts colleges into wider view, and the challenge of faithfulness in a post-Christian world drew Protestant educators into wider conversations with others committed to integrating faith and learning.

Even a brief overview of Christian liberal arts colleges suggests points to ponder. First, America's earliest colleges perpetuated Christian and classical models of education as old as Western universities. Standing within this tradition, Puritans insisted that Christ was the essential foundation for the liberal arts and for professional studies. As American Protestants looked West, they took on the enormous challenge of spreading Christian liberal arts colleges across the nation's vast expanse because they believed such colleges would form virtuous and democratic citizens capable of leading the nation toward a glorious future. The first American brand of the Christian liberal arts college embraced the Bible, affirmed the gospel, and anticipated America's role in ushering in the kingdom of God. Early Christian colleges promoted social justice, championed opportunities for women and other minorities, and engaged public issues—tasks that certainly remain relevant across generations in places where the gospel shapes both mind and heart. But Christian liberal arts education proved difficult to sustain, and in the late nineteenth century, several concerns combined to produce widespread change. These revolved broadly around finances and control, theology, and curriculum, issues that present perennial challenges.

After the Civil War, dissonant voices clamored for attention: biblical scholarship and scientific discoveries questioned the assumptions behind Christian liberal arts education. People attuned to the work of modern scientists and biblical scholars abandoned familiar ways of reading the Bible in favor of approaches to Christianity that accommodated modern science and theology. Accelerated immigration added millions of non-Protestants to the population. Among some conservative Protestants, premillennialism—a radically different view of the times, God's kingdom, and American destiny—displaced the quest for a Christian America. The widely shared assumptions about the Bible, Christian faith, and the United States that had energized the founding of Christian liberal arts colleges devolved into the rancor remembered as the Fundamentalist-Modernist controversy.

At the same time, influential educators enacted long-discussed curricular revisions that fundamentally put into practice new assumptions about truth and transformed colleges into modern universities. Under the strong hand of President Charles Eliot, Harvard paved the way, relinquishing the time-honored assumptions about learning that guided colleges across the country. One assertion after another in Eliot's widely circulated 1909 address "The Religion of the Future" illustrated implications of this distinguished Unitarian's views for historic Christian educational practice: "Religion is not a fixed but a fluent thing"; or, "The religion of the future will not be based on authority, either spiritual or temporal. The decline of reliance upon absolute authority is one of the most significant phenomena of the modern world."[18]

Pre–Civil War American Christian liberal arts colleges adopted goals that were at once private and public. In general, their promoters held certain assumptions about God, country, and destiny. When these assumptions faltered toward the end of the nineteenth century in response to enormous social and intellectual changes, the relevance of Christian liberal arts colleges to a new era came under review. Close ties to a particular public agenda complicated identity when the agenda no longer commanded loyalty. Economic challenges made attractive incentives that promoted efficiency at the expense of historic evangelical affirmations. Changes effected to secure funding over time effectively altered identity. Enthusiasm for new assertions about truth marginalized Christian liberal arts colleges.

The Common Sense Realism that undergirded nineteenth-century evangelical certainty met its match in the new learning: it was dismissed as old-fashioned and outmoded. In time even its apologists recognized the inadequacy of its guiding assumptions. Historian George Marsden pointed out the dire consequences: "Almost without warning . . . the place of biblical authority in American intellectual life was in a complete shambles."[19] The "new learning" and the new cultural consensus presented Christian liberal arts colleges with two stark choices: a separate path, or fresh engagement facilitated by a rigorous reflection on the meaning of integrating faith and learning for God's glory.

Unanticipated intellectual and cultural upheavals, then, set the stage for ongoing grappling with the purpose and possibilities of the Christian liberal arts college in modern America.

---

[18]Charles W. Eliot, *The Religion of the Future* (Boston: John Luce, 1909), 4, 8.
[19]George Marsden, "The Bible, Science, and Authority," in *The Bible in America*, ed. Nathan Hatch and Mark Noll (New York: Oxford University Press, 1982), 94.

THEOLOGICAL CONVICTIONS

This book is about a particular kind of college education: *Christian* liberal arts education. As we have seen, the long and noble tradition of liberal education began with the ancient Greeks and Romans. Yet for nearly two millennia, the Christian community has embraced this tradition as its own and developed it along biblical lines; in recent centuries the Christian tradition of liberal education has found a place in America and begun to spread to other places. What distinguishes Christian liberal arts education, of course, is its worldview. In this section we introduce some of the basic theological principles that comprise the Christian worldview; later on we will describe the skills that a liberal education develops, showing the difference that "thinking Christianly" makes to the study of particular arts and sciences as we integrate learning with faith.

A worldview is simply a way of looking at life—the structure of understanding that we use to make sense of our world. According to James Olthuis, it is "the set of hinges on which all our everyday thinking and doing turns."[1] To use a different analogy, worldviews are the spectacles through which we look at the universe. Or perhaps it is better to compare our worldview to our eyes themselves, because we see everything through our own lenses and interpret our experience accordingly.

Ideally, your worldview is a carefully reasoned framework of beliefs and convictions that gives a true and unified perspective on the meaning of existence. Unfortunately, many people take a view of the world that leaves God out of the picture entirely. For example, the Oxford professor and evolutionary biologist Richard Dawkins maintains that because there is no God, "there is at bottom no design, no purpose, no evil, no good—nothing but blind, pitiless indifference."[2] If Dawkins is right, and no ultimate meaning exists, then what is the purpose of a liberal educa-

---

[1] James Olthuis, "On Worldviews," in *Stained Glass: Worldviews and Social Science*, ed. Paul A. Marshall, Sander Griffioen, and Richard J. Mouw, Christian Studies Today (Landham, MD: University Press of America, 1989), 29.
[2] Richard Dawkins, *River Out of Eden: A Darwinian View of Life* (New York: HarperCollins, 1995), 133.

tion? Only what human beings are able to make of it for themselves: this represents a common humanistic response among secular thinkers who lack eternal hope. In the end, we are left with little more than the ancient dictum of Protagoras: "Man is the measure of all things." If there is no God, reasoned the French existentialist Jean-Paul Sartre, then "man is nothing else but that which he makes of himself."[3]

All of this stands in sharp contrast to the Christian intellectual tradition, which is grounded in the triune God—Father, Son, and Holy Spirit. The existence of the living God liberates us from all merely human worldviews by giving us a true perspective on everything. This is because God has more than a point of view: he has a complete view. As the Creator who made all things and the Savior who is redeeming all things through Jesus Christ, God is the ultimate frame of reference for all human thought and action. This leads the pastor-scholar John Piper to conclude that "all understandings of all things that leave him out are superficial understandings, since they leave out the most important reality in the universe."[4] But when we begin with God, taking "every thought captive to obey Christ" (2 Cor. 10:5), we have the proper starting point for seeing the world the way it really is.

A Christian worldview begins with God, but it does not end there. Happily, God has revealed his purposes in his Word—the Scriptures of the Old and New Testaments. There we discover vital truths: why God made the world in the first place, including the people he designed in his image (creation); what has gone wrong with the world because of human sin (the fall); how the world is being rescued through the incarnation, crucifixion, and resurrection of Jesus Christ (grace); and how God will make everything right in the end (glory). This fourfold structure to the story of salvation—creation, fall, grace, and glory—goes back at least as far as the great fourth-century African theologian Augustine. It helps us understand who we are—not simply molecules in motion, but the crown of creation. It also explains why things have turned out so badly in every area of human life, as well as what God intends to do about it.

[3]Jean-Paul Sartre, "Existentialism and Humanism," in *The Modern Tradition: Backgrounds of Modern Literature*, ed. Richard Ellmann and Charles Fiedelson Jr. (New York: Oxford University Press, 1965), 828.
[4]John Piper, *A God-Entranced Vision of All Things: The Legacy of Jonathan Edwards* (Wheaton, IL: Crossway, 2004), 24.

Best of all, this framework gives us hope for the restoration of all things in Jesus Christ.

As we shall see, each of these four doctrines has profound implications for the liberal arts and sciences. The doctrine of creation affirms the goodness of everything that God has made, opening up the scientific exploration of the universe and teaching us to see the world as something "charged with the grandeur of God," as the poet Gerard Manley Hopkins describes.[5] The truth that we are all made in God's image shows us that by God's common grace, we can appreciate and learn from the insight and artistry of non-Christians as well as from Christians. God's redemptive work in Christ enables the liberal arts to fulfill their purpose as the *liberating* arts, which, in spite of our sin, can free us to develop our intellectual and artistic gifts to their fullest potential. Indeed, it is only a God-grounded, Bible-based, Christ-centered view of the world that enables us to make best use of the liberal arts through the integration of our learning with our faith, to the glory of God.

---

[5]Gerard Manley Hopkins, "God's Grandeur," in *The Top 500 Poems*, ed. William Harmon (New York: Columbia University Press, 1992), 792.

CHAPTER FOUR

LIBERAL ARTS EDUCATION AND THE DOCTRINE OF HUMANITY

Roger Lundin

You stir man to take pleasure in praising you, because you have made us for yourself, and our heart is restless until it rests in you.
—AUGUSTINE, *CONFESSIONS*

As a deer pants for flowing streams,
    so pants my soul for you, O God.
My soul thirsts for God,
    for the living God.
—PSALM 42:1–2

"Midway in our life's journey," writes Dante Alighieri in the first sentence of *The Divine Comedy,* "I went astray / from the straight road and woke to find myself / alone in a dark wood."[1] In the opening lines of this classic work, the fourteenth-century Italian poet offers a sober assessment of the human condition, as he outlines the contours of a Christian doctrine of humanity. That he is able to do so in a little more than a hundred lines of poetry is as much a testimony to the clarity of his Christian view of human nature as it is a tribute to his skill as an artist. To be human, this great poem asserts, is to awaken and find yourself lost and lonely on the journey of life. To Dante as a poet and as a Christian, this sudden, stunning awareness marks the first step on a pilgrimage of repentance and renewal intended to lead the sinner back to God.

In beginning its account of experience *in medias res*—"in the middle of things"—Dante's *Comedy* follows a pattern adopted by writers of epics since the time of Homer. The abrupt entry into the middle of a life

---

[1]Dante, *Inferno*, trans. John Ciardi (New York: Modern Library, 1996), 3.

story—"Midway in our life's journey, I went astray"—serves two crucial purposes. First, in introducing us to a situation marked by turmoil and discord, it speaks to our sense that our lives are somehow not as they should be but fall short of the ideal. In turn, that sense of failure and incompleteness prompts a series of questions: How did this man, or how did all of us, get into such a predicament? Is it possible for things to be made right? If we are lost, how can we find our way back to the right path?

It is pertinent to ask these questions about the stories we read but even more important to pose them to the lives we lead. The Christian faith offers vigorous responses to such questions, and in this chapter we will see how a doctrine of humanity might inform a Christian liberal arts education. We will begin by looking at what the Bible and the Christian tradition have to say about human nature. We will then turn to the question of human destiny, and our thinking will be guided by Augustine's claim that our hearts are restless until they find their rest in God.

CREATION, FALL, AND THE KNOWLEDGE OF GOD

On the question of human nature, two scriptural passages provide a remarkably concise summary of the biblical view. The first comes from the opening chapter of Genesis, in which we hear that on the sixth day, "God created man in his own image, . . . God saw everything that he had made, and behold, it was very good" (Gen. 1:27a, 31). The second is found in the apostle Paul's description of the law and its relationship to grace: "For there is no distinction: for all have sinned and fall short of the glory of God" (Rom. 3:22b–23).

The passage in Genesis declares that all things in creation, including human beings, stand distinct from God as realities that bear the marks of his handiwork. In a number of religious traditions, and in Christian heresies such as Gnosticism, the material world is seen as the inferior creation of a lesser god, but the Bible spurns such claims, and so has the church throughout its history. The Old and New Testaments declare human life to be the gift of a gracious God, and they see the mystery, beauty, and order of the world as testimony to God's glory. "The heavens declare the glory of God," the psalmist writes, "and the sky above proclaims his handiwork" (Ps. 19:1).

What the heavens declare and the sky proclaims, says John Calvin, our hearts also confirm. Because we are made in God's image, we long to learn of his world and hunger to know him and rest in him. In the first sentence of his *Institutes of the Christian Religion*, Calvin sketches a Christian view of humanity and knowledge: "Nearly all the wisdom we possess, that is to say, true and sound wisdom, consists of two parts: the knowledge of God and of ourselves." Like Dante before him, Calvin concludes that our knowledge of ourselves may lead us at last to God, for it "not only arouses us to seek God, but also, as it were, leads us by the hand to find him."[2]

Calvin and the psalmist raise the question of what we might learn of God's truth through the study of nature, history, and human experience, which serve as the subject matter, after all, of a liberal arts education. Christian views of human ability to discover the truth have varied significantly over the centuries. In the main, however, the church has affirmed that what we learn through such study may be sufficient to meet our ordinary needs but remains powerless to reconcile us to God. For that, we require another type of knowledge, which is revealed to us through the witness of God's Word to the crucified and risen Christ.

To ground its confidence in our capacity to discover truth through the study of God's world, the church through the ages has turned repeatedly to the opening verses of John's Gospel: "In the beginning was the Word, and the Word was with God, and the Word was God. He was in the beginning with God. All things were made through him, and without him was not any thing made that was made" (John 1:1–3). Through Jesus Christ, the whole of creation came into being, and that creation bears witness to God and to the beauty and order at the heart of things. "Look at the structure of the universe," Augustine says in a meditation on these verses. Although our studies of the heavens, the earth, and our own hearts and histories cannot in themselves discover the truth of the gospel, they may point us to the power and majesty of the One who is revealed there: "See what was made by the Word and then you will recognize what the nature of the Word is."[3]

---

[2]John Calvin, *Institutes of the Christian Religion*, ed. John T. McNeill, trans. Ford Lewis Battles (Philadelphia: Westminster, 1960), 1:35, 37.
[3]Augustine, *Tractates on the Gospel of John, 1–10*, trans. John W. Rettig (Washington, DC: Catholic University of America Press, 1988), 49.

NATURE AND GRACE

Dante grounded his trust in life's meaningfulness in a complex under-standing of the dynamic interplay of nature and grace. Medieval Christianity taught—and modern Catholicism continues to teach—that through a study of the natural world, the social order, and the structures of the human mind, we may learn substantial truths about God's pur-poses for our lives. This knowledge is only partial, but it is in harmony with what God reveals to us in Jesus Christ. "The unity of truth is a fundamental premise of human reasoning," explains Pope John Paul II. "It is the one and the same God who establishes and guarantees the intel-ligibility and reasonableness of the natural order of things upon which scientists confidently depend, and who reveals himself as the Father of our Lord Jesus Christ."[4]

According to this line of thought, we till the field of nature in order to prepare the ground for the growth of grace. In *The Divine Comedy,* for example, the Latin poet Virgil represents the pinnacle of human reason and stands as the best that a human being might become through the use of his natural powers. As Dante's guide, Virgil is able to lead the poet into the depths of hell and on the ascent through purgatory, but when they reach the peak of Mount Purgatory, he must transfer Dante to the care of Beatrice. Only she, who serves as the bearer of grace and the messenger of revelation, has the capacity to guide the penitent sinner through paradise. Beatrice thus completes the journey that Virgil had begun. As both pilgrim and poet, Dante "knew . . . that the peculiar effect of grace is not to vindicate nature or to suppress it, but to perfect it."[5] To the Catholic poet, grace may need to correct, adjust, and supple-ment the work of nature, but the most important point is that it works in concert with nature rather than in opposition to it.

In contrast to the medieval view of grace perfecting nature, many Protestants have embraced an equally sweeping but less intricately structured doctrine, that of *common grace*, to describe what can be known of God independent of revelation. This doctrine holds that in the wonders of nature and through the workings of conscience, God reveals

[4]John Paul II, *Fides et Ratio: On the Relationship between Faith and Reason* (Washington, DC: USCCB, 1998), 51–52.
[5]Etienne Gilson, *Dante and Philosophy*, trans. David Moore (New York: Harper, 1963), 187.

truth in some measure to all human beings. Advocates of common grace argue that throughout history the church has searched for those points at which it can make common cause with philosophy, the arts, and the sciences. Although sin has skewed the world and clouded our judgment, we are still able to discover "a continued revelation through nature and the reason, in heart and conscience, . . . an illumination of the Logos, a speech from the wisdom of God through the hidden working of grace."[6]

Both the Catholic view of nature and the Protestant doctrine of common grace give Christians a warrant to explore boldly and fearlessly the workings of the natural world and the works of human culture. A Christian liberal arts education builds upon a foundational trust in a God who endows his creation with order and purpose and who gives us the capacity to learn of those ordered purposes through the study of what God and his creatures have made.

STRIKING THE UNEVEN BALANCE

At this point, a word of caution is in order. Despite the many positive things a Christian doctrine of creation and common grace may imply about our capacity to know as well as our ability to create, the reality of sin remains. Even as the grace of God undergirds creation and culture, so does the waywardness of sin work to undermine them. Whether we dwell within the church or live beyond its walls, all of us are lost in our sins, and each of us wanders "alone in a dark wood."

In our state of darkness and confusion, we need illumination of the kind the doctrine of original sin can provide. This doctrine teaches that from the first parents of the human race down to us, the children of today, all human beings have sinned and fallen short of God's glory. That news is hard to hear, but it has a clarifying power. In the mid-twentieth century, American theologian Reinhold Niebuhr cited approvingly the judgment that "the doctrine of original sin is the only empirically verifiable doctrine of the Christian faith."[7] Whatever their view of God may have been, many great writers over the centuries would no doubt have agreed with this conclusion.

---

[6]Herman Bavinck, "Calvin and Common Grace," in *Calvin and the Reformation: Four Studies*, ed. William Park Armstrong (New York: Revell, 1909), 103.
[7]Reinhold Niebuhr, *Man's Nature and His Communities: Essays on the Dynamics and Enigmas of Man's Personal and Social Existence* (New York: Scribner, 1965), 24.

There are profound points of contact, for example, between the doctrine of original sin and the central insights of tragedy. One case, that of Shakespeare's *King Lear*, shows this relationship with particular clarity. At the midpoint of the play, the aged king is staggering across the fields of England at night, exposed to the fury of a violent storm. Having been abandoned by two of his daughters, the king and father must confront his own pride and folly. He has banished the daughter who loves him, Cordelia, and the daughters he has trusted, Goneril and Regan, have betrayed him and left him to find his way in the wind and the rain and the darkness.

In his anguished madness, Lear puts Goneril and Regan on trial in a mock proceeding on the heath. As he "interrogates" the absent Regan, he cries out, "Is there any cause in nature that makes these hard hearts?" Lear's question is not answered until the end of the following act, when Cordelia returns in an effort to save him. As Lear awakens, he tells her,

> I know you do not love me; for your sisters
> Have (as I do remember) done me wrong.
> You have some cause, they have not. (Act 4. Scene 7. Lines 73–75)

To this confessional plea, Cordelia can only respond, "No cause, no cause." Just as there has been "no cause" that has compelled her sisters to treat their father so cruelly, so too is there no cause that makes Cordelia love him. Evil and love alike are deep mysteries anchored in the unfathomable freedom and folly of the human heart.[8]

Through its view of sin, a Christian doctrine of humanity provides a potent tool for the analysis of human action and culture that takes place throughout a liberal arts education. Herman Melville spoke bluntly of this power in an 1850 review of a collection of short stories by Nathaniel Hawthorne. As he seeks to account for Hawthorne's exceptional powers of character depiction, Melville concludes they derive their force from an appeal "to that Calvinistic sense of Innate Depravity and Original Sin, from whose visitations, in some shape or other, no deeply thinking mind is always and wholly free." With its sober assessment of human nature, Christianity offers exceptional resources to anyone seeking to take the measure of the human condition. "For, in certain moods,"

---

[8]William Shakespeare, *King Lear*, ed. Alfred Harbage (New York: Penguin, 1970), 110, 146–47.

Melville concludes, "no man can weigh this world, without throwing in something, somehow like Original Sin, to strike the uneven balance."[9]

THE ENDS OF LIFE

The doctrines of creation and original sin speak to the origins of human nature, but what about the purpose and meaning of human life? What relevance does the question of the meaning or goal of human life have for a Christian liberal arts education? And in personal terms, what does God intend for me to make of the life he has so generously given to me?

While other chapters discuss the doctrine of redemption, our interest here is focused on what we know of human nature and human destiny in the contexts of social life and personal development. We are concentrating, that is, less on what theologians call *eschatology*, the doctrine of last things (death, judgment, eternal life), and more on *teleology*, or the study of the ends for which God created human beings and toward which he intends them to strive.

Teleological thinking reached its peak in the Middle Ages. Under the considerable influence of Aristotle, figures such as Thomas Aquinas and Dante developed a complex philosophy of the human subject. Their view held that God plants within each human being seeds of development that can flower, with proper care, into the full bloom God has in mind for every human life. To be human is to possess both a given nature—essentially good but flawed and fallen—and a potential destiny, which encompasses the virtuous ends God means for us to pursue. For medieval Christianity, "there is thus a purposeful order to the processes of nature in a well-ordered cosmos made intelligible by the Unmoved Mover and permeated by a love that the most Christian of poets, Dante, was to interpret as the 'Love that moves the Sun and the Stars.'"[10]

Medieval teleology developed an elaborate hierarchy of goals and capacities meant to situate the myriad facets of personal development that it sought to foster. This system found its perfect embodiment in the intricate architectural structure of *The Divine Comedy*. Protestant teleology seems stark and simple in contrast. Compare, for example, the levels in Dante's hundred-canto *Comedy* with the first question and answer

[9]Herman Melville, *The Complete Shorter Fiction* (New York: Knopf, 1997), 238.
[10]Seyyed Hossein Nasr, *Religion and the Order of Nature* (New York: Oxford University Press, 1996), 88.

of the Westminster Shorter Catechism (1647): "*Question. 1. What is the chief end of man? Answer*: Man's chief end is to glorify God, and to enjoy him forever."

In its brevity, Westminster's definition of the "chief end of man" has the ring of Augustine's declaration in the *Confessions*: "You have made us for yourself, and our heart is restless until it rests in you."[11] Augustine envisions a common goal for all human lives, but countless different roads within Christian experience may lead to it. Unlike the teleology of medieval Christianity, the Augustinian concept of the *end* of human striving implies nothing hierarchical about the structures of personal and social life, nor does it delineate any specific distinctions among the human virtues. For Augustine, it is enough to say that human beings are restlessly destined for God and generously open, in their service to God and others, to a host of possibilities and practices in their lives.

The open-ended quality of Protestant teleology proved well suited for the cultural environment of the early modern world. New views of individual liberty and self-definition were burgeoning in that era, and as it leveled the hierarchical orders of medieval Christianity, the Reformation began to place an unprecedented emphasis upon self-formation and exploration. The closing lines of John Milton's *Paradise Lost* (1667) give us a striking sense of the bittersweet possibilities of these new freedoms. Having sinned and having been judged by God, Adam and Eve wend their way out of the garden of Eden. Their journey will plunge them into loneliness and sorrow but also lead them through freedom to hope:

> They looking back, all th'Eastern side beheld
> Of Paradise, so late their happy seat,
> Wav'd over by that flaming Brand, the Gate
> With dreadful Faces throng'd and fiery Arms;
> Some natural tears they dropp'd, but wip'd them soon;
> The World was all before them, where to choose
> Their place of rest, and Providence their guide:
> They hand in hand with wand'ring steps and slow
> Through Eden took their solitary way.[12]

---

[11]Augustine, *Confessions*, trans. Henry Chadwick (Oxford: Oxford University Press, 1991), 3.

[12]John Milton, *Paradise Lost and Paradise Regained*, ed. Christopher Ricks (New York: New American Library, 1968), bk. 12, lines 641–49.

HUMAN NATURE AND THE LIBERAL ARTS

Christianity's balanced doctrine of humanity offers fruitful resources for the Christian student of the liberal arts. Its nuanced understanding of sin provides a compelling interpretive key to the conflicted course of human history. It shines light upon the darkened reality of individual and corporate evil, and as Shakespeare and Melville attest, it can strike the uneven balance for the student seeking to weigh the world of human action.

At the same time, a Christian doctrine of humanity testifies to the power of truth to shine forth in all manner of persons and places, cultures and ages. For two thousand years, we Christians have affirmed both our belief in the Word through whom all things came to be and our confidence in our God-given capacity to discern the truth wherever we come upon it.

Yet our capacities here are limited by the fact that we are finite and fallen. In our sinful state, we require the gift of grace and the miracle of revelation to complete our knowledge of ourselves and of God. The doctrines of redemption and reconciliation speak most fully to this facet of God's work and truth, yet a Christian view of humanity also has much to contribute to our understanding on this front.

This is especially the case with the history of the church's reflection on the questions of the ends for which God has created human beings. Both the hierarchical world of Catholicism and the vistas of modern Protestantism draw upon Augustine's insight that we as human beings remain disturbingly unsettled until we reach and rest in God.

A Christian liberal arts education is particularly well equipped to address the sense of excitement and anxiety that marks the modern search for identity. If our true end is to glorify God and enjoy him forever, we are free to travel many different paths to that goal. Yet especially as we prepare to enter adulthood, the prospect of our journey down those open roads can seem daunting. Faced with a bewildering abundance of options for our lives, we need, now more than ever, clear perspectives to guide us on our pilgrimage. To that end, a Christian liberal arts education grounds us in the truths of the Christian faith even as it orients us to the world that lies all before us. As our restless hearts make their way through the world, such an education can illuminate the darkness and point us to the end, which is—and who is—Jesus Christ.

CHAPTER FIVE

FAITHFUL CHRISTIAN LEARNING

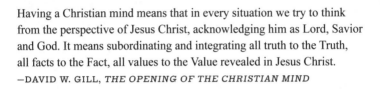

Jeffrey P. Greenman

Having a Christian mind means that in every situation we try to think
from the perspective of Jesus Christ, acknowledging him as Lord, Savior
and God. It means subordinating and integrating all truth to the Truth,
all facts to the Fact, all values to the Value revealed in Jesus Christ.
—DAVID W. GILL, *THE OPENING OF THE CHRISTIAN MIND*

You shall love the Lord your God with all your heart and with all your soul and
with all your strength and with all your mind, and your neighbor as yourself.
—LUKE 10:27

I was raised by churchgoing parents in the Episcopal Church. As an
infant, I was baptized, and soon after I howled loudly in protest about
being left in the church nursery. I still have my perfect attendance pin
(three years straight!) from Sunday school. I was confirmed at age
twelve. Throughout high school, I attended church consistently with my
parents. I never rebelled against them, the church, or God.

My family could be called "observant Christians." Ours was more
than a nominal faith. We attended worship, participated in church programs, and helped out with various ministries. Christianity was an
important part of our lives. Christian faith prompted us to say grace
before meals, encouraged us to be upright and compassionate people,
and prompted an attitude of service toward others. I am immensely
grateful for my family's valuable religious heritage.

After high school I attended a small, church-related liberal arts college in the Midwest. I admired the liberal arts ideal of a well-rounded
education that wrestles with life's big questions, pursues learning for its
own sake, and fosters an ability to think critically. During my undergraduate days I had friends whose Christian faith was central and pervasive

to them in ways that were unfamiliar to me. As I got to know them, I came to see that their faith guided their whole way of life, not just the spiritual aspects of life. They talked about how a desire to follow Jesus was motivating them in their choices. They described the importance of prayer for major decisions. They had a focus for their lives and unusual resiliency. I was impressed and puzzled by these people. They had a more personal experience of Christianity than I did. What was I missing? I became a seeker after God, or at least after something deeper in Christian faith than I'd experienced before.

In this spiritual condition I began my graduate studies at Oxford University. A few weeks later I heard a sermon proclaiming, in simple and straightforward terms, that Jesus was alive. The preacher explained that being a Christian meant having a personal faith in Jesus Christ as Lord and Savior. I joined in a prayer of commitment to Christ, asking forgiveness for my sins. Right after the service, I signed up to participate in a small group of people who had professed faith in Christ that morning. I had never been part of such a thing. It was remarkably formative in deepening my new faith. There I began to pray and to read the Bible for myself for the first time.

The next week, I joined a discussion group offered by the church called "Christians in Philosophy." The group aimed to help students pursuing a degree in philosophy to approach their studies in ways that were consistent with Christian faith. It sounded intriguing. The basic question was, "What does our faith in Jesus have to do with what we are studying?" I had no idea where to begin. Our group started out by discussing a book by Harry Blamires, *The Christian Mind*. It was the first "Christian" book I had ever read. I still return to it often. Very few books I have encountered since have made such a profound impact on my life. In my view, it is a modern classic that every Christian college student could benefit from reading.

The book begins with a stinging critique of Christians who have forsaken their minds to subtle but powerful influences. Blamires claims,

> As a *thinking* being, the modern Christian has succumbed to secularization. He accepts religion—its morality, its worship, its spiritual culture, but he rejects the religious view of life, the view which sets all earthly

issues within the context of the eternal, the view which relates all human problems—social, political, cultural—to the doctrinal foundations of the Christian Faith, the view which sees all things here below in terms of God's supremacy and earth's transitoriness, in terms of Heaven and Hell.[1]

Quickly I realized that Blamires was talking about me. My churchgoing upbringing had hardly begun to shape my intellectual development or my mental habits. I had learned the doctrinal foundations of Christianity in my confirmation class, but no one had ever suggested that Christian beliefs had anything to do with social, political, or cultural matters. Reading Blamires proved to be a personal turning point in reorienting my goals and purposes as a student. Looking back, I realize that my story of growing into a more deeply Christian way of engaging in academic study, and of embracing the value of liberal arts education, can offer Christian college students today a vision for an integrated spiritual-intellectual experience of faithful Christian learning.

THINKING IN THE LIGHT OF FAITH

Blamires defines the Christian mind as "a mind trained, informed, and equipped to handle data of secular controversy within a frame of reference that is constructed of Christian presuppositions. The Christian mind is the prerequisite of Christian thinking. And Christian thinking is the prerequisite of Christian action."[2] The Christian mind is contrasted with a secular mind, whose frame of reference is "bounded by the limits of our life on earth; it is to keep one's calculations rooted in this-worldly criteria."[3]

According to Blamires, Christians too often operate with the same mental outlook and categories as non-Christians. The problem is that Christians may behave or pray or worship Christianly but, for example, when we "talk politics with the politician" or "social welfare with the social worker," usually we have "emptied our brains of Christian vocabulary [and] Christian concepts" and "thus we have stepped mentally into secularism."[4] In particular, Blamires laments that Christians discuss issues of public life with the same pragmatic and utilitarian approaches

---

[1]Harry Blamires, *The Christian Mind* (London: SPCK, 1963), 3; emphasis original.
[2]Ibid., 43.
[3]Ibid., 44.
[4]Ibid., 38–39.

that dominate secular thinking. His point is that secular studies of any topic can be valuable, but they will not be sufficient.

In contrast, Blamires calls for thinking in a Christ-centered way about every area of life: "There is nothing in our experience, however trivial, worldly or even evil, which cannot be thought about christianly."[5] This undertaking involves much more than merely "secular thinking trimmed with pious platitudes."[6] Blamires advocates an undertaking that is far more demanding than simply adorning fundamentally secular thinking with a few decorative Bible verses. It goes beyond sorting out a cohesive set of theological doctrines (difficult as they might be). It means putting those beliefs to work, thinking through their implications for every dimension of our lives.

Putting the case positively, Blamires calls for "flooding" any and every topic of inquiry with "distinct and distinctive light" that comes from Christian convictions. According to his approach, those basic yet remarkably powerful theological convictions include the following:

- a "supernatural" and eternal orientation;
- "an acute and sensitive awareness of the power and spread of evil upon the human scene";
- the notion of "divine revelation as the final touchstone of truth";
- a submission to God and acceptance of the "authority of his revelation, his commandments, and his Church";
- a concern for the human person and the "sacredness of human personality";
- and, a "sacramental cast" that affirms "life's positive richnesses as derived from the supernatural."[7]

After reading Blamires, our discussion group turned to some writings by C. S. Lewis. There I found a similar insight, for which Blamires had prepared me. Lewis wrote: "I believe in Christianity as I believe the sun has risen. Not only because I see it, but because by it I see everything else."[8] The notion that the truth of Christianity could enable

---

[5]Ibid., 45.
[6]Ibid., 41.
[7]Ibid., 67, 86, 107, 136, 156, 173.
[8]C. S. Lewis, "Is Theology Poetry?" in *The Weight of Glory and Other Addresses* (New York: HarperCollins, 1980), 140.

someone to consider literally anything and everything from a distinctive standpoint was completely new to me.

What I learned from Blamires was that Christianity is much bigger and more radical than I had realized. Christian faith is not confined to Sunday observances or even affirming right beliefs about God. Nor is it simply about recognizing the overtly spiritual aspects of life or about being a good person. Rightly understood, *every* aspect of life is spiritual. My compartmentalized, Sunday-oriented faith quickly became overturned. Everything now belonged to God. My conversion meant turning everything I had done, was doing, and wanted to do in the direction of Christ. Faith is to be at the center of our lives, giving focus and direction to everything we do. I remember discovering for the first time the apostle Paul's words in 2 Corinthians 5:15—words which were revolutionary and remarkably liberating for me—that the purpose of Christ's saving action was "that those who live might no longer live for themselves but for him who for their sake died and was raised."

LOVING GOD WITH OUR MINDS

Living for Christ, not simply for oneself, is a radical message. I learned that Christian faith involves both eternal salvation *and* an active (and potentially costly) allegiance to Christ in everyday life. The two are inseparable. It means accepting the call to give ourselves fully and unreservedly to God and to enlist in his service and to walk in his ways. Before my conversion, I had considered my academic career as all about me, earning high grades and winning academic awards. Now I was asking how my studies could be turned toward living for Christ and serving him.

What propelled me forward in grasping these challenges was reckoning with the Great Commandment. Jesus teaches, "You shall love the Lord your God with all your heart and with all your soul and with all your strength and with all your mind, and your neighbor as yourself" (Luke 10:27). Surely I had heard that verse sometime in my churchgoing youth, but, if so, its significance never registered with me. Now I saw that it was utterly fundamental to Jesus's message about discipleship. Christians are meant to love God supremely: thoroughly, not partially; actively, not passively; intentionally, not accidentally; and consistently, not sporadically. One commentator on this verse writes, "God's claim on us reaches to every area of our experience, to our innermost being (heart); our lives—what gives us our individual identity (soul); our energy, strength, resolve and resources (might); and our understanding and intellectual capacities (mind). No part of ourselves is to be withheld from God."[9]

Moreover, the commandment teaches that loving God is not at odds with loving our neighbors. Discipleship does not demand that we disregard the needs of others, or retreat from the world, or concern ourselves only with fellow believers. In fact, if we are to love our neighbors wisely and well, we must first love God, who is to be placed first in our priorities. Nor is loving God solely a matter of pious sentiment, simply cultivating holy feelings as if what we do with our minds does not matter to God. Here Blamires's point that Christian thinking is a prerequisite for Christian action should remind us that we cannot love our neighbors with our "strength," through appropriate service and ministry, without using the insight and wisdom that comes from loving God with our minds.

THINKING CHRISTIANLY ABOUT THE LIBERAL ARTS

All disciples are called to love God with their minds. Consequently, authentic discipleship is never anti-intellectual. The need for ongoing Christian learning is a direct implication of faith. Although it is not widely enough recognized, the challenge of cultivating a mature ability to think Christianly about every area of reality belongs to the entire church. It applies to all Christians, no matter what we do with the bulk of our time during the week.

These insights enabled me to see that the Great Commandment provides a compelling rationale for Christians to undertake liberal arts education. The liberal arts tradition at its best endorses the intellectual and moral formation of the whole person, seeking to prepare men and women with the knowledge, character, and skills to become responsible citizens and public leaders in all walks of life. If we consider from a biblical standpoint such a way of conceiving the liberal arts, it is clear that Christian liberal arts offers a profound expression of its transformative

---

[9]R. Alan Culpepper, *The Gospel of Luke*, The New Interpreter's Bible, vol. 9 (Nashville: Abingdon Press, 1995), 227.

ideal and its overarching purpose. Loving God with heart, mind, and strength expresses the Bible's most thoroughly holistic concept, and loving our neighbors as ourselves expresses the Bible's most comprehensive vision for service in God's world.

Therefore, the Christian liberal arts are for the sake of love—learning to grow into the most comprehensive love of God and to be equipped for the most comprehensive love of our neighbors. Accordingly, the entire breadth of academic learning in the humanities, arts, social sciences, and natural sciences opens up as the Christian's context for learning to cultivate a Christian mind, thinking Christianly about God, his world, and his creatures so that we might honor, serve, and glorify God in word and deed.

Loving God with our minds entails learning from God's "two books," the Book of Scripture and the Book of Nature. The foundation of the entire Christian liberal arts enterprise is becoming biblically rooted in our ways of thinking and theologically formed to grasp the implications of our beliefs for every dimension of life. Learning from the Book of Nature, Christians discover God the Creator's work through astronomy's study of the starry heavens above and through geology's study of the shifting tectonic plates below. We gain insights into God's creatures through sociology's analysis of urbanization, through history's narration of the rise and fall of the Roman Empire, and through theater's depiction of varied human experience in all its richness and complexity. To love God fully, we need to understand God and his creation; to love and serve our neighbors, we must understand them in diverse ways—socially, politically, economically, linguistically, culturally, historically, and artistically.

The value of a Christian mind cultivated through liberal arts education becomes acutely important once we recognize that the vitality and effectiveness of the church's mission in the world depends upon the whole people of God becoming representatives of Christ in every sphere of society. Christians are not merely to be morally upright people or productive citizens of an earthly society, but God's representatives wherever they live and work—the citizens of an eternal kingdom. The church's mission belongs to every Christian, right where we are, not simply to specialist "full-time missionaries." The apostle Paul writes,

"Whatever you do, whether in word or deed, do it all in the name of the Lord Jesus, giving thanks to God the Father through him" (Col. 3:17 NIV). To do something in the "name of Jesus" means doing it on his behalf, as his commissioned agent or personal representative. Acting in "the name of Jesus" requires thinking with the mind of Christ through the particular complexities of each situation of action and decision that we face, whether our daily tasks involve starting a new business, teaching first-graders to read, or serving as an elected official. Theologian Georgia Harkness contends that in doing so "it is the business of the Church to hold every proposed line of action up to Christian scrutiny—to throw the searchlight of the gospel upon every issue which affects the lives and destinies of persons in God's world."[10] Christian liberal arts education affords the opportunity to be well prepared with the faith-informed knowledge and disciplined habits of mind necessary to take up Blamires's challenge to "flood" any and every topic of inquiry with the "distinct and distinctive light" that comes from Christian convictions.

Thinking Christianly is not an optional nicety relegated to bookish followers of Christ; it is essential to the missionary vocation of each Christian and to the church's credibility in public life. Thus understood, it would falsely limit the scope of the command to love God with our minds if we applied it primarily or exclusively to those whose daily work involves chiefly intellectual labor. But it does apply in a particularly acute way to students and professors whose particular vocations require focused and sustained study. I propose that such people pursue what I call "faithful Christian learning" as the particular fulfillment of our general calling to love God with our minds. Students should seek to be faithful to Christ in their specific courses of learning in order to be faithful to Christ over the entire course of a lifetime.

Christian students are invited to see all their studies, in whatever academic fields may best match their gifts and interests, as an expression of personal allegiance to Christ. The apostle Paul speaks to every student's deepest motivation when he says, "Whatever you do, work at it with all your heart, as working for the Lord, not for human masters" (Col. 3:23 NIV). Education becomes a context for exercising faith as a form of reliance

---

[10]Georgia Harkness, *The Church and Its Laity* (Nashville: Abingdon, 1962), 132.

upon God's grace to be sufficient for our intellectual as well as our personal needs. We should consider ourselves ready for every challenge that comes with genuine academic inquiry since we can stand firm on the presupposition that Christian faith provides a compelling, unrivalled account of the truth in a wide-ranging frame of reference that applies to all of reality. Holding these factors together enables our studies to become genuinely Christian learning—learning undertaken as an intentionally spiritual pursuit, motivated by a desire to grow in the love of God, grounded in God's truth, and aimed at being equipped for faithful service to Christ as a representative of his kingdom, wherever his calling might lead.

Faithful Christian learning, so defined, can give meaning and focus to one's college years. It is not something achieved conclusively during a few precious college years, but it can be accelerated dramatically when those years are well spent. However, faithful Christian learning really is a lifelong challenge. We will always have more to learn about God, about his written word in Scripture, and about the ever-changing natural and cultural worlds around us. Developing faith-informed thinking is a gradual process requiring patience and persistence. It is best undertaken in the company of wise mentors within the fellowship of the praying and witnessing church. And it is crucial to remember that loving God with all of our capacities—heart, soul, strength, and mind— does not allow us to focus on intellectual development to the neglect of all else or to elevate intellectual achievement to the most important aspect of Christian faith. Your college years will be spent most valuably through engagement, both inside and outside the classroom, which simultaneously attunes your inner life through prayer and worship, orients your life concerns and passions toward God, and develops practical skills through experiential learning in active service to your neighbors.

The journey into faithful Christian learning in a liberal arts context involves the daring venture of whole-life discipleship in response to the Great Commandment. Whether at the beginning, middle, or end of this journey, it is appropriate to meditate on and pray the words of Frances Havergal's famous hymn: "Take my life, and let it be consecrated, Lord, to Thee. . . . Take my intellect, and use every power as Thou shalt choose."

CHAPTER SIX

LIBERAL ARTS AS A REDEMPTIVE ENTERPRISE

Wayne Martindale

The end then of learning is to repair the ruins of our first parents by regaining to know God aright, and out of that knowledge to love him, to imitate him, to be like him . . . by possessing our souls of true virtue, which being united to the heavenly grace of faith make up the highest perfection.
—JOHN MILTON, *OF EDUCATION*

The first man was from the earth, a man of dust; the second man is from heaven. . . . Just as we have borne the image of the man of dust, we shall also bear the image of the man of heaven.
—1 CORINTHIANS 15:47–49

While Hitler's military machine was crushing its neighbors and the fate of Great Britain and the world was an open question, C. S. Lewis's Oxford students wanted to know if and how they could justify going to college instead of to war. Was taking time for study a moral option when former collegians were falling daily? Lewis raised the bar by pushing the question further. For Christians who know that each person advances daily to the moment of judgment, determining an eternal destiny of heaven or hell, how can we consider spending even a single peace-time hour "on such comparative trivialities as literature or art, mathematics or biology?"[1]

For the Christ-following student who has never asked this question, it is high time to put it on the table, for, at any given moment, the answer may well be to stop what you are doing in order to proclaim the gospel explicitly in word and deed—in a particular situation or perhaps as a life calling. For the serious disciple, spreading the good news

---

[1] C. S. Lewis, "Learning in War-Time," in *The Weight of Glory and Other Addresses* (New York: HarperCollins, 2001), 49.

should be a given. Nevertheless, the question remains: Can we read, write, and think to the glory of God, and, if so, how can our study of various disciplines at a liberal arts college advance the good news of Jesus Christ? As Scripture shows and the examples of Milton, Lewis, and Paul illustrate, we must prepare ourselves for God's service by rigorous discipline of spirit, mind, and body precisely because we care about souls.

THE LIBERAL ARTS AND ORIGINAL SIN

Paradise has been lost; the world is in ruins, and we are all "bad to the bone." Though many have tried to make heaven on earth, all have failed. The doctrine of original sin is no mere theological opinion. From Adam and Eve's disobedience onward, humanity has always wanted to captain its own destiny. History abounds with examples, whether Rousseau's cultivation of innate human goodness in the education of Emile, or the Communist Revolution's promise of a classless society in Russia, or the Nazi Party's propaganda in support of a pure Aryan race. All of these operated on the premise that it was possible to alter society toward perfection by humanly directed means.

But the myth of utopian progress is a powerful lie. Bitter disillusionment and horror has been the common fate of every utopian program. Nor will studying the best of the world's human accomplishments in the arts and sciences make us ultimately good. France's philosophers on individual rights did not stop the guillotine; Russia's great literary writers on the human spirit did not stop the Gulag; and Germany's great musicians did not stop the concentration camps. We must not look to another ethical and cultural makeover by strictly human means, as T. S. Eliot cautions:

> Any machinery, however beautiful to look at and however wonderful a product of brains and skill, can be used for bad purposes as well as good: and this is as true of social machinery as of constructions of steel. I think that, more important than the invention of a new machine, is the creation of a temper of mind in people such that they can learn to use a new machine rightly. . . . We cannot be satisfied to be Christians at our devotions and merely secular reformers all the rest of the week, for there is one question that we need to ask ourselves every day and about

whatever business. The Church has perpetually to answer this question: to what purpose were we born? What is the end of Man?[2]

Similarly, this point is starkly made in Lewis's "Christianity and Culture": "The Christian knows from the outset that the salvation of a single soul is more important than the production or preservation of all the epics and tragedies in the world."[3] The salvation of souls is "the real business of life" and our only means of "glorifying God because only saved souls can duly glorify Him."[4] At first blush, this might seem anti-intellectual, but most assuredly it is not.

CHRIST THE ONLY FOUNDATION

We cannot fix the world on our own, but God certainly can and will create a new heaven and a new earth without our help or hindrance.[5] In the meantime, we are not to sit on our thumbs. Sloth is one of the deadly sins. When God put Adam and Eve in the garden of Eden, he set them to work with both brain and brawn. They tended the garden, named and ruled the animals, and worshiped God. The creation mandate to steward the gifts of God has not lapsed. In God's design, the choices of this life and our "Christian walk" reverberate and redouble down the generations and throughout eternity. "We are his workmanship, created in Christ Jesus for good works, which God prepared beforehand, that we should walk in them" (Eph. 2:10).

How, then, can the study of liberal arts be a redemptive enterprise? Where did the human aspiration for the good, the true, and the beautiful come from? As Genesis proclaims, and Augustine explains, God created all things good, including reason, imagination, and emotion, along with our physical bodies. The natural world also reflects the mark of the Maker. God, our good, true, and beautiful creator, has placed a longing for himself and his attributes in each one of us. Yet, in this fallen world we must always choose to live for him or for something else. All of God's gifts to us, including education, may be used for good or evil. But for the mind given over to Christ, wonder and the occasion for worship

---

[2]T. S. Eliot, *Christianity and Culture* (New York: Harcourt Brace Jovanovich, 1977), 77.
[3]C. S. Lewis, "Christianity and Culture," in *Christian Reflections* (Grand Rapids, MI: Eerdmans, 1994), 10.
[4]Ibid., 14, 26.
[5]For examples, see these verses: 1 Cor. 15:22–24; 2 Cor. 5:1–2; Rev. 21:1–4.

are ever at hand. The glory of earth's Creator shimmers still in every stone and star, and in each human face. As Paul says, when it comes to God, no one has an excuse because his "invisible attributes, namely, his eternal power and divine nature, have been clearly perceived, ever since the creation of the world" (Rom. 1:20).

To restore the ruins, personally and in the world, we cannot begin with culture or education or force of will. We begin with metamorphosis: the radical transformation of an underwater tadpole into an air-breathing frog, of a caterpillar into a butterfly, of a sinner into a saint. The English word *metamorphosis* is a transliteration of the same Greek word Paul uses when he instructs us: "Do not be conformed to this world, but be *transformed* by the renewal of your mind" (Rom. 12:2). For education to be redemptive, we need to acknowledge that we are "dead" in our sins until we are made "alive" in Christ, not by anything we do, but by the pure gift received in faith (see Eph. 2:8–9). We must realize, by faith, that our ability to make ourselves good or better or free through learning will not be sufficient. We need God to change us from within before we can truly learn with a soulful understanding of things. So, we begin by begging God to remake us (not merely to patch us) by the power of his Holy Spirit—metamorphosed by the very presence of Christ himself, dwelling within us.

John Donne prays for this sort of transformation in his Holy Sonnet 14, using the analogy of the tinker (the mender of metal pots) in reference to God. He writes, "Batter my heart, three-personed God; for you / As yet but knock, breathe, shine, and seek to mend; / That I may rise and stand, o'erthrow me, and bend / Your force to break, blow, burn, and make me new."[6] Donne's paradox of being crushed to be remade, of being brought low to stand, wonderfully expresses the mystery of God in saving and sanctifying us. Donne captures in these few lines not only the biblical truth that every person has a sin nature, but that the fullness of the Trinity is, and has forever been, at work in creation and in re-creation.

We are creatures, and God is our creator. But if we do not take the radical and foundational step of seeking "new birth," if we are not

---

[6]John Donne, "To E. of D. with Six Holy Sonnets," in *John Donne: A Critical Edition of the Major Works*, ed. John Carey (Oxford: Oxford University Press, 1990), 177.

transformed by Christ, we cannot make the educational choice and redemptive act of bringing "every thought captive" to him (2 Cor. 10:5). At their founding, America's colleges and universities promoted this precondition of higher learning, as demonstrated in the earliest known account of Harvard (1642): "Let every student . . . consider well the main end of his life and studies is to know God and Jesus Christ which is eternal life, John 17:3, and therefore to lay Christ in the bottom, as the only foundation of all sound knowledge and learning."[7] This is wisdom; repairing the ruins begins with faith in Christ.

BUILDING ON THE FOUNDATION

In *The Future of Christian Learning*, Mark Noll assesses the history and present state of Christian higher education, asserting that we need both "real learning" and "real Christianity." Real learning must include "curiosity and openness toward human and natural phenomena," a critical eye to assumptions (especially of our own subculture, lest evangelical words and behaviors become another legalism), "a strong commitment to empirical research," and the humility to learn from "as wide a community of learners as possible." Real Christianity, Noll insists, must be fully Trinitarian, recognizing God the Father as creator and sustainer, Jesus as savior and redeemer, and the Holy Spirit as judge of sin and righteousness.[8]

The New Testament call to worship God with mind, heart, and soul is universally binding. If all must worship God with their minds, some must give direction. From Moses to Daniel to Paul, God called some who had rigorous (often secular) formal educations to use their minds and educations in his service. As C. S. Lewis told his students, it is impossible to have no culture but very possible to have an inferior one; likewise, it is impossible to have no aesthetic and intellectual life but very possible to have a depraved mind and imagination. "If all the world were Christian," Lewis explained, "it might not matter if all the world were uneducated." However, Lewis understood that a depraved world desperately needs well-educated Christians. He continues, "To be

---

[7] Kelly Monroe Kullberg, ed., *Finding God at Harvard*, rev. ed. (Grand Rapids, MI: Zondervan, 2007), 17.
[8] Quoted in *The Future of Christian Learning: An Evangelical and Catholic Dialog*, ed. Thomas Albert Howard (Grand Rapids, MI: Brazos, 2008), 28.

ignorant and simple now . . . would be to throw down our weapons, and to betray our uneducated brethren who have, under God, no defense but us against the attacks of the heathen. Good philosophy must exist, if for no other reason, because bad philosophy must be answered."[9] For those whose circumstances and abilities allow it, the "learned life" is not an option, but a "duty."[10]

For example, the great accomplishments in both politics and poetry by the seventeenth-century Puritan John Milton could not have been made except by someone steeped in the broadest and deepest education possible. In his famous essay "Of Education," Milton asserts that a liberal education should prepare the student "to perform justly, skillfully, and magnanimously all the offices, both private and public, of peace and war."[11] Milton devoted himself to liberal arts learning, describing his own "appetite for knowledge" as "voracious"—so much so that during his teenage years, he rarely left his studies before midnight. Milton plowed through all the fields of learning in his day, quite literally from agriculture to zoology, learning many languages, ancient and modern, especially focusing on the biblical languages. He did not, however, neglect the practical studies, making time for hunting, farming, engineering, and navigation. Similarly, Milton believed in stewardship of the body, promoting good diet and rigorous exercise.

No time was wasted in Milton's educational scheme: students who were "unsweating themselves" after exercise would make the most of their time by listening to or making music with "solemn and divine harmonies."[12] For Milton, God supremely demonstrates comprehensive wisdom and skill in creation, and therefore Milton advocates striving for comprehensive knowledge and skill as creatures made in God's image.

REIMAGINING THE RUINS

Always sensing that the educated pose a particular threat to unjust power, dictators have routinely attempted to control the thinking of their oppressed subjects. For example, Rameses II, who held the Israelites in

---

[9]Lewis, "Learning," 58.
[10]Ibid., 59.
[11]John Milton, "Of Education," in *John Milton: Complete Poems and Major Prose*, ed. Merritt Y. Hughes (New York: Odyssey Press, 1957), 632.
[12]F. E. Hutchinson, *Milton and the English Mind* (New York: Collier, 1962), 35–36.

bondage until God delivered them through Moses, kept scores of writers busy making up bogus stories about his exploits and covered the landscape with huge statues of himself, pretending to be divine. Similarly, in his letter to the Colossians, written during the reign of Caesar, Paul describes how the emperor's likeness was everywhere.

But Christians can use their knowledge and creative skill to promote a different agenda—that of God. Writing from prison in Rome, Paul affronted the most powerful ruler of his day by writing a subversive poem about his true king—Jesus.

> He is the image of the invisible God
> the firstborn of all creation
> for in him were created all things
> in heaven and earth
> things visible and invisible
> whether thrones or dominions
> whether rulers or powers
> all things have been created through him and for him
>
> And he is before all things
> and in him all things hold together
> And he is the head of the body, the church
>
> He is the beginning
> the first born of the dead
> so that he might come to have first place in everything
> for in him all the fullness
> was pleased to dwell
> and through him God was pleased to reconcile to himself all things
> whether on earth or in heaven
> by making peace through the blood of his cross.[13]

Paul wanted the disciples of Jesus to re-imagine the question of sovereignty in their lives. Likewise, Christian college students today have a profound challenge before them—always to place Christ first in their daily commitments and activities, attempting to see the world with new eyes that provide fresh spiritual insight. As Brian Walsh and Sylvia

---

[13]This poetic formatting of Col. 1:15–20 comes from Brian J. Walsh and Sylvia C. Keesmaat, *Colossians Remixed: Subverting the Empire* (Downers Grove, IL: InterVarsity, 2004), 83.

Keesmaat encourage, we must "re-imagine the world as if Christ, and not the powers, were sovereign."[14]

Without shared values we cannot have a shared vision of learning. The goal of a Christian liberal arts education is to put into practice Jesus's summation of all the law and prophets: to love God and love our neighbor. Likewise, Milton's goal for education encourages Christians to "repair the ruins" of original sin by offering our intellectual gifts and studies to our creator in our desire "to love him, to imitate him." As one prominent theologian plainly puts it, "Christians should know what their universities are for. They are to shape people in the love of God."[15]

Disciplined study is not the easy way out of the Christian life. Paul records that he would prefer to die at once, for "to die is gain." But he accepts his labors, for "to live is Christ" (Phil. 1:21). The great Russian novelist Dostoyevsky, in criticizing his young Christian hero Alexey for being too much like a certain kind of youth, describes him as

> honest in nature, desiring the truth, seeking for it and believing in it, and seeking to serve it at once with all the strength of his soul, seeking for immediate action, and ready to sacrifice everything, life itself, for it. Though these young men unfortunately fail to understand that the sacrifice of life is, perhaps the easiest of all sacrifices, and that to sacrifice, for instance, five or six years of their seething youth to hard and tedious study, if only to multiply tenfold their powers of serving the truth and the cause they have set before them as their goal—such a sacrifice is utterly beyond the strength of many of them.[16]

Alexey reminds us of our own culture, which fosters instant gratification at the cost of a dedicated life.

What if this were the last hour before Jesus comes again? As a student you may well ask, "Do I want to be reading a book or writing an essay when the curtain falls on the last scene of my own human drama?" If we may eat and drink to the glory of God, as the apostle Paul tells us

---

[14]Ibid., 84.
[15]Stanley Hauerwas, quoted in Jerry Pattengale, "What Are Universities For?," review of *Debating Moral Education: Rethinking the Role of the Modern University*, ed. Elizabeth Kiss and J. Peter Euben, *Books and Culture* (July/August 2010): 26. Kiss and Euben also give four key components of a moral education: (1) knowing what a university is for, (2) pursuing "high ideals," (3) exposing "moral evasions," and (4) developing "a capacious moral imagination," 30.
[16]Fyodor Dostoyevsky, *The Brothers Karamazov: A Novel in Four Parts and an Epilogue*, trans. Constance Garnett (New York: Macmillan, 1922), 22.

we must, and if we believe that being a student actually is a calling, our spiritual vocation from God, then surely the answer is "Yes!" In "The World's Last Night," C. S. Lewis muses on the end of the world and a variety of final earthly actions, offering these poignant words: "Happy are those . . . laboring in their vocations, whether they were merely going out to feed the pigs or laying good plans to deliver humanity a hundred years hence from some great evil. . . . No matter; you were at your post when the Inspection came."[17]

Have you sensed the prompting of God to study at a Christian liberal arts college? Then your post is the library and classroom, and your desk is your altar.

---

[17]C. S. Lewis, "The World's Last Night," in *The World's Last Night: And Other Essays* (San Diego: Harcourt, 1988), 111.

CHAPTER SEVEN

LOVING GOD AS THE KEY TO A CHRISTIAN LIBERAL ARTS EDUCATION

Duane Litfin

Affection is responsible for nine-tenths of whatever solid and durable happiness there is in our lives.
—C. S. LEWIS, *THE FOUR LOVES*

May the Lord direct your hearts to the love of God.
—2 THESSALONIANS 3:5

Of all the commandments, a lawyer once asked Jesus, which is greatest? Jesus answered by citing Deuteronomy's ancient *Sh'ma*. This is the greatest, he said: "You shall love the Lord your God with all your heart and with all your soul and with all your strength and with all your mind" (Luke 10:27).

This greatest of commandments is the key to making sense of a "Christian liberal arts education." Without it we can scarcely imagine what this unlikely combination of words might mean, but stipulate this commandment's driving force and all becomes clear. We discover both the essence of, and, equally important, the most profound motive for, a passionate pursuit of Christian learning.

How so? To borrow Shakespeare's famous line, "Thereby hangs a tale." To see how this works, let us start at the beginning.

A FAILURE OF LOVE

Everyone knows, at one level or another, that there is a God. How do they know this? "God has made it plain to them," says the apostle Paul. "For since the creation of the world God's invisible qualities— his eternal power and divine nature—have been clearly seen, being understood from what has been made, so that men are without excuse" (Rom. 1:19–20 NIV).

Now, to be sure, as the apostle also observes, a great many people suppress this knowledge (v. 18), exchanging the true for the false out of a preference for worshiping the created thing rather than the Creator (v. 25). But it's no use; we all remain accountable for the knowledge God has granted us—the knowledge that he exists and is powerful in ways only a divine maker could be. This is the very Creator the Great Commandment bids us love without reservation.

But here the plot thickens. He exists and he is immeasurably powerful, but how are we to *love* such a one as this? What is there to love? Astonishment, yes. Awe, certainly. But *love*? Is this Creator a person or merely a force? A "he" or an "it"? Does, or even can, my welfare matter to him/it? What is there about this Creator that should call forth affection from me? The truth is, the more I learn about "what has been made," the more difficult such a notion becomes.

Consider this: one group of scientists has estimated that there are in the range of 10^{80} elementary particles (protons, neutrons, electrons) in the observable universe.[1] These particles are capable of interacting with one another at the incredible rate of up to 10^{43} interactions per second, and there have elapsed more than 10^{16} seconds since the beginning of the cosmos. This means that the total number of potential particle interactions that could have occurred in the observable universe since the beginning is 10^{139}.

A number such as this is, of course, incomprehensible to ordinary minds. To say it is a large number is like saying the oceans have some water in them. Multiply trillions upon trillions, and we still do not come close. If 10^2 equals 100, and 10^3 equals 1,000, then 10^{23} equals a 1 with twenty-three zeroes behind it (100,000,000,000,000,000,000,000). Now continue until you have 139 zeroes in that line-up. There you have the maximum number of particle interactions that could possibly have taken place since the beginning of the observable universe. It is a number normal human minds cannot even imagine.

Yet the Creator we are called to love is the one who fashioned every

---

[1]Stephen C. Meyer, *Signature in the Cell* (New York: HarperCollins, 2009), 216–17.

one of those particles. What is more, he is the one who knows intimately each of those 10^{139} particle interactions, whether actual or possible. Not one has ever escaped his notice. He has from the beginning supervised every blink of every one of the universe's protons, neutrons, and electrons; he knows each and all of their movements exhaustively. Yet such knowledge does not begin to exhaust *him*. He is all-knowing and infinitely powerful.

I confess that if these sorts of things were all I knew about God— "his eternal power and divine nature," as the apostle summarizes it— my first reaction would not be to *love* such a creator. He (or it) is too far beyond my grasp, too inconceivable. As a broken, finite creature I quickly drown, succumbing in only the first fathom of the unfathomable depths of this vision, overwhelmed by the sheer, incomprehensible boundlessness of what I am trying to imagine. My emotional computer crashes; the screen goes dark.

The cosmos provides more than enough to fill me with awe and even dread when I consider such a creator—but love? To fear such a one makes sense; to avoid at all costs encountering him makes even more sense; to cower before him should I be forced to meet him, this makes the most sense of all. But to *love* him? For that I need more than the cosmos can give me. What I need is *special revelation*.

THE FACE OF LOVE

God has provided us what we need. Far beyond what we can discover from the sheer nature of things, God has over time revealed himself in a variety of ways. But his surpassing revelation occurred when he himself joined the created order by taking upon himself flesh. As the apostle John tells it, "In the beginning was the Word, and the Word was with God, and the Word was God. . . . And the Word became flesh and dwelt among us, and we have seen his glory, glory as of the only Son from the Father, full of grace and truth" (John 1:1, 14).

We quote the Bible here because, after the Living Word, God's inscripturated Word is our second-most-important revelatory source. Within its pages God reveals to us what we could never otherwise have gleaned: namely, his attributes, his ways, his purposes, his will, his view of things. We find there a history of his actions in the world and an interpretation of what those actions mean. Most importantly, we discover all these summed up in the person of the incarnate Word, Jesus Christ.

In these living and written Words, then, God has granted us the special revelation we need. There he reveals himself as the one who is worthy not merely of our astonishment but of our unreserved devotion. Our awe at what we can know of God from nature is not thereby diminished; it is translated from fear inducing to love producing. This mysterious God, the awesome, infinite creator of the universe, turns out to be a God of mercy and grace, one who cares about *us*. He has given himself, both to us and for us, in the person of his Son. If we wish to know more of what he is like, he tells us, look to Jesus. And when we do so, the Great Commandment—to love this God with all we are and have—is transformed from an alien duty into a magnificent privilege.

THE NATURE OF GOD

This privilege lies at the center of a Christian liberal arts education. Such an education, whether pursued for a few years in a formal curriculum or explored for a lifetime along a thousand different avenues, is simply—nothing more, nothing less—an exercise in living out Christ's Great Commandment.

Understanding this linkage begins with Scripture. The Bible, significantly, never tries to prove the existence of God; the cosmos does that effectively enough. The Bible simply assumes what can be known from nature and moves on from there, providing us vast expanses of revealed truth we could not otherwise know. We start with the Bible because it is from this special revelation that we discover the key things our Creator wills us to grasp.

Most importantly, of course, the Scriptures tell us about God himself. We already knew he is divinely powerful, but from the Bible we learn much more. We discover, in classical terms, his *simplicity* (he is indivisible); his *unity* (he is one); his *infinity* (he is without boundaries); his *eternity* (he transcends time); his *immutability* (his essence does not change); his *omnipresence* (he is everywhere present); his *sovereignty* (he reigns supreme); his *omniscience* (he knows all things, actual and possible). God is *just* (he is the very measure of fairness); he is *love* (he eternally gives of himself); he is *truth* (he is the gauge of all that is true); he is *free* (he is bound by none other); he is *good* (all that he does is worthy of approval); he is *holy* (he is utterly free of sin); he is *righteous* (he is the standard of all that is right); he is *personal* (he is the one in whose image we are made).

But there is more. From the Bible we learn that our Creator is a *tri-unity*. Who could have guessed? Here we meet one of the great mysteries of God. Early Christians wrestled with the Scriptures for centuries, seeking to capture in words what the inspired writings were teaching about the triune nature of God. What they produced, and what none afterwards have been able to improve upon, is the classic doctrine of the Trinity. God is one and indivisible, they said, but in the unity of the Godhead there are three eternal and coequal persons who have always existed in loving communion: God the Father, God the Son, and God the Holy Spirit.

Of the three persons of the Godhead, the Father in one sense receives the least attention in the Scriptures. The ancient creeds thus abbreviate what they affirm about him: "I believe in God the Father Almighty, Maker of heaven and earth."[2] But this impression is misleading, first, because all of the biblical teaching summarized above speaks of him; and, second, because of the iconic role that the Father assigned the Son.

A Christian liberal arts education is, as the phrase has it, "Christ-centered." Why should this be? Because in the drama of the unfolding creation, the Father placed the Son in the center-stage spotlight. Jesus repeatedly attributed his words and works to the Father. So fully did the incarnate Son embody the Father that he could say, "Anyone who has seen me has seen the Father" (John 14:9 NIV). How could this be? Because, Jesus said, "I and the Father are one" (John 10:30). Jesus does not eclipse the Father; he reveals him. In looking to Jesus we see not only him; we see the Father as well. According to the Scriptures, the Son is:

Creator of all things. It was expressly the Son "through whom" the Father effected the creation of the world: "In these last days [the Father] has spoken to us by his Son, . . . through whom also he created the world" (Heb. 1:2). In fact, as the apostle John insists, this was without

---

[2]Apostles' Creed. See also the creeds of the First Council of Nicaea (325) and the First Council of Constantinople (381).

exception: "All things were made through [the Son], and without him was not any thing made that was made" (John 1:3).

Sustainer of all things. As the world's creator the Son is not only "before all things," but "in him all things hold together" (Col. 1:17). He who created the world is also the one who sustains it. It is the Son, we are told, who "upholds the universe by the word of his power" (Heb. 1:3).

Goal of all things. This same Son is also the goal of all things. Not only were all things created "*by* him"; they were also created "*for* him" (Col. 1:16). From the beginning it was the Father's purpose that the Son should be appointed "heir of all things" (Heb. 1:2). Somehow, in ways we can scarcely imagine, the universe is groaning toward the Son, leaning into its eschatological fulfillment in him. He is at once its destination and its destiny, its goal and its blessed hope.

Redeemer of all things. And to all this, of course, must be added the Son's role as redeemer. The creation could be salvaged from its sin and brokenness only by God himself becoming part of it. This task was assigned to the second person of the Godhead: "When the fullness of time had come, God sent forth his Son" (Gal. 4:4).

This is the incomparable story of Christmas, the account of the Son's incarnation: "Behold, the virgin shall conceive, and bear a son, and they shall call his name 'Immanuel' (which means God with us)" (Matt. 1:23). The Son undertook this assignment in order to give himself on our behalf: "Though he was in the form of God, [the Son] did not count equality with God a thing to be grasped, but emptied himself, by taking the form of a servant, being born in the likeness of men. And being found in human form, he humbled himself by becoming obedient to the point of death, even death on a cross" (Phil. 2:6–8).

Judge of all things. These words from Philippians continue: "Therefore," because the Son had fulfilled the Father's assignment to the uttermost, "God has highly exalted him and bestowed on him the name that is above every name, that at the name of Jesus every knee should bow, in heaven and on earth and under the earth, and every tongue confess that Jesus Christ is Lord, to the glory of God the Father" (vv. 9–11). "Behold," says John, "He is coming with clouds, and every eye will see Him, even they who pierced Him. And all the tribes of the earth will mourn because of Him" (Rev. 1:7 NKJV). On that day history will have reached its crescendo. The redeeming work of the Son will be completed. The heavens and the earth will be refashioned, and the Son will present to the Father a people for his name and a creation made new (1 Cor. 15:24).

It was the Father's express design and delight, his *good pleasure,* that the second person of the Godhead should play this preeminent role in the creation (Col. 1:18–19; see also Phil. 2:11). The Bible reveals the Son as the primary—though not exclusive—agent for virtually everything in creation. When John says, "No one has ever seen God; the only God, who is at the Father's side, he has made him known" (John 1:18), he is speaking of Jesus, and his point is that the Son preeminently manifests the Father to the world: "No one knows the Father except the Son and anyone to whom the Son chooses to reveal him" (Matt. 11:27). The Son is the prime interface, the central point where the universe and the Godhead meet. He is the Godhead's unique mediator for dealing with the world: its formation, its sustenance, its redemption, and its restoration.[3]

The assignment in the world of the third person of the Trinity— the Holy Spirit—is multifaceted: regenerating, indwelling, sanctifying, sealing, revealing, empowering, comforting, illuminating, even creating (Gen. 1:2; Ps. 104:30). But as with the Father, the work of the Spirit received relatively scant attention in the ancient creeds. This was no doubt due to the Spirit's own focus on the Son.

As theologian John Stackhouse says, "The Holy Spirit remains . . . a relatively minor, shadowy figure in the New Testament compared with the center stage, fully lit person of Jesus."[4] But that is by design. The central aim of the Spirit is not to draw attention to himself; it is to show us the Son, to "glorify" him (John 15:26; 16:14). Stackhouse's reference to the "fully lit person of Jesus" suggests the image of a floodlight shining on a church steeple at night. The floodlight is not designed to draw attention to itself but to display the steeple. So also, the Father-assigned role of the Spirit is not to garner attention to himself but to reveal and

---

[3]For a fuller exploration of this point see Duane Litfin, *Conceiving the Christian College* (Grand Rapids, MI: Eerdmans, 2004), 34–63.
[4]John Stackhouse, *Evangelical Landscapes: Facing Critical Issues of the Day* (Grand Rapids, MI: Baker, 2002), 168–69.

glorify the Son. The Spirit is scarcely slighted when we look to the Son; it is his essential role to help us do precisely that.

Thus does God's special revelation reveal him as a loving, triune God who is worthy of our love. No longer is he dimly grasped as a frighteningly anonymous First Cause; he has shown himself to be our heavenly Father. He loses none of his incomprehensible power, but now we see that he wills to exert that power on our behalf through the Spirit. He loves the world and the race he created so much that he was willing to join it, experiencing its full pain in order to rescue it from its rebellious ways. He is God with the face of Jesus. Only a bitter, rebellious spirit, resentful that God is God and we are not, could keep us from loving such a creator as this.

A CHRISTIAN LIBERAL ARTS EDUCATION

Learning to love this God with all we are and have is what a Christian liberal arts education is about. It is an exercise in applying all of ourselves—spirit, intellect, emotions, even our bodies—to an engagement with the Creator and his creation.

In this engagement God's special revelation, centering on the person of Jesus Christ, is our starting point, for, like our sun, not only can we see *it,* but *by it* we are enabled to see everything else more clearly. So it is that we study not only God and his ways but also what he has made: the natural world, history, society, the arts, the realm of ideas, the church, culture, politics, the future, ourselves. Nothing is without interest to us because nothing is without interest to him. All these and more are dimensions of the world God has made, the world he loves and is in the process of redeeming. We honor and learn of him by honoring and learning of it, the work of his hands.

This is our calling. We know this because of another truth that, without the Bible, we could never have guessed: God has set us humans, his unique image bearers, as his vice-regents in creation. He has made us its stewards and he calls us to participate in its redemption. Thus we study to understand and fulfill our role as stewards. We study each of the world's dimensions for its own sake and in its own way, because each is fascinating in its own right. But we also study them because, as we do so in the light of God's Word, we learn more of him. This in turn prompts within us, when we allow it, still deeper responses of godly love: "O LORD, our Lord, how majestic is your name in all the earth!" (Ps. 8:1).

If one cares nothing for Christ's Great Commandment, a community dedicated to this sort of learning will likely hold little attraction. But if we do take this commandment seriously, a living, learning, serving community—such as a Christian college—offers a splendid opportunity to develop a heart directed toward loving God with abandon. What is more, as that directed heart develops, we also discover—not incidentally, but as a natural consequence—a growing desire to obey Jesus's second greatest commandment: "You shall love your neighbor as yourself."

Therein also hangs a tale, but for another time.

HABITS AND VIRTUES

At its best, liberal education is intended to promote *the good life*. Quintilian, the first-century teacher and contemporary of the apostle Paul in Rome, believed that a liberal arts education must be practiced, not merely purchased. Therefore, serious students must cultivate particular habits of mind and body and soul that will lead them toward noble goals. Liberal learning, then, requires students to exercise humanizing habits that contribute to well-being—both for individuals and society.

Emphasizing the centrality of virtue (character formation) in the expression of standards for learning and life achievement, dedicated teachers of the liberal arts promoted specific moral and spiritual aims through daily literacy activities: reading, writing, speaking, and listening. They also modeled virtuous behavior themselves, believing, as Homer did, that every teenager needs a mentor, just as Telemachus needed Mentes (the very name from which we derive the word *mentor*) in order to discover his true identity as the son of Odysseus. Modeling virtue and practicing virtuous habits serve as integral parts to the process of person formation.

Similarly, early Christians identified themselves as "people of the Way." They connected themselves so intimately with the life and teachings of Jesus that they sacrificially gave up all they had to be followers of the One who promised not the good life but abundant life, both now and forever, in the new heavens and the new earth. Followers of Christ have always distinguished themselves as in the world but not of it, intent on a purpose greater than themselves, and moving in a direction that Jesus himself described as the narrow road (Matt. 7:14). As the early proponents of pagan liberal arts advocated a message of learning for the benefit of the elite, the proclaimers of the gospel preach a message of learning that goes beyond status and power and privilege. Authentic Christian liberal arts education uses ancient instructional methods, but it promotes a different end: the development of whole and effective people who live for a kingdom that is not of this world.

Christian liberal arts education emphasizes the personal cultivation of virtues as a central objective. Understood historically as "standards guiding the pursuit of excellence," virtues come in two forms: Christian and intellectual. The Christian virtues include *the cardinal virtues* of temperance, prudence, restraint, and justice, along with *the theological virtues* of faith, hope, and charity. It is important to note that these virtues do not emerge automatically upon conversion. The Christian virtues, like the intellectual virtues, must be properly understood and skillfully developed. The intellectual virtues, which, according to some scholars, comprise almost fifty in number, by their very nature must be exercised. This is why liberal arts learning is not simply an education to gain knowledge; rather, it is an education to put knowledge into practice.

Cultivating the spiritual and intellectual virtues as a means of pleasing God, students participate in a radically transforming approach to learning that, in fact, should change people for a lifetime and beyond.

CHAPTER EIGHT

THE LOST TOOLS OF LEARNING AND THE HABITS OF A SCHOLARLY MIND

Marjorie Lamp Mead

Education is simply the soul of a society as it passes from one generation to another. . . . It is a truth, however sad and strange, that we cannot give what we have not got, and cannot teach to other people what we do not know ourselves.
—G. K. CHESTERTON, *ILLUSTRATED LONDON NEWS*

If you indeed cry out for insight,
    and raise your voice for understanding;
if you seek it like silver,
    and search for it as for hidden treasures—
then you will understand the fear of the LORD
    and find the knowledge of God.
—PROVERBS 2:3–5 (NRSV)

Over half a century ago, Christian lay apologist Dorothy L. Sayers stated unabashedly, "The sole true end of education is simply this: to teach men how to learn for themselves."[1] In declaring the supremacy of self-education, Sayers affirmed her belief in the importance of a liberal arts education, whereby a student acquires trained habits of the mind that transfer effectively to all areas of life.

Sayers herself proved to be a sterling example of this standard. Homeschooled until the age of fifteen, educated at a recognized boarding school, and then the recipient of the Gilchrist scholarship to Somerville College, Oxford, Sayers ultimately earned an undergraduate degree in

---

[1] Dorothy L. Sayers, "The Lost Tools of Learning," in *The Poetry of Search and the Poetry of Statement* (London: Victor Gollancz, 1963), 176.

modern languages, with First Class honors, from the university.[2] After leaving Oxford, Sayers used her exceptional intellect and education to forge a successful and accomplished career in various fields, including advertising and the theater, along with her achievement as the highly regarded author of the Lord Peter Wimsey detective novels. Her capstone literary accomplishment, however, was her vibrant translation of Dante's *The Divine Comedy*—a fourteen-year labor that required the full depth and breadth of her scholarly training as well as her own developed talents as a creative writer and translator.

A lifelong proponent of the liberal arts, Sayers returned to Oxford on her forty-first birthday to participate in a celebration honoring her former tutor. In her talk at this gathering, she addressed the concerns of those who rather flippantly dismissed their university education as having done them no good in terms of the "rough and tumble of post-war conditions."[3] Citing her own experience in the business world, Sayers strongly disagreed with this critique of higher education, maintaining that Oxford and Cambridge graduates had actually done very well in commercial enterprise, bringing with them the academic skills they had acquired at university—proficiencies such as "the scholar's habit of orderly thinking," the ability to handle words, and the "scholar's habit of looking upon knowledge of any sort as a thing to be freely shared without jealousy."[4]

Sayers maintained that these academic abilities, in company with a scholar's insatiable desire to learn, served as great preparation for the mastery of new tasks and unfamiliar jobs. Contrary to popular opinion, she believed that a high-quality liberal arts education actually ended up being excellent vocational training as well—not in terms of the acquisition of specific technical competencies but rather in the development of the foundational abilities required to master these skills.

Through both her experience and her words, Sayers serves as a powerful model of what the liberal arts can do to prepare an individual

---

[2]Even though Sayers completed all the requirements for her degree work in 1915, women were not then eligible for a formal degree from Oxford University. But in 1920, Oxford passed a statute that officially received women into full membership. Thus, on October 14, 1920, Dorothy Sayers was in the historic first group of women graduates to receive their BA and MA from the university.
[3]Dorothy L. Sayers, "Toast of the University" (unpublished manuscript), June 13, 1934, The Marion E. Wade Center, Wheaton College, Wheaton, IL, DLS MS-221, 5.
[4]Ibid., 7.

to enter into the challenges of life from a position of stren;
tise. As a college student preparing for your future, it is c
essential questions, including the following: How should I l
myself for a lifetime of work—and leisure? In what way will   ..veral
arts contribute to the quality of my being? Given the volatile nature
of business today, how do I best prepare myself for a career path that
will almost inevitably involve fluctuating job markets and changing
demands for skills? Valuable insights into these types of questions can
be found by looking more closely at Dorothy Sayers's own exploration
of these issues as a model for the liberally educated Christian.

WHAT IS RIGHT WITH THE LIBERAL ARTS?

The value of scholarly habits that come from liberal learning would
prove to be an enduring theme in Sayers's life and writings. In 1935,
one year after her Oxford talk, in an article titled "What Is Right with
Oxford?," Sayers elaborated on these key traits, detailing "scholarly
judgement that can settle any doctrine upon the evidence, without haste,
without passion, and without self-interest . . . integrity of mind that
money cannot buy . . . humility in face of the facts that self-esteem cannot corrupt; these are the fruits of scholarship, without which all statement is propaganda and all argument special pleading."[5] In other words,
Sayers regarded scholarly *integrity* as a safeguard against the temptation
to issue statements that are false; in the same way, scholarly *judgment*
enables an individual to discern falsehood in assertions made by others.

In sum, Sayers viewed the attributes of a liberally educated person
as being vital to critical thinking—eventually resulting in an individual
who is not only skilled in the use of words but, even more importantly,
skilled in the understanding of them. Having herself contributed to the
marketing techniques employed by advertisers, and with post–World
War I awareness of the potency of political propaganda, she was concerned that too many people no longer had the capability of distinguishing truth from falsehood, or even "disentangling fact from opinion and
the proven from the plausible."[6] In fighting against this loss of critical thinking, Sayers regarded a liberal arts education as a significant

---

[5]Dorothy L. Sayers, "What Is Right with Oxford?" *Oxford* 2 (Summer 1935): 37.
[6]Sayers, "The Lost Tools of Learning," 157.

protection against this "pathetic helplessness under the domination of words."[7] In today's world, Internet "myths" are a perfect example of this type of semantic distortion: imaginary statements that all too easily become self-perpetuating fabrications that prove nearly impossible to defeat, even when set side by side with the truth. Sayers believed that a liberally educated person is defended against deceptive tactics and thereby able to discern truth from lies.

REASSERTING "THE LOST TOOLS OF LEARNING"

In 1947, more than a decade after her talk on the importance of an Oxford education, Sayers returned once again to speak to a university gathering—this one comprised of faculty and students involved in a summer vacation course on education. In this address, she presented her concerns that education was failing in its true object: the development of citizens who are "fitted to preserve their intellectual freedom amid the complex pressures of our modern society."[8] To remedy this situation, Sayers proposed a return to the medieval model of education.

This talk, titled "The Lost Tools of Learning," went on to become a phenomenon when, in the 1980s, it so captured the imagination of educators in the United States that it gave rise to the Classical Christian movement, which continues to thrive today. Lest one be tempted to dismiss this essay as having value only for a small number in the Christian community, it should be noted that in 1979 the *National Review* republished Sayers's piece for the second time (having first offered it in 1959), observing that "in our 23 years of publishing, no article has provoked so great a demand for reprints as this one."[9] In addition, numerous other examples could be cited of schools—secular and religious, state and private, as well as homeschools—that have applied this essay with success to the shaping of an educational curriculum.[10]

This popular demand for Sayers's ideas is a noteworthy and unexpected legacy for an academic talk encouraging a return to the medieval

---

[7]Sayers, "What Is Right with Oxford?," 37.
[8]Sayers, "The Lost Tools of Learning," 156.
[9]Anon., editorial note in "Table of Contents," *National Review* 31 (January 19, 1979): 58.
[10]For examples of the successful implementation of this model in various contexts, see David B. Warner, "The Context and Legacy of Dorothy L. Sayers' 'The Lost Tools of Learning,'" in *Proceedings of the Dorothy L. Sayers Society* (1994): 41–53.

model of education—written by an author who, by her own admission, had "extremely limited" experience as an educator herself. However, in approaching this subject from the perspective of a student rather than a teacher, Sayers was able to share the methodology she had found to be most beneficial and effective when she was being taught. This educational approach, she felt, was best encapsulated in a medieval conception of the liberal arts, which included the trivium and quadrivium.

THE TRIVIUM AND QUADRIVIUM

The term *liberal arts* originated with the ancient Romans, and in the fifth century it became standardized by Martianus Capella in *De septem disciplinis* (*On the Seven Disciplines*), which describes the study of a set curriculum of disciplines or subjects that were gathered into two basic divisions: the trivium and the quadrivium. The trivium was comprised of three parts: grammar, dialectic (or logic), and rhetoric, and was intended to teach students how to learn as well as to give them the tools by which they could analyze and master other subjects. In other words, the trivium was the preparatory work that enabled the student to approach the serious study of other subjects.

Specifically, in the study of *grammar*, the student would acquire language skills including the following: reading notable texts with comprehension; understanding language and its structure with application; and writing particular kinds of expression with skill. In the study of *logic*, the student would learn to reason correctly by analyzing arguments, subsequently developing the ability to construct an appropriate response, culminating in the ability to determine whether something is true or false, knowing how to obtain facts relevant to the argument, and developing the discernment to be able to determine why a statement is indeed true or false. Finally, in the study of *rhetoric*, the student would acquire the ability to debate either verbally or in writing, and just as important, to be skilled in evaluating one's own work and the work of others, using the facts obtained in logic, and, finally, drawing upon this knowledge and developing the ability to persuade others in argument.

Successful completion of the skills of the trivium ("the three ways") prepared students for the quadrivium ("the four ways"), as well as the study of other specific subjects. In the medieval scheme, the four subjects of the quadrivium included arithmetic, geometry, music, and astronomy. While today's educational curriculum has obviously broadened well beyond these original four, the goal of the traditional liberal arts education remains the same: to prepare the younger members of the community for the responsibilities of life by nurturing the necessary skills, and also to pass along the values and beliefs held by the community that will enable them as adults to live their lives with thoughtfulness and integrity.[11]

MORE THAN "LOST TOOLS"

We have already noted that these lost tools of learning are not primarily focused on content but rather intended to help individuals *learn how to learn*. But as significant as these skills may be in the life of an individual, they are not intended to be an end in and of themselves. Having once acquired these tools, it is important to note that substantive content—what in Sayers's model might be termed *the quadrivium*—is also essential for the development of a balanced and prepared intellect.

Indeed, in spite of her clear emphasis upon the lost tools, Sayers believed just as firmly in the critical importance of acquiring foundational knowledge. For example, much of her speaking and writing about the Christian faith dealt with the lack of theological content that directly weakened the faith of those within the church. She frequently cautioned that all too many Christians do not know the basic doctrines of their faith, resulting in a deficiency that compromises their ability to function effectively in the world in which they live or even to intelligently express the reality of their faith to others. Princeton theologian Richard Osmer expresses this critical need well: "To put it simply, you cannot think, speak or act unless you have something to think, speak or act with. Unless explicit attention is given to the acquisition of biblical and theological knowledge, the members of the church will not be capable of using the faith to interpret their lives or their world. They will employ concepts from other areas of life in which they do have competence."[12]

C. S. Lewis also spoke to the issue of the acquisition of knowledge in a sermon he gave at Oxford during World War II. It might be

---

[11]It should be noted that in her essay "The Lost Tools of Learning," Dorothy Sayers focuses particularly on the trivium and virtually ignores the quadrivium.

[12]Richard R. Osmer, "The Case for Catechism," *The Christian Century* 114 (April 23–30, 1997): 412.

surprising to some that in the midst of war, with the grave uncertainty this entailed, Lewis chose to underscore the essential importance of obtaining a liberal education. In this sermon to Oxford undergraduates and faculty, Lewis addressed a hypothetical question: "How can one be so frivolous as to commit time and effort to university studies in the midst of war?" Lewis's response was both firm and affirming:

> Neither conversion nor enlistment in the army is really going to obliterate our human life. . . . If you attempted, in either case, to suspend your whole intellectual and aesthetic activity, you would only succeed in substituting a worse cultural life for a better. . . . If you don't read good books you will read bad ones. If you don't go on thinking rationally, you will think irrationally.[13]

Lewis went on to make clear that he believed that the study of philosophy, history, and other worthy subjects is a vital part of our development to think critically—no matter what external realities surround us.

An easy application of this principle can be found in examining the most effective way to conduct Internet searches. The more you know about a subject (i.e., the quadrivium's content), the more easily you can define terms that will enable your online search to be most productive. Likewise, as you filter the results of your search, your ability to distinguish the relevant from the insignificant (i.e., utilizing critical judgment, one of the lost tools of the trivium) is essential to obtaining a successful result—the alternative being an exceedingly long and therefore useless list of possible sources. Without sufficient knowledge, we do not know what questions to ask; but without critical judgment, we are unable to intelligently evaluate the answers we uncover. Both are essential.

Learning how to learn and to think critically and also having adequate knowledge to interpret and understand the world and its challenges are not luxuries, but rather essential and basic responsibilities of every individual who desires to live a full and meaningful life—just as these elements are essential requirements of the Christian faith. Those who abdicate these responsibilities are not immune from the dangers and limitations of a nonintellectual life, for as Sayers, Osmer, and Lewis

---

[13]C. S. Lewis, "Learning in War-Time," in *The Weight of Glory: And Other Addresses* (New York: Macmillan, 1949), 46.

warn, this only results in the substitution of an inferior intellectual understanding, given that no individual can function fully without employing critical thinking and judgment at various junctures. Thus, we observe that even as the lost tools serve as the preparatory work to help us learn, in turn, as we acquire knowledge, these core skills are strengthened and we are able to apply them with ever-increasing insight and wisdom.

DEVELOPING THE LOST TOOLS AND OTHER HABITS OF A SCHOLARLY MIND

So where do you begin on this lifelong process of learning to learn? First, it is key to assess your own expertise in terms of the practical skills that Sayers terms the "lost tools" of learning—and then enlist help in developing any of those abilities in which you are deficient. If you are not certain how well you think, read, write, and speak, consider asking a supportive teacher or friend to aid in making this assessment.

Having evaluated the areas you would like to develop, make use of the academic support that may be available to you: a tutor, a study group, a writing center, and so on. Any and all of these resources can help you improve your underdeveloped "tools." And in doing so, if you understand that these abilities are lifelong tools, you will not mistakenly view them as skills to be conquered simply to fulfill an academic requirement. In other words, "testing out" of freshman writing is not the same thing as possessing mature writing skills that translate successfully to coursework—and to future interests and jobs.

Take advantage of the numerous opportunities offered to you in an academic community. First and foremost, do not neglect the courses you are enrolled in; take your responsibilities as a student seriously. Achieving the credit hours but walking away from a class without having actually learned something substantive is an opportunity squandered. Attend optional evening lectures that expose you to new topics and ideas; you will learn much by exploring areas other than your own particular interests. In the same way, consider using your electives to venture outside your chosen discipline. Have lunch with a professor and talk about his or her intellectual passions, as well as your own. Allow the books you read, both inside and outside of class, to become part of your intellectual landscape. Do not forget to read for fun. But most of all, after graduation persist in cultivating your mind as much as you continue nurturing other aspects of your person.

WHAT CAN A LIBERAL ARTS EDUCATION DO TO ME?

If we are to be successful (and motivated) in this lifelong process of learning to learn, it is essential that we understand what a liberal arts education might instill in us. As noted previously, a liberally educated person—someone possessing the core skills of the trivium and the foundational knowledge of the quadrivium—is uniquely equipped to master the technical elements of a range of jobs. Rather than being viewed as training for a single career, the liberal arts should instead be understood as essential preparation for the wide variety of work that may lie ahead. But the richness of a liberal arts education provides infinitely more in terms of the whole development of the individual person. According to philosopher Arthur Holmes,

> Liberal learning concerns itself with truth and beauty and goodness, which have intrinsic worth to people considered as persons rather than as workers or in whatever function alone. . . . Liberal learning therefore takes the long-range view and concentrates on what shapes a person's understanding and values rather than on what he can use. . . . The question to ask about education is not, "What can I do with it?" . . . The right question is rather, "What can it do to me?"[14]

In other words, unlike vocational training, which seeks to produce particular skills and train an individual for specialized employment, the liberal arts work to shape an individual to live life fully, both while at labor and also while at leisure.

While some people are born with an innate desire to learn about truth, beauty, and goodness, for others this passion must be awakened. In this endeavor, the liberal arts can also be of help. For it is often within the educational setting that many individuals are first exposed to the depth and breadth of the creative arts, the fascinating expanse of the natural world, the wonder of story, the significance of philosophy and history, and so on. In the same way that exposure to good food can awaken a healthy appetite, so too can students benefit from the opportunity to

---

[14]Arthur F. Holmes, *The Idea of a Christian College*, rev. ed. (Grand Rapids, MI: Eerdmans, 1991), 28–29.

experience a wide array of academic subjects. In part, this is a key purpose for general education courses within the college curriculum, as they are often the reason many incoming freshmen who expected to major in one subject find themselves drawn to an entirely different discipline once they have actually experienced it.[15]

Dorothy Sayers's emphasis on the importance of the trivium should not be overlooked in this discussion of outcome, however; for as previously noted, these lost tools of learning are precisely the skills that enable us to fully apprehend the knowledge we acquire in the quadrivium. If the educational process places too much emphasis upon the subject matter and does not give sufficient attention to the skills required to learn, then the end result will be a student who knows facts but has failed "to learn how to learn." As Sayers warns, "To learn six subjects without remembering how they were learnt does nothing to ease the approach to a seventh; to have learnt and remembered the art of learning makes the approach to every subject an open door."[16] It is through this open door that true learning takes place.

Understood rightly, a liberal arts education, including *both* the trivium and the quadrivium, is not only a rigorous and disciplined preparation for life but also the springboard for a glorious endeavor wherein we learn to see life with new eyes—to value what is present in the vast created world around us rather than to be limited only to those things we have previously known or understood. Once we are able momentarily to step outside our lone perspective and open ourselves to the understanding offered us in the words or images or teachings of others, we are then ready to look, listen, and receive to a degree that was not possible before. In so doing, we are changed—as we come to experience the mind of our divine Maker coming ever more fully alive in us.[17]

---

[15]Dorothy Sayers would also add that even as we necessarily specialize within a particular subject, maintaining our exposure to the great breadth of the liberal arts curriculum is essential to our ability to learn from one another and from other disciplines.

[16]Sayers, "The Lost Tools of Learning," 174.

[17]For more on Sayers's understanding of God and the creative mind at work, see her volume *The Mind of the Maker* (London: Methuen, 1941).

CHAPTER NINE

HOW TO READ A BOOK

Alan Jacobs

Some books are to be tasted, others to be swallowed, and
some few to be chewed and digested; that is, some books are
to be read only in parts; others to be read, but not curiously;
and some few to be read wholly, and with diligence and attention.
—FRANCIS BACON, *OF STUDIES*

In reading this, then, you will be able to understand my insight into the
mystery of Christ, which was not made known to men in other generations as
it has now been revealed by the Spirit to God's holy apostles and prophets.
—EPHESIANS 3:4–5 (NIV)

In the essay from which I have taken my epigraph, Francis Bacon
provides a brief, crisp survey of the challenges facing the person who
would be studious. Bacon's language sounds, to the modern ear, solemnly old-fashioned; it comes from a very different world than ours—
or so it might seem. But as the historian Ann Blair has commented,
Bacon's advice was a response to the early modern era's "information
overload"—an overload created by the recent invention of the printing
press. With books, pamphlets, and broadsheets rolling off the presses
day after day, the European world, long used to the stately pace of hand-
copied texts, had a great deal of adjusting to do. Within living memory
of people in Bacon and Shakespeare's generation, books had been rare
and scarce; but now, quite suddenly, there were more books than anyone
could read in a lifetime.

To anyone striving to handle the fire hose of information blasting
from our computer screens every day, this must sound like a familiar
story. But that just means that Bacon's advice is even more valuable
now than it was four hundred years ago. If we want to learn how to read
books, Bacon's model serves as a wonderful guide—for readers in general and even for Christian readers in particular, as we shall see.

DISCERNMENT

The first point we will want to note is that not all books deserve the same attention from us. Readers must be discerning in this matter. Note that Bacon does not tell us to read only the greatest books, to live on a diet of masterpieces; rather, he assumes that we will read books of varying quality. Why? Why shouldn't we read the best and only the best?

The poet W. H. Auden once wrote, "When one thinks of the attention that a great poem demands, there is something frivolous about the notion of spending every day with one. Masterpieces should be kept for High Holidays of the Spirit."[1] The word "frivolous" is particularly interesting here: Auden thinks that it would be rather silly to think that we can just sit down any old time and rise to the challenge of a great poem or novel or work of philosophy. Their greatness depends in large part on their determination to challenge us: by forcing us to think thoughts that never would have crossed our minds, by forcefully plunging us into alien experiences, or by gently touching our hearts, such works disrupt the familiar rhythms of our lives. Immanuel Kant once wrote that reading David Hume woke him from a "dogmatic slumber."[2] That's what all great books do to us—but it's hard on the system to be so awakened, and we're not up for that every day.

Moreover, often we read not to be profoundly moved, or even to be entertained, but for plain old information. And this is by no means shameful: as Bacon says, some books are just to be "tasted," that's all, or—dare we say it?—*skimmed*. It may seem scandalous for an English professor to acknowledge the legitimacy of skimming, but I will do more than that: I will confess to being quite an accomplished skimmer myself.

Skimming is really the first stage in the discernment I am recommending: we skim a book to find out whether it appears to be genuinely substantive—to find out whether it deserves more than a skim. And not all books *do* deserve more. Sometimes this is because they are not very good; but sometimes because only a small part of what they contain is needful to a particular reader at a particular time. For instance, I own a very large history of Europe that I have never read from cover to cover but have used several times to learn about a particular European country at a particular point in its

---

[1]W. H. Auden, "Making, Knowing and Judging," in *The Dyer's Hand* (New York: Random House, 1962), 37.
[2]Immanuel Kant, *Prolegomena to Any Future Metaphysic* (1783), trans. and ed. Gary Hatfield (Cambridge, UK: Cambridge University Press, 2004), 10.

history. I have skimmed it—"tasted" it, as Bacon would say—and I have a pretty good idea of what's in it, in case I need to return to it some day.

You should rarely *plan* to skim. First impressions can be misleading, and it can also be hard for us to know just what knowledge we need until we read seriously for awhile; moreover, to offer attention to a book (as we shall soon see) is a way of acting charitably toward its writer. For all these reasons it is best to start a book intending to read it "wholly, and with diligence and attention." But if the book proves to be less useful than you had hoped, it is no crime to abandon word-by-word reading and try to glean the major ideas. (One useful technique is to read the first and last sentences of each paragraph.) Sometimes this is all you will need to do; sometimes you will realize that the book deserves careful reading after all; and sometimes the skimming will show you that you don't need to read the book at all. There are no hard-and-fast rules about such things, but you need to be aware of your own temperament—are you naturally impatient and quick to abandon what doesn't immediately grab you?—so you can become discerning in your reading. Skimming *will* be done; it's best that we learn to do it well.

But then, Bacon says, there are those books that deserve to be "swallowed": not sampled on the tongue, so that we know what their flavor is, but sent right down the hatch. Bacon is probably referring to those books that we need to read from beginning to end, the ones we read simply in order to receive the information they contain. Much textbook reading is like this: you need to read it straight through, and you need to remember what you've read, but the book itself is essentially dispensable—it's a vehicle for data. Reading a textbook is often a kind of *uploading*, and successful uploading can be quite a challenge, as anyone who has crammed for an exam knows.

Most students develop, over time, and usually with a good deal of suffering, strategies for reading such books. The strategies often involve highlighters and index cards and sometimes messages scribbled on the inside of a forearm. We won't worry too much about those strategies right now, because whatever they happen to be in your case, they can be strengthened (or perhaps corrected) by reflection on Bacon's third and most important category of reading material.

"Some few," Bacon says, are "to be chewed and digested; that is,

. . . read wholly, and with diligence and attention." Such books provide significant intellectual, and perhaps spiritual, nourishment: we are stronger and healthier and wiser for reading them. But how do we really chew and swallow a book so that we get the maximum nourishment from it? Three things are needful: attentiveness, responsiveness, and charity.

ATTENTIVENESS

Attentiveness has always been hard, though it is probably harder for us than for any people in human history. As the novelist Cory Doctorow writes, "The biggest impediment to concentration is your computer's ecosystem of interruption technologies."[3] And it's not just your computer but also your smartphone, your iPad, and who knows what else. Our reliance on these gadgets—and I say "our" advisedly, being someone just as dependent on them as you—leaves us in a state of what Linda Stone has called "continuous partial attention."[4] Such a state isn't *always* bad; there are pleasures and benefits to being in a high-speed multitasking groove, and if Katherine Hayles is right, this can itself be a kind of attention—"hyper" attention as opposed to "deep" attention.[5] But the more consistently we immerse ourselves in this "ecosystem of interruption technologies," the harder it becomes to live and think any other way. That is why Nicholas Carr writes:

> The problem today is not that we multitask. We've always multitasked. The problem is that we're always in multitasking mode. . . . As a result, we devote ever less time to the calmer, more attentive modes of thinking that have always given richness to our intellectual lives and our culture—the modes of thinking that involve concentration, contemplation, reflection, introspection. The less we practice these habits of mind, the more we risk losing them altogether.[6]

Our always-on multitasking, our continuous partial attention, makes it hard to read books, and it may cause trouble in other areas of

---

[3]Cory Doctorow, "Writing in an Age of Distraction," *Locus*, January 2009 (http://www.locusmag.com/Features/2009/01/cory-doctorow-writing-in-age-of.html).
[4]Stone coined this term while working as a researcher for Microsoft. She offers a brief and clear explanation of it on her website (http://lindastone.net/qa/continuous-partial-attention/).
[5]N. Katherine Hayles, "Hyper and Deep Attention: The Generational Divide in Cognitive Modes," *Profession* (2007): 187–99.
[6]Nicholar Carr, "Hypermultitasking," *Rough Type* blog, December 10, 2009 (http://www.roughtype.com/archives/2009/12/hypermultitaski.php).

life as well. In the 1930s the Jewish-Christian thinker Simone Weil gave a lecture to some French school girls on the spiritual value of academic study, and in the process gave this wise counsel:

> The love of our neighbor in all its fullness simply means being able to say to him: "What are you going through?" It is a recognition that the sufferer exists, not only as a unit in a collection, or a specimen from the social category labeled "unfortunate," but as a man, exactly like us, who was one day stamped with a special mark by affliction. For this reason it is enough, but it is indispensable, to know how to look at him in a certain way. This way of looking is first of all attentive.[7]

Weil goes on to argue that in school we can practice the art of attentiveness, and having learned it, transfer it to God and our neighbors. The person who knows how to *attend* can pray better, listen better, and yes, read better.

It makes sense to think of the books that we are reading as our neighbors: we might not ask them, "What are you going through?" but we really would do well to ask them, "What do you have to say to me?"—and then stay for an answer.[8] This requires a determination to make our attention as full as we can make it, not partial, which, in turn, requires us to shut down the computer and put the phone (set to "silent") well out of reach. After all, how would you feel if you were opening your heart to a friend who claimed to be listening but never stopped texting or updating his Facebook page? Attentiveness is an ethical as well as an intellectual matter; it's about treating our neighbors as they deserve as much as it's about getting facts into our heads.

RESPONSIVENESS

This brings us to the matter of responsiveness. Mikhail Bakhtin, a Russian polymath who was perhaps the greatest literary theorist of the twentieth century, once commented that in any given conversation the real initiator is the person who listens, not the one who speaks.[9] After

---

[7]Simone Weil, "Reflections on the Right Use of School Studies with a View to the Love of God," in *Waiting for God* (New York: Harper Perennial, 1973), 115.

[8]Francis Bacon's essay "Of Truth" (1625) begins thus: "*What is truth?* said jesting Pilate, and would not stay for an answer."

[9]Mikhail Bakhtin, "Discourse in the Novel," in *The Dialogic Imagination: Four Essays*, ed. Michael Holquist, trans. Caryl Emerson and Michael Holquist (Austin, TX: University of Texas Press, 1981), 280.

all, who would ever speak unless he or she believed that someone would be listening? It is the listener who *elicits* the speech, brings it forth. The speaker counts on a responsive listener. In the same way, a writer counts on a responsive reader.

Furthermore, Bakhtin argues, such a response needs to be more than a mere passive reproduction of the author's intention. That kind of reading "contributes nothing new to the word under consideration. . . . Such an understanding never goes beyond the boundaries of the word's context and in no way enriches the word." Note Bakhtin's core assumptions: that when we speak we want our listeners to "contribute something new" to what we have said and thereby "enrich" our words. Those assumptions may be a little surprising at first, but if we think about actual face-to-face conversations we've had with our friends about important issues, we'll realize that Bakhtin is right. When you're pouring out your heart to others, you don't want them just to nod and repeat your last few words. You want them to offer their own words, as an indication that they have heard you and *thought* about what you've said—have processed it in some meaningful way.

This is what writers want also: for you to "enrich their words" with your own responses. And this is the main reason to read books, especially difficult and challenging books, with a pencil in your hand: not primarily so that you can remember what you've read—though that is nice—but so you can register your reaction. If you are surprised, indicate it with an exclamation point; if you are confused, give the margin a question mark; if you are impressed, a star shows it. (Those are my key symbols, along with a few others. Every careful reader develops his or her own symbolic language: recently I heard of a young woman who marks passages she particularly likes by drawing great big hearts around them.)

Disagreement prompts response, too—in my case often in words rather than symbols: *NO,* I write, or *WRONG.* Often more detailed refutation is needed, so the margin or the white space at the bottom of the page gets filled up, and in some cases the blank pages at the end of the book. But this too is a sign of respect: when I register and explain my disagreement in a book, I demonstrate that I am paying attention and that I *care* about what the author is saying—I want (as the author wants) to get it right. Responsiveness, even critical responsiveness, is a token of respect and engagement. And yes, writing in your books will help you remember what you've read.

CHARITY

Charity is the one thing most needful for us—in both a universal and a distinctively Christian sense. The philosopher Donald Davidson writes that when we are reading or listening to other people, we operate with a "principle of charity" according to which we assume that they are basically coherent.[10] That is, when we run across an unclear or imprecise statement, we construe it so that it makes some kind of sense. According to Davidson, that's just what people *do*; it's how we get along with one another, conversationally speaking.

I think Davidson is right about what we do, but ascribing charity to such an involuntary action may not be right. Since people usually *do* make sense when they speak, if I assume that the next person I talk to makes sense too, I am just using basic inductive reasoning. It would be strange to do otherwise. But charity in the Christian sense is anything but natural, automatic. It's something we won't even begin unless we are highly conscious of the need for it, which might lead us to ask: In what ways does reading call for charity, and why?

Reading calls for charity because everything we do calls for charity—if by "charity" we mean, as we should, Christian love. Jesus says, "You shall love the Lord your God with all your heart and with all your soul and with all your mind. This is the great and first commandment. And a second is like it: You shall love your neighbor as yourself. On these two commandments depend all the Law and the Prophets" (Matt. 22:37–40). Note: *all* the Law and the Prophets are governed by this twofold commandment. And if, as I suggested earlier, it makes sense to say that a book we are reading is, for the duration of the reading experience, our *neighbor*, our obligation to be charitable is even stronger.

Now, charity toward what we read does not mean being nice to what we read. (Jesus himself was unfailingly charitable but not always very nice.) Sometimes charity requires us to be challenging and at times even skeptical. For example, the charitable Christian reader wouldn't pick

---

[10]Donald Davidson, "On the Very Idea of a Conceptual Scheme," in *Inquiries into Truth and Interpretation*, rev. ed. (Oxford: Clarendon Press, 1984).

up a copy of Hitler's *Mein Kampf* and say, "Well, I'm sure there must be something in what you say." That would be loving neither to God nor to our neighbor. Earlier I referred to the need for discernment about the informational value of books, but we need discernment even more when we strive to assess the moral or spiritual character of what we read—and of its likely effect on our own moral and spiritual character. The Scripture says, "Beloved, do not believe every spirit, but test the spirits to see whether they are from God" (1 John 4:1)—and this requires a degree of self-testing as well. Just as when deciding whether to skim, we need to be aware of our own temperamental tendencies—to impatience, perhaps—we also need to know our own spiritual strengths and vulnerabilities.

This does *not* mean that we are to set aside every book that we deem unedifying, for there can be very good reasons for reading work that has an unsound and unhealthy spirit. Often such reading is a powerful way of coming to understand the world to which we must respond. But it does mean that we need to work hard to discern those spirits, within a context of prayerful and honest self-assessment.

So if we determine to read a book, what does it mean to read it charitably? Well, charity begins with the two traits we have already mentioned: attentiveness and responsiveness. I have said that those traits are *ethically* important, and they are so because they contribute to charity. We show our willingness to love by our active, alert awareness of what's going on in a book. Having achieved that (as best we can, anyway), we should ask ourselves these questions: How can I read this book in such a way that I grow in the love of God? How can I read it so that I grow in the love of my neighbor? Do I see in its events a pattern of thought or action I should follow? Do I learn something from it about fallen or redeemed human nature? Does it offer me the opportunity to reflect on the glory of creation, or "the fair beauty of the Lord"?[11] Through it, can I see into my own heart—is it a mirror for me?

These are hard questions, and can be tiring even to think about. *Do I have to do all that when I read?* No, you don't—you *can't*. None of us can. My suggestion is not that you force yourself to ask such questions

---

[11]Psalm 27:4, in *The Book of Common Prayer*.

of every book you read but simply that you be *open* to such questions—
that you allow them to enter your heart and mind. It would be a good
spiritual discipline to begin each session of reading with a very brief
prayer—"Lord, may I hear the word you have for me in this book"—and
then to stay for an answer.

WHIM

As I draw this essay to a close, let me turn to a matter that, in my mind,
is very important indeed—but not nearly as solemn as what we've been
talking about over the past few pages. Recalling Auden's warning that
masterpieces of literature should not be our steady diet, we should
affirm the great value of reading just for the fun of it. The poet Randall
Jarrell tells the story of meeting a literary critic who said that every year
he reread his favorite book, Rudyard Kipling's novel *Kim*, just because
he wanted to. Though a critic, he had never written anything about *Kim*,
nor did he ever plan to. That one book he read, Jarrell says, "at whim,"
and Jarrell ends his essay by exhorting us all to "*read at whim!*"[12]

In my experience, Christians are strangely reluctant to take this
advice. We tend to be earnest people, always striving for self-improve-
ment, and can be suspicious of mere recreation. But God doesn't just
create, he takes delight in his creation, and expects us to delight in it
too; and since he has given us the desire to make things ourselves—
has allowed us to be "sub-creators," as J. R. R. Tolkien says[13]—we may
rightly take delight in the things that we (and others) make.

Reading for the sheer delight of it—reading at whim—is therefore
one of the most important kinds of reading there is. By all means strive
to be a better reader, to grow in attentiveness, responsiveness, and charity; but whatever you do, don't forget to allow yourself to have fun.

---

[12]Randall Jarrell, "Poets, Critics, and Readers," in *No Other Book: Selected Essays*, ed. Brad Leithauser
(New York: Harper, 1999), 229; emphasis original.
[13]Tolkien develops this idea of writing as "sub-creation" chiefly in his long essay "On Fairy Stories," first
published in *Essays Presented to Charles Williams*, ed. C. S. Lewis (Grand Rapids, MI: Eerdmans, 1966),
38–89.

CHAPTER TEN

WRITING FOR LIFE

Sharon Coolidge

I write entirely to find out what is on my mind,
what I'm thinking, what I'm looking at, what I'm seeing,
and what it means.
—JOAN DIDION, "WHY I WRITE"

Whatever you do, do all to the glory of God.
—1 CORINTHIANS 10:31 (NASB)

Did you ever wish you could avoid taking freshman writing? After all, you studied English every year in high school and had to write good essays to get into college. While we all might sympathize with the impulse to take courses that seem more interesting, I confess to cringing whenever I hear a student ask, "How can I get out of taking writing?" Perhaps even more frustrating are e-mails like the one I received recently that asked the same question. The e-mail was written with no capital letters, several run-on sentences, and almost every comma error that could be squeezed into one short note. The tone and attitude implied that taking writing was not only unnecessary but a great inconvenience. Unfortunately, I have often had similar conversations with soon-to-be-graduating seniors who delayed taking writing, hoping it would simply go away.

Although I answer patiently, I try to redirect the conversation to a discussion of why writing matters—because it does matter, enormously. Writing is not just something you do in college; it is an essential lifelong skill and the mark of a liberally educated person. Writing well involves discovering new thoughts and conveying them effectively and persuasively. At a personal level, your writing reflects who you are.

THE IMPORTANCE OF WRITING WELL

If Arthur Holmes is right, and liberal arts education is eternally important because it helps you develop into the person God wants you to be,[1] then learning to write well is an essential part of that process. The very act of writing will help you clarify and develop your ability to think. Writing forces you to solve problems and find creative solutions. C. Day Lewis understood well that writing involves more than simply translating your ideas into words and transmitting them to others: "If it were clear in my mind, I should have no incentive or need to write about it. We do not write in order to be understood; we write in order to understand."[2] Writing involves evaluating others' ideas and discovering your own thoughts as you shape them into words, sentences, and paragraphs that can persuade a reader. Because learning how to write also strengthens your ability to think, a writing class early in your college career will help you maximize your liberal arts education and will benefit you long after you graduate.

Writing is an important public skill, involving a social transaction between you and your reader. How you present yourself in writing may determine how others will judge you. In college, your teachers will use your writing on tests and papers to evaluate your mastery of the material and your ability to think. After graduation, your most important act of persuasion may be the letter you send to a prospective employer, seeking a job. Will your letter convey effectively who you are and why you are the right person for the job? Would the student who e-mailed me trying to get out of writing receive serious consideration for any job that involved communication? How you write matters.

The other side of the social equation is your ability to influence others through your writing. Can you persuade others to see an issue from your point of view? Can you write effectively enough to secure a grant or have a proposal accepted? Can you write a succinct report for your boss that effectively summarizes your work? Can you communicate with the public in a way that instills trust? I recall a letter I received from one of my son's elementary teachers, full of grammatical errors. Immediately, my trust in her teaching abilities eroded. Communicating ideas at church or articulating your faith also requires strong writing. Writing teaches you how to value others, to understand

---

[1]Arthur F. Holmes, *The Idea of a Christian College* (Grand Rapids, MI: Eerdmans, 1975), 45.
[2]C. Day Lewis, *The Poet's Task: An Inaugural Lecture Delivered Before the University of Oxford on 1 June 1951* (Oxford: Clarendon Press, 1951), 15.

their perspectives, to anticipate their responses, and to care enough to communicate clearly. How you engage others in your writing is not only a part of a liberal arts education, but it is also a key part of becoming an effective Christian, able to serve Christ and his kingdom.

From the beginning God has used words and writing to communicate with us. Genesis tells us that God spoke and brought the universe into being, and John 1 connects that word with Christ himself: "In the beginning was the Word, and the Word was with God, and the Word was God." He gave the law to the Israelites by writing with his finger on the tablets of stone (Ex. 31:17). He spoke his word to prophet after prophet—"Write this down"—to call the Israelites back to repentance and to help them remember his deeds. In the only account of Jesus writing, John tells us that Jesus wrote twice on the ground with his finger when defending the woman taken in adultery. When Jesus taught, he used parables, metaphors, and stories to instruct, and the Gospels all record Jesus quoting from the written Old Testament. When Jesus was tempted in the wilderness, he quoted Deuteronomy to rebuke Satan ("Man does not live by bread alone, but . . . by every word that comes from the mouth of the Lord," Deut. 8:3). And on the cross, his last words came from the Psalms, "My God, my God, why hast thou forsaken me?" (Ps. 22:1 KJV). Jesus clearly valued the written word.

The Bible is God's written word to us, and he chose to work through human authors, each with their own cultural context and limitations. He also chose to work through an array of different genres: history, narrative, letters, apocalyptic visions, prayers, proverbs, and poetry. Through his inspired Word, he communicates to us who he is, how much he loves us, and how we can be reconciled to him. Words matter to God, and they should matter to us. In church we use words and writing to pray, to worship, to instruct, and to communicate with each other. In our daily lives, we use writing to glorify God, to explain our faith, to persuade others, and to witness to the truth of God's Word. Because our ability to write is a gift from God and reflects who we are as persons made in his image, we should develop that gift and use it for God's glory—not our own. Good writing can and should be both an act of stewardship and an act of worship, and that means taking the task of learning to write seriously, following the principles outlined in the rest of this chapter.

BE AUTHENTIC

Often I get "perfect" five-paragraph papers that are written in a bland academic voice and that are largely a patchwork of quotations and facts with no real point or argument. To some degree, each of these characteristics is a sign of inauthentic writing. If you want your writing to matter, you need to start by having something worthwhile to say, as Wendell Berry suggests: "What gets my interest is the sense that a writer is speaking honestly and fully of what he knows well."[3]

When you have the opportunity to choose your topic, choose something you care deeply about and think through what you really want to say. When a teacher assigns the topic, find a narrow angle that genuinely interests you and shape it into a focused and arguable thesis. Take your time in framing your argument, since research shows that students often make key mistakes at this stage. Brainstorm, outline, research, talk to people—whatever helps you to sharpen and deepen your thinking. Speak the truth you want to speak, not what you think others want to hear. College writing involves more than following a formula and spewing information; it demands commitment, critical thinking, and careful argument.

Authenticity requires humility rather than perfectionism. Sometimes when we read writers we admire, the writing looks so easy, so perfect, that it sounds as though it emerged fully formed, like Athena from the head of Zeus. When we compare their writing to ours, we can easily become paralyzed with feelings of inadequacy. But even if the final product makes writing look easy, it is always the result of hard work and significant rewriting. Author Gwendolyn Brooks described writing as a "delicious agony,"[4] and sportswriter "Red" Smith envisioned it as sitting down at a typewriter and opening a vein.[5] As you write, you need to recognize your limitations, but don't let them paralyze you or tempt you to cheat. Although some people seem able to compose in their heads, everyone needs to do some kind of significant prewriting planning. Start early, discover what you want to say, work for your own voice, and over time your own strong style will emerge.

---

[3]Wendell Berry, "Some Thoughts I Have in Mind When I Teach," in *Writers as Teachers, Teachers as Writers,* ed. Jonathan Baumbach (New York: Holt, Rinehart & Winston, 1970), 23.
[4]Gloria Wade Gayles, ed., *Conversations with Gwendolyn Brooks* (Jackson: University Press of Mississippi, 2003), 159.
[5]Quoted in John Brady, *The Craft of Interviewing* (New York: Vintage, 1977), 202.

Authenticity also demands complete honesty. I grieve over the increase in plagiarism I see as students naively or intentionally incorporate chunks of material (more from online sources than from books) or submit papers purchased or copied from the Internet. I realize from conversations with students that they may feel overwhelmed, inadequate, or panicked because they waited too long to start the project. I also realize that sometimes students don't see the Internet as something they need to document. But plagiarism (presenting something as your own that you have taken from someone else) is a huge breach of integrity and has no place in any writing, much less at a Christian college. When you plagiarize, ultimately the person you cheat most is yourself.

KNOW YOUR AUDIENCE

As a teacher of writing, I receive hundreds of student papers. Most of them are easy to understand, but occasionally I get papers that are genuinely difficult to read: papers with an unclear thesis, ideas that jump around, confusing sentences, densely elevated diction, and often obscure references. The reader must take huge leaps of faith between ideas and unpack each sentence before moving on. This kind of writing suggests one thing: the student is writing primarily for himself and not for a reader, and he leaves himself open to misunderstanding. Albert Camus has articulated the challenge every writer faces: "Those who write clearly have readers; those who write obscurely have commentators."[6] Any writer who is self-reflective wants to communicate clearly and be understood—and that involves putting the reader first.

A good writer never assumes the reader will read past the first sentence. As a writer, you have no control over what your reader is doing prior to reading your paper, but your task is to grab your reader's attention, as Barbara Tuchman clearly understands: "I . . . want the reader to turn the page and keep on turning to the end."[7] A reader who has to struggle over every idea and sentence will almost certainly put it down, and you will have lost the opportunity to communicate. While some might want to blame the reader for difficulties in understanding, the

---

[6]Albert Camus, *Notebooks, 1942–1951*, vol. 2, trans. Justin O'Brien (Lanham, MD: Ivan R. Dee, 2010), n.p.
[7]Barbara Tuchman, "Biography as a Prism of History," in *Practicing History: Selected Essays* (New York: Ballantine, 1982), 89.

problem almost always originates with the writer. Most readers have simple expectations: the writing should be interesting, organized, clear, and smooth. Good writing involves both wise strategy and loving the reader enough to meet those simple expectations. F. L. Lucas identifies the best strategy for achieving clarity: write "to serve people rather than to impress them."[8] Write in such a way that you are able to compel your readers to read—not because they must—but because they want to.

Student writers often make a second audience-related mistake: writing only for a reader who already agrees with them. This results in one-sided arguments, shallow explanations, and support that is shaky, at best. Or it can result in a paper that sounds polemical, preaching only to the choir. This problem becomes especially prevalent when students are writing about issues related to faith or morality. If your reader already agrees with you, all you are doing is reaffirming a shared belief without digging deeply or thinking critically. But if you think about your reader as someone who doesn't share your particular belief, you have a persuasive challenge on your hands. You will need to think through your position carefully, recognize where your argument seems controversial, anticipate counter arguments, and shape strategies for addressing them. Your rhetorical task is to hook your readers, compel them to read, and convince them that your argument has merit. You can do this only if you see your readers as people who need convincing.

STRIVE FOR CLARITY AND SIMPLICITY

Respecting your reader's need for clarity requires several conscious choices. The point you want to make should be clear and forceful. Too often a thesis simply announces a topic ("Saving the earth is important") or "maps out" the structure of the paper ("An understanding of the problems involved in good ecology is important before we can consider solutions"). Before writing your thesis, mentally complete the sentence, "The point I want to make is . . . " Take this idea, word it as sharply and powerfully as you can, and use this as the claim your paper will prove or demonstrate. Going through this step not only will help you keep focused but will give your reader a clear sense of where you are headed.

---

[8] F. L. Lucas, *Style* (London: Cassell, 1955), 76.

Shape your paper as an unfolding argument, not as a static outline to be filled in, with every paragraph following a rigid pattern. In a strong paper, each topic sentence and paragraph needs to build momentum and propel your main argument forward. Within each paragraph, articulate your claims, develop the reasons that explain them, and select the best examples or statistics to support them. Then order and build your points (from weakest to strongest) and work out the full implications for the claims you are making. Good paragraphs don't just happen; they must be shaped intentionally to move the reader smoothly through your argument and on to the next point.

Clarity also involves making conscious choices at the sentence level. When we speak, we rely on gestures, intonation, and volume to punctuate our points. But the reader has only black words on a white page—nothing more. How you craft your sentences and connect them can direct how your reader will read what you have written. Jumping around in your argument and using short disconnected sentences only increases the opportunity for misunderstanding. To help your reader read as you have intended, you can use several strategies: shaping your argument and your sentences to move from information your reader already knows to new information, providing smooth transitions between points, designing parallel or contrasting sentences, and varying sentence lengths. This kind of conscious shaping will help your reader better understand your intention.

Choosing your words carefully also makes a difference. George Orwell compares jargon and general, abstract language to a snowfall that blurs the sharp outlines of the landscape.[9] Unconscious and vague writing can easily obscure our meaning. Academic settings often tempt us to write in the technical vocabulary of our disciplines or strive for a high, formal style we associate with intelligence. Christian settings sometimes tempt us to use evangelical jargon or insider language ("born again," "abide in Christ," "blessed"). By using jargon, we don't have to be specific about what we mean. Clear thinking, however, forces a good writer to choose words actively, finding fresh ways to talk about our faith or express ourselves academically. Instead of relying on phrases

---

[9]George Orwell, "Politics and the English Language," *Horizon* 13, no. 76 (1946): 252–65.

that come ready to hand, choose words that are fresh and vigorous, capturing exactly what you want to say.

Even punctuation is a matter of clarity and choice. Although students often view punctuation as either a minefield or something they can ignore, good punctuation serves as road signs for the reader, pointing the way to your intended meaning. Punctuation helps connect thoughts in an orderly fashion, but it also helps emphasize contrasts and parallels and mark new directions. Used in this way, punctuation can be one of the writer's most important tools to highlight ideas and guide the reader.

REVISE, REVISE, REVISE

All good writers revise. Research on how both professional and student writers revise reveals interesting findings. Students generally make minor changes: substituting one word for another, correcting grammar errors, adding a sentence here and there—small fixes. But mature writers make global revisions: eliminating whole sections, reshaping, writing new material—all based on their purpose for the piece. Isaac Bashevis Singer acknowledged that "the wastebasket is a writer's best friend."[10] The best-selling novelist James Michener confessed, "I have never thought of myself as a good writer. . . . But I'm one of the world's greatest rewriters."[11] Such wholesale re-visioning of a paper or essay, however, is difficult for students. It means cutting words and sections you have worked hard to write, a form of self-sacrifice that doesn't come easily. It is also difficult because students seldom start soon enough to do major revisions.

After you have written, let the paper sit for a while—a few days if possible. Then read it out loud, noting where the language sounds vague, the argument unconvincing, or the rhythm awkward. You can train your ear to hear many of the problems in your writing. You just need to schedule the time to address them. Rightly understood, rewriting is essential for discovering your true voice and developing what you really want to say. There is no shortcut.

Learning to write well is an academic skill, but it is also a part of our Christian calling. Henri Nouwen recognized that writing fundamentally

---

[10]Quoted in Steven D. Price, ed., *1001 Smartest Things Ever Said* (Guilford, CT: Lyons Press, 2005), 260.
[11]A. Grove Day, *James A. Michener* (New York: Twayne, 1964), 135.

involves self-discovery and fosters both personal and spiritual development: "Writing is a process in which we discover what lives in us. The writing itself reveals what is alive. The deepest satisfaction of writing is precisely that it opens up new spaces within us of which we were not aware before we started to write. To write is to embark on a journey whose final destination we do not know."[12] Just as your liberal arts education is a step in the process of becoming the person God wants you to be, so learning to write well is a step in discovering who you are and learning what it means to be a precise and mature thinker. You will write your whole life. Write with integrity, creativity, and authenticity, and do this—as you should do everything else—to the glory of God. When you take a writing course in college, don't think of it as "getting it out of the way." Instead, recognize it for what it is: an invitation to begin a lifelong journey of self-discovery.

---

[12]Henri Nouwen, "Theology as Doxology: Reflections on Theological Education," in *Caring for the Commonweal: Education for Religious and Public Life,* ed. Parker J. Palmer, Barbara G. Wheeler, and James W. Fowler (Macon: Mercer University Press, 1990), 107.

CHAPTER ELEVEN

LISTENING, SPEAKING, AND THE ART OF LIVING

Kenneth R. Chase

Nothing commends the gospel more eloquently than a transformed
life. . . . We are charged to behave in a manner that is worthy of
the gospel of Christ, and even to "adorn" it, enhancing its beauty by
holy lives.

—JOHN STOTT, *THE MANILA MANIFESTO*

How beautiful upon the mountains
    are the feet of him who brings good news,
who publishes peace, who brings good news of happiness,
    who publishes salvation,
    who says to Zion, "Your God reigns."

—ISAIAH 52:7

Many people care little about beautiful lives. They care, rather, about
looking beautiful, or about the gossipy details of those celebrities who
are advertised as beautiful. On the flipside of this preoccupation with
appearances is the too frequent fascination with lives that revel in ugli-
ness, as we find in entertainment focused on adultery, murder, betrayal,
and revenge. Toggling our attention between the appearance of beauty
and a fascination with evil leaves little room for contemplating a life of
authentic attractiveness.

LIVING BEAUTY

Although we know, somewhere deep inside us, that appearing beautiful
is a highly fragile phenomenon, we often repress the fear of our own
mortal decay by focusing on the temporary pleasures that looking good
or enjoying evil can bring us. Yet when we are honest with ourselves,
we know that living well requires more than just a pretty face. We want

143

to be beautiful people—people who live harmoniously with others and our environments, whose external appearance becomes more appealing through the vibrancy of our daily encounters.

By engaging in high quality speaking and listening, we provide for ourselves and others the best possible circumstances—the richest and most fertile soil—in which beautiful lives can take root and grow. We use lots of terms to describe the quality of life we build as we improve our speaking and listening—*effective*, *successful*, or *accomplished*—but I choose *beauty* as a way of pointing to communication that is far more than a mechanical process of receiving and distributing information. We are not smartphones, capable only of uploading and downloading data. Rather, our communication shapes identities, relationships, and cultures. How we communicate ought to be fully consistent with God's design for personal and social growth.

We live beautiful lives when our bodies and souls mesh with God's ultimate reality; this is a life of wholeness and depth, of rightness and wisdom. Rather than fading with time, this beauty grows and develops, as if we are learning an intricate dance choreographed to the rhythms of God's creation. When our speaking and listening are fitted well to the Spirit's movement, we are glimpsing the beauty of life well lived, and we are giving a glimpse of beauty to all who have eyes to see and ears to hear.

LIVING ELOQUENCE

Ancient communication theorists used the term *eloquence* for those sweet spots in time when a speaker's character and words fit beautifully into the complex circumstances of the listeners. Cicero, the first-century BCE Roman orator whose eloquence defined Latin style for more than a millennium, celebrated the communication ideal of uniting eloquence with wisdom ("the tongue with the brain").[1] His ideal was adapted for Christian education by Augustine, who considered the Christian Scriptures to be the model of eloquent wisdom for all humanity.[2] Augustine's influence bequeathed the ideals of wisdom and eloquence

---

[1]Marcus Tullius Cicero, *On the Orator*, trans. H. Rackham, Loeb Classical Library (Cambridge, MA: Harvard University Press, 1942), 3.60–61.
[2]Augustine, *On Christian Doctrine*, trans. D. W. Robertson Jr., Library of Liberal Arts (Indianapolis: Bobbs-Merrill, 1958), 4.5.7–4.6.10.

into Christian liberal arts education extending all the way through the Renaissance, and beyond.

Cicero's primary insights into education were not his own, though. He inherited them from the greatest educator of fourth-century BCE Athens, Isocrates, whom many recognize as the "father" of the liberal arts.[3] Isocrates believed that speaking well through the union of eloquence and wisdom was the pinnacle achievement of higher education. In his view, orators shaped politics and law by artfully intertwining Athenian culture, history, and values into a compelling call for wise action. Therefore, Isocrates taught his students to respect their heritage, to live up to the highest moral standards of their society, and to persuade their listeners to attain a higher level of personal and political achievement. Isocrates pushed his students to live as eloquently as they spoke. Eloquence, then, was not artificially enhanced prose but a way of speaking into life that required a corresponding way of living. One's life was to embody the beauty of one's language so that speakers became what they proclaimed.

Isocrates's eloquence demanded a deep harmony between speaker and listener, which he described as a relationship of *charis* (Gk: favor, grace, or honor).[4] Speakers were to generate messages from a listening posture that linked communicators together in the mutual offering of kindness and the expression of gratitude. The economy of *charis* was Isocrates's own version of the circle of life. Orators received a favored and honored education that, in turn, allowed them to favor their teachers and audiences with wise persuasion. As orators gave their speeches back to the community, the citizens bestowed afresh upon them civic honor and gratitude.

Isocrates contrasted his *charis* model of communication with the materialistic models of his rival Athenian educators: a student paid a teacher to learn the art of persuasion in order to reap material benefits from listeners. That crass economic exchange was not a harmony of listening and speaking but an exploitation of communication in which grace was absent and personal gain trumped all virtue.

---

[3]Bruce A. Kimball, *Orators and Philosophers: A History of the Idea of Liberal Education* (New York: Teachers College Press, 1986), 19, 33.
[4]Yun Lee Too, *A Commentary on Isocrates' Antidosis* (Oxford: Oxford University Press, 2008), 128–29.

The New Testament also locates communication in a relationship of *charis*, but it is more radical than Isocrates's version. The *charis* we Christ followers receive is not due to our acts of kindness toward others but to God's kindness toward us. Isocrates's *charis* was an "I'll scratch your back; you scratch mine" arrangement with the goal of achieving honor and respect in the Athenian community. In contrast, Christ's *charis* is lavish and undeserved, far exceeding whatever honor we could give back to him. Therefore, to be eloquent communicators within Christ's *charis* means that we are recipients first, beneficiaries of his kindness. For good reason, then, James tells us to listen more than speak (James 1:19). Our speaking ought to originate out of the "wisdom from above," which is "peaceable, gentle, open to reason, full of mercy and good fruits, impartial and sincere" (3:17). Speaking must emerge from listening, and listening should characterize the very core of our being.

If we truly speak according to God's wisdom, we will bring beauty into our interactions with others. We will fit our talk into the reality of God's peace and love. We will weave our own words into ongoing conversations, building upon what has been given to us as we shape the conversations yet to come. As the ancient Hebrews used to say, "A word fitly spoken is like apples of gold in a setting of silver" (Prov. 25:11). Speaking and listening, according to God's *charis*, is beautiful. This work of grace leads us to a deep enjoyment of friendship, of our capacity to influence others, and of learning rooted in the goodness of God's creation.

Listening

How do we achieve the eloquence worthy of God's own abundant grace? We must be clear about the basic logic of communicating well. Listening is the priority at all times. First and foremost, we must be listening to God. Through his Word he redeems us and releases us from the fears and insecurities that prevent us from listening lovingly to others, even those with whom we disagree. Being open to God translates into being open—and humble—toward the people whom he loves. This becomes the basis for an exceptional Christian liberal arts education. Grounded in listening to God, the student becomes open to the ways God works through history, literature, philosophy, science, communication, and the arts.

In short, the beautiful listener seeks an ever-increasing awareness and insight into the ways that people throughout history and from around the globe speak about themselves, the world, and each other. Every element of a college education becomes an opportunity to listen; we listen to our textbooks, to our professors, to each other. And the medium through which we learn ought not change the priority of listening. If we are exploring websites, we listen; if we are in the chemistry lab, we listen; if we are on a geology field trip, we listen; if we attend a campus lecture, we listen. A liberal arts education promotes listening as a mode of active awareness and eager discovery.

This type of listening is neither passive nor boring. Good students are not pawns, following directions mindlessly; nor are they lifeless sponges, merely absorbing information. Listening well requires a reflective mind alert to multiple voices; it requires giving attention to the many nuances of a speaker's words, to the interplay of sounds within an orchestra, to the dialogue of ideas within a good book, to the ways a message fits (or fails to fit) people and circumstances. Listening to God is the baseline for this best type of listening. The sixty-six books of Scripture fall into multiple genres with multiple human voices, all divinely inspired to be God's Word to us. As we listen closely to one of the inspired authors—say, for example, the apostle Paul—we do so in the context of the other books, knowing that Paul was himself shaped by listening to the Old Testament, to the other apostles, and to Jesus himself. We also listen to Scripture in the context of a local church, and this local church is part of the church universal, whose voice echoes throughout history as a shaping influence on Christian life today. Listening well, then, requires attentiveness to multiple voices and their broader contexts.

Since most people are not naturally inclined to listen well, improving listening requires practice and know-how. How do we listen?

Physically and mentally prepare. In face-to-face communication, listening well means we posture toward others with physical directness and eye contact.[5] In many cases, it also means turning off the cell phone. Giving full attention is a deeply spiritual act, an act of *charis*, for we are

---

[5] Lynn O. Cooper and Trey Buchanan, "Listening Competency on Campus: A Psychometric Analysis of Student Listening," *The International Journal of Listening* 24 (2010): 149–50.

considering others to be worth our time and energy. We choose to love the speaker, or the artist, or the author by choosing to be fully present. This is doubly important when reading a challenging book or sitting in a large lecture hall, cases in which we find it much easier to turn away from the other and toward the comfortable routines of our own ideas and agendas or the convenient distractions of text messages.

Be hospitable toward the message. Make room for others in your mental life by looking for the best in what you receive. Give their verbal and visual messages some elbow room within your assembled thoughts and beliefs. This is hospitable listening, welcoming the other as an act of love. Paul's description of love in 1 Corinthians 13:4–5 can serve as our template: "Love is patient and kind; love does not envy or boast; it is not arrogant or rude. It does not insist on its own way; it is not irritable or resentful." As we sync our lives with these qualities of love, we will listen more patiently, more selflessly, more justly.

Use tactics to maintain attentiveness. We can use basic interaction skills to sustain our concentration and commitment to others.[6] These skills include the following:

- Restating the message in your own words. The work of *paraphrasing* can be done out loud in a conversation, as part of the give and take, or through silent repetition while listening to a lecture or viewing a film. You can insert restatement into the conversational flow as a question: "Do you mean . . . ?"; a suggestion: "You seem to be saying . . . "; or an agreement: "I agree with your view that . . . " To enjoy a more collaborative interaction, rephrase and extend what you have heard rather than merely parroting the words back to the speaker.

- Providing bits of feedback. Respond to the speaker verbally ("OK," "Uh-hum," "That's right," "Amen") and nonverbally (nodding, smiling). Because such feedback is minimal, it does not interrupt or distract the speaker. These *minimal encouragers* tell the speaker that you are fitting into the conversation, seeking to provide a full hearing. One of the best ways to encourage a speaker is to use the simple phrase, "Say more." Use it when you want to deepen the conversation.

[6]John Stewart and Carole Logan, "Empathic and Dialogic Listening," in *Bridges Not Walls: A Book About Interpersonal Communication*, 8th ed., ed. John Stewart (Boston: McGraw Hill, 2002), 208–29.

Test the message. We are not blank slates, as if every time we listen, the speaker is creating in us a new mind. Rather, we bring to every encounter multiple experiences and viewpoints. Thus, listening well requires that we use skills in reasoning and discernment to evaluate messages. Taking notes or jotting down key ideas starts the process. Sifting the message in terms of the broader contexts—of Scripture, other cultures, family and friends, trustworthy knowledge—advances the process. Checking arguments and noticing evidence are additional ways to take the messages seriously. Accepting any single message without *critical thinking* betrays the larger task of listening to the multiple voices that shape self and represent God's work in the world. To take a speaker seriously means valuing the person as contributing to the broader human conversation. Gullibly accepting a speaker's message elevates that one voice above all others in our lives, demeaning those from whom we already have received much. We need not accept at all those messages that violently or coercively strip us of our ability to live Christ's love.

Speaking

We typically—and unfortunately—associate eloquence only with a certain type of persuasive flamboyance or a high-sounding speech style. Considering that the apostle Paul seemingly rejects eloquence as unsuitable for proclaiming the gospel, the faulty association is not surprising (1 Cor. 2:1–5). The best sort of eloquence, though, is exceptionally well fitted to the message, speaker, listeners, and occasion; it neither violates the power of the gospel nor distracts hearers from the Spirit's whispers. Paul was not denouncing this healthy practice but the showy performances of Corinth's competitive orators.[7]

Eloquence, rightly done, is vital in lots of different circumstances: we have eloquent everyday conversations by simply speaking right words at right times; we produce eloquent essays by capturing some insight in a way that gives the reader an "aha" moment; we give eloquent speeches that directly, but convincingly, structure arguments for audiences. When a person's hospitable listening is combined with a facility for effective speaking, the resulting discourse produces connections that

---

[7] Anthony C. Thiselton, *The First Epistle to the Corinthians*, New International Greek Testament Commentary (Grand Rapids, MI: Eerdmans, 2000), 204–5.

make a difference. Dinner chats move beyond the trivial, relationship partners work through conflict for mutual growth, and sermons bring listeners into a fresh awareness of God's Word.

Because listening is an active engagement with God's reality, speaking from within this receptiveness can be both surprising and disturbing. Sometimes, of course, we talk just to enjoy being with others—we pass time, hang out, or battle loneliness. On other occasions, though, we must not settle for the routine. One of the greatest American communicators of the nineteenth century modeled how sharp criticism might be the best fit for a given circumstance. The former slave Frederick Douglass rarely hesitated to speak the truth about the cruel injustice of the American slave trade. In his famous 1852 Fourth of July oration to a northern abolitionist society, he proclaimed that calmly worded argumentation and genial appreciation were inappropriate. "At a time like this," he exclaimed, "scorching irony, not convincing argument, is needed." He powerfully identified the hypocrisy of white Americans who celebrated their freedom and then expected slaves to join in. His irony was pointed and unflinching:

> What, to the American slave, is your 4th of July? I answer: a day that reveals to him, more than all other days in the year, the gross injustice and cruelty to which he is the constant victim. To him, your celebration is a sham; your boasted liberty, an unholy license; your national greatness, swelling vanity; your sounds of rejoicing are empty and heartless; . . . your prayers and hymns, your sermons and thanksgivings, with all your religious parade, and solemnity, are, to him, mere bombast, fraud, deception, impiety, and hypocrisy.[8]

These words, indeed, exhibit highly stylized eloquence, but they are appropriate for the evil described, given the oratorical standards of the day.

Douglass's oration shows all the marks of effective persuasion. Douglass was a highly credible speaker, sharing his audience's values (and their Christian faith) and pushing them to a deeper embrace of freedom and courage. His slave experience provided a distinctive level of competency and served as a resource for potent emotional appeals. He also argued well, despite his protestations to the contrary. His irony arose from

---

[8]William L. Andrews, ed., *The Oxford Frederick Douglass Reader* (Oxford: Oxford University Press, 1996), 118–19.

within a lengthy defense of America's ideals and a withering exposé of slavery's brutalities. Douglass wove together these persuasive resources (character, emotion, argument) into an indictment of audience and culture. His eloquence fit well the deeper truths shaping both speaker and listener.

The same persuasive resources that Douglass used are available to all speakers. Although we are unlikely to match his oratorical prowess, we can embrace a liberal arts education that cultivates the quality of our character, the depth of our emotional understanding, and the strength of our argumentation. We must add to these resources the speaking skills necessary to connect persuasive resources with audience understanding.

Overall Structure. Since people tend to think in terms of story lines, whether it is the story of a life, a significant relationship, a nation, or salvation, we should develop each of our own particular formal speeches (such as an oration, a sermon, a business presentation, or a lecture) with narrative sensibility. To invite listener attention, every speech should have a beginning, a middle, and an end. In the Western world, the middle part typically involves a series of main points, logically ordered, to help the listeners follow the speaker's linear development of ideas. In the global South, speakers stick more closely to traditional storytelling, weaving narratives together to lead listeners in a discovery process.

Content Development. Our speech should be carefully linked with our listeners' existing knowledge and beliefs. In storytelling, this means that details must resonate with audience experiences to provide a vicarious reality. Listeners should see and feel what the speaker sees and feels, so eloquent speakers connect new information to audience understanding through analogies, references to specific locations, vivid descriptions, and familiar concepts.[9] In argumentation, the speaker's claims must be connected with evidence acceptable to the listeners. Recognized experts and trustworthy news sources give an audience the strongest incentive to follow the speaker's reasoning. Statistics and other factual data should be pulled only from published sources that have strong editorial boards checking for accuracy.[10]

[9]Ruth Ann Clark, *Persuasive Messages* (New York: Harper & Row, 1984), 67–86.

[10]Because the Internet is a magnet for erroneous information, speakers can find reliable data through websites vetted by experts. For links to hundreds of reliable sites, see http://FactCheckEd.org or http://www.ipl.org.

Vocabulary. Not every utterance must be eloquent, but speakers too often take informal chatter as the norm for all communication, disregarding the more beautiful work that can be done through conscious attention to the occasion. We can select words carefully to demonstrate a loving regard for the fuller reality of a conversation and the dignity of others. Neglecting word choice weakens arguments, makes a story less compelling, and potentially insults listeners. For most college-aged speakers, eliminating filler words and vocal pauses (*like, just, you know, um*) is crucial for a job interview, an oral presentation, or professional-quality broadcasting.

Speakers also should avoid obscene and coarse language. These words typically are abusive toward others and reflect a broader disregard of the *charis* that gives life and love. Thus, when Paul says to put away "obscene talk from your mouth," he places this command in the broader context of new life in Christ and the additional command to be thankful (Col. 3:8, 15–17). Our vocabulary should demonstrate respect for the dignity of each person and gratitude for our Lord's gift of speech. Filling conversations with expletives or junk words is, in most cases, neglecting one of the most extraordinary gifts given to persons for advancing God's purposes in his creation.

LIVING DIGITAL

Our changing communication environment adds new challenges for the eloquent communicator. About a third of US teens send more than one hundred text messages (SMS) daily, and the majority of teens report that they are more likely to contact friends through messages than by any other means. In 2010, US SMS users from all age groups sent over 187 billion messages per month. But the US is not the leader in cell phone communication; cellular mobile networks cover almost 90 percent of the world's population with nearly six billion global cellular subscriptions. Nearly five-and-a-half trillion text messages were sent around the world in 2009.[11]

---

[11]This data on digital communication is from (in order): "Teens, Cell Phones and Texting: Text Messaging Becomes Centerpiece Communication," Amanda Lenhart, Pew Research Center, last modified April 20, 2010 (http://pewresearch.org/pubs/1572/teens-cell-phones-text-messages); "U.S. Wireless Quick Facts: Year-End Figures," CTIA Wireless Association, accessed May 20, 2011 (http://www.ctia.org/media/industry_info/index.cfm/AID/10323); "Mobile Broadband Subscriptions to Hit One Billion in 2011," The International Telecommunication Union, Dec. 5, 2011 (http://www.itu.int/ITU-D/ict/facts/2011/material/ICTFactsFigures2011.pdf); "SMS Continues to Confound Expectations as Worldwide Messaging Revenues Set to Exceed USD 233 Billion by 2014," Portio Research, accessed August 11, 2010 (http://www.portio-research.com/news.html).

As we know too well, the rapid exchanges of brief messages easily distract us. Add dozens of daily text messages into the mix of video games, television, iPods, Facebook, and Twitter, and communicators face an uphill battle in the quest to listen attentively to God and others. A shortened attention span is a likely consequence of heavy dependence on digital speaking and listening, but it is not necessarily the most damaging consequence. For many, instant digital contact with an increasing number of people shifts communication further away from the economy of *charis* and into an "economy of attention."[12] Knowing that we can be texted at any time increases our appetite to be contacted, to be acknowledged, to be kept within the attention span of our peers. The absence of messages can become an unsettling background noise of anxiety: "What if others no longer think about me?" The potential of being forgotten—a fear always lurking in the dark corners of our existence—becomes in the digital age a fear faced every hour, or every half hour, or every few minutes.

Maintaining ourselves as the focus of others' attention pushes us further away from the deeper beauties of *charis*. Digital messaging is speed dependent and location independent. So, we often send messages in haste and without any sense of how the message fits with persons or occasions. Through digitized social media, personal disclosures, rants, pictures, and gossip circulate to unknown and unseen people who can exploit the information or be harmed by a vile rumor. The simple pleasures of a digital confession turn painful quickly, cutting into the reputation or safety of the one who posts and the unseen reader.[13] Such messages flow not from the heart that listens first to God and others but from psychological wounds not yet healed or from the illusion that digital disclosure is naturally eloquent and, hence, always desirable.

The antidote to digital attention disorder is not to smash our smartphones or boycott the web. It is, rather, to let Christ's grace saturate all our communication. Taking countercultural action by occasionally abstaining or fasting from digital communication could provide the

---

[12]I borrow this phrase from Richard Lanham, *The Economics of Attention: Style and Substance in the Age of Information* (Chicago: University of Chicago Press, 2006).

[13]Paula S. Tompkins, *Practicing Communication Ethics: Development, Discernment, and Decision Making* (Boston, MA: Allyn & Bacon, 2010), 224–25.

needed perspective on the role of electronic messages in a beautiful life. Texting, after all, is only a means to an end. The end is not our popularity, nor is the end the false comfort of a thousand Facebook friends. In all our interactions, including digital, we should be open to the presence of God's goodness and mercy, accepting with gratitude the relationships we have and exhibiting selfless love in placing others' interests above our own. Loving in the digital era may also require the courage to insist on accurate information, which is crucial for the peaceful resolution of conflict and the promotion of honest politics. These ends cannot be achieved when we let anxieties and jealousies drive our digital interaction. Rather, God's undeserved favor toward us frees us to fashion a new digital eloquence that builds intentional relationships, celebrates beauty in life and culture, and holds earthly authorities accountable to God's justice.

LIVING PROPHETICALLY

Writing to the Romans, Paul brings the eloquence of Isaiah to bear on the gospel of Christ: "How then will they call on him in whom they have not believed? . . . As it is written, 'How beautiful are the feet of those who preach the good news!'" (Rom. 10:14–15). In ancient civilizations, watchmen kept a sharp eye for runners in the distance who brought reports of battles, approaching enemies, or good fortune. Long before fiber-optic networks, submarine cables, or communications satellites, human feet channeled messages to the awaiting cities.[14] Although communication technologies have changed, Isaiah's prophetic message—of peace, of salvation, and of God's righting the world—remains urgent. The prophecy of global redemption is fulfilled in Christ, and as Christ's followers we are commissioned to speak forth the eternal beauties of God's justice and love, addressing the complex challenges of a world still affected by the evil that harms persons, corrupts governments, derails peace, and seeks to crucify Christ again and again, whether by blaspheming his name or persecuting his church. By cultivating a listening orientation to the world and directing our speech accordingly, we are well equipped to have beautiful feet, living an eloquent life as a worthy response to Christ's abundant grace.

---

[14]For more on the image of feet in Scripture, see Leland Ryken, James C. Wilhoit, and Tremper Longman III, eds., *Dictionary of Biblical Imagery* (Downers Grove, IL: InterVarsity, 1998), 280.

CHAPTER TWELVE

EDUCATING FOR INTELLECTUAL CHARACTER

Jay Wood

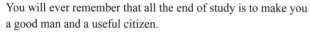

You will ever remember that all the end of study is to make you
a good man and a useful citizen.
—JOHN ADAMS, FROM A LETTER WRITTEN TO HIS SON

Make every effort to supplement your faith with virtue,
and virtue with knowledge.
—2 PETER 1:5

Many Christian colleges claim that the best education does more than
impart information and skills. At their best, they also strive to shape
a student's character. Indeed, this conviction that the best education
includes personal formation stretches back to the very first schools in
the West.[1] The Christian college where I teach stands squarely in this
tradition. Its catalog explicitly states that "our mission as an academic
community is not merely the transmission of information; it is the development of whole and effective Christians who will impact the church
and society worldwide for Christ and His Kingdom." We also have a
community covenant that explicitly lists these priorities. The covenant
calls each member of the campus community to a lifestyle that involves
"practicing those attitudes and actions the Bible portrays as virtuous and
avoiding those the Bible portrays as sinful [vicious]." Among the virtues
listed under the heading "Living the Christian Life" one finds the following: love, justice, kindness, compassion, self-control, forgivingness,
chastity, and patience.

Curiously, most Christian colleges, including mine, lack any explicit

[1]See Pierre Hadot's *Philosophy as a Way of Life* (Malden, MA: Blackwell, 1995). Hadot argues that the
ancient schools of Skepticism, Epicureanism, and Stoicism were as concerned with personal transformation
(*askesis*) as their Platonic and Aristotelian predecessors.

mention of specifically *intellectual* virtues and practices. Moral and theological virtues and vices receive the lion's share of attention. Few evangelicals speak of prudence, humility, courage, and caution as intellectual virtues, nor are advisory notes sounded against such intellectual vices as close-mindedness, testimonial bias, gullibility, self-deception, and other traits that hinder our intellectual growth and pursuit of intellectual goods.[2] A complete Christian liberal arts education must include training in how to foster intellectual virtues as well as how to avoid or conquer intellectual vices. Such training, however, depends on the simultaneous formation of one's moral and theological character. This is because virtuous cognitive functioning requires the cooperation of our wills; our appropriate desires, loves, and emotions (and the moral virtues that correspond to them) must be successfully recruited to bring about Christian intellectual transformation.

INTELLECTUAL POWERS AND INTELLECTUAL GOODS

Humans possess a unique repertoire of cognitive powers. Unlike the beasts, humans have cognitive powers, allowing us to infer, introspect, recall, intuit, and learn (among other abilities). These powers allow us to gain intellectual goods unavailable to the beasts, such as reflective knowledge, wisdom, understanding, and rationality. To be sure, animals have knowledge of an *unreflective* sort. My dog knows where its food dish is and knows the location of the squirrel it vainly chases around the backyard, but it lacks any reflective access to these bits of knowledge. Animals cannot summon reasons to support their knowledge, nor defend it against objection, locate it as arising from reliable cognitive powers, nor situate it in a broader intellectual or narrative framework.[3] Lacking reflective knowledge, animals cannot acquire understanding, wisdom, and rationality.

Christians appreciate the central place our distinctively human cognitive capacities for knowledge, wisdom, and understanding receive throughout Scripture, since our ability to acquire these goods is part of

---

[2]Intellectual goods such as wisdom, knowledge, and understanding are qualities of mind better to have than to lack, from an epistemic point of view.
[3]Ernest Sosa distinguishes the "apt belief" that animals possess from the "reflective knowledge" possessed by humans. See *A Virtue Epistemology: Apt Belief and Reflective Knowledge*, vol. 1 (Oxford: Oxford University Press, 2007), esp. chap. 2.

what makes us God's image bearers. God knows and understands, and so do we, albeit as befits our finite and creaturely status. To live into the fullness of all that God intends for us to be, we must seek and secure various intellectual goods. A father's counsel in Proverbs 5:1–2 urges, "My son, be attentive to my wisdom, incline your ear to my understanding, that you may keep discretion, and your lips may guard knowledge." Likewise, Paul tells the believers in Colossae, "We have not ceased to pray for you, asking that you may be filled with the knowledge of his will in all spiritual wisdom and understanding" (Col. 1:9). Scripture teaches that God has created us with a unique repertoire of cognitive powers so that we may become wise knowers, filled with understanding. God also imparts to us gifts of wisdom and understanding beyond what we can achieve by our own efforts, that we might grow fully into his divine image and so live full, robust, human lives now and in the life to come.

While Scripture repeatedly mentions such goods as wisdom, knowledge, and understanding, it does not formally define them. Indeed, the fact that these terms are so frequently bundled in Scripture might convey the idea that these are merely three words to describe the same thing—a kind of Hebrew parallelism. But this cannot be the case, inasmuch as Scripture also tells us that we can have knowledge without wisdom and understanding, as Paul says of the "knowledge" that "puffs up" (1 Cor. 8:1). Where Scripture remains silent, philosophers rush in to fill the definitional void. A brief, though contestable, account of some chief intellectual goods seems in order.

Let's begin with *knowledge*. Everyone agrees that we cannot know what is in fact false. Nobody knows that Sydney is the capital of Australia, for example. Knowledge is intimately bound up with the truth—so much so, that knowledge is sometimes simply defined in terms of our having successfully tracked the truth. Human knowers are persons who have made successful—though not necessarily exhaustive or infallible—cognitive contact with reality.

The intellectual virtue of *prudence*, or practical wisdom, concerns a disposition to think well that we might live well, successfully negotiating the particular problems and demands we face. Of course, in the Hebrew-Christian tradition, right thinking and right living have chiefly to do with living in right relation to God, to neighbor, to oneself, and to creation. Wisdom in this tradition is not concerned merely with abstract, esoteric, or other-worldly knowledge, as was the case with some Greek philosophy; rather, it has a very practical, real-world orientation. Prudent persons not only apprehend the content of wisdom, but they are also reliably disposed to live it out in their daily lives.

The intellectual good of *understanding* has to do with seeing relations or connections between concepts, claims, and other things. One might know some propositional truths about Mozart's *Requiem*, but this does not guarantee that one thereby understands how the voices, words, instruments, rhythms, tonalities, and other musical elements should coalesce into a first-rate performance. Understanding, then, is a synthesizing intellectual good; it allows us to see how things fit together and function, and thus how a whole constitutes something more than the sum of the parts.

Finally, there is *experiential acquaintance*, an intellectual good that consists of knowing through direct perceptual encounters. For instance, someone who has never tasted bananas will never know what they are like, regardless of how many true propositions he or she might read about them. To memorize more facts about the Sistine Chapel than any other human, yet never to have visited it—never to have felt its cool marble, seen its stunning masterpieces, or inhaled its odors of the centuries—is to lack an important kind of knowledge. This is especially true of our knowledge of persons, both human and divine. The demons are said to believe correctly various truths about God, but they are not experientially connected to God's love and goodness and thus fail to love and worship him.

So God has equipped us with cognitive powers capable of acquiring various intellectual goods. But having properly functioning faculties is no guarantee of our securing the intellectual goods at which they naturally aim. René Descartes, the father of modern philosophy, wrote: "For to be possessed of good mental powers is not sufficient; the principal matter is to apply them well. The greatest minds are capable of the greatest vices as well as of the greatest virtues."[4] Superstition, dogmatism,

---

[4] René Descartes, "Discourse on the Method," in *Philosophical Works of Descartes*, vol. 1, trans. Elizabeth Haldane and G. R. T. Ross (Mineola, NY: Dover Publications, 1955), 82.

willful naïveté, self-deception, and a host of other common intellectual vices threaten success in our intellectual endeavors. To counter these everyday barriers to knowledge and understanding, serious Christians must train themselves in intellectual virtue.

INTELLECTUAL VIRTUES IN GENERAL

A virtue is an acquired habit of excellent functioning in some area of life that is challenging and important. We customarily think of virtues in connection with the moral life. Self-control of our appetites, fair dealing with fellow citizens, and management of routine fears require that we cultivate temperance, justice, and courage, respectively, if we are to live excellent lives. Just as one swallow does not a summer make, so one act of self-control, or compassion, or generosity does not a moral virtue make. No one is counted as virtuously generous for having once dropped five dollars into a Salvation Army kettle at Christmas. Rather, as Aristotle taught, one must be reliably disposed to give the right amount, to the right person, for the right reason, in the right circumstances. This is not easy, requiring as it does the successful integration of heartfelt regard for the beneficiary, right judgment, and well-timed, tactful action. Virtues are deeply anchored habits of the whole person that we can be reliably counted upon to display in appropriate circumstances. Virtues (and vices, unfortunately) thus become ingredients of our character, of who we are at our core.

We are not born morally or intellectually virtuous, nor does virtue develop in us automatically. Traits such as generosity, forgivingness, and intellectual humility form no part of our straight-from-the-factory, standard-issue equipment. In fact, Christianity teaches that our default mode as humans tends in opposite directions, toward stinginess, grudge bearing, and intellectual pride. This is why the apostle Peter commands that we make every effort to add to our faith virtue (2 Pet. 1:5). Intellectually, this means that the renewal by the transformation of our minds, of which Paul also speaks (see Rom. 12:1–2), calls us, among other things, to exchange self-deception for unflinching honesty about our faults, close-mindedness for a willingness to hear thoughtful objections to our preferred ways of thinking, and biased or prejudicial reading for charitable and interpretively sensitive reading of authors with whom we disagree.

While Scripture clearly teaches that we are reasoning beings, it also stresses that we are not purely cerebral, cogitating machines, like *Star Trek*'s Spock or Data. We are instead complex beings that combine intellectual, emotional, and appetitive elements. In Genesis, God laments concerning man that the thoughts of his heart were only for evil (Gen. 6: 11–12). In the Gospels Jesus talks of understanding with our hearts, and of our hearts being slow to believe (Mark 10:5; Luke 5:22). Paul likewise speaks of "having the eyes of your hearts enlightened, that you may know what is the hope to which he has called you" (Eph. 1:18). Here, the heart refers to the center of our loves, cares, concerns, emotions, and desires: what we collectively refer to as "the affections." Scripture's assigning to the heart cognitive tasks such as believing, understanding, and knowing points to the intimate connection between heart and head in gaining intellectual virtues and intellectual goods.

The clear teaching of Scripture is that we function optimally in intellectual pursuits, especially those that concern moral, religious, and interpersonal knowledge and understanding, only when our affections are rightly ordered, when we love the things God loves. Plato taught that the heart's highest quarry and the mind's summit meet in the Form of the Good, thereby requiring that one's moral and emotional nature mature alongside the intellect. A. G. Sertillanges puts the point nicely: "The true springs up in the same soil as the good: their roots communicate. . . . By feeding the mind on truth one enlightens the conscience, by fostering good one guides knowledge."[5] Christians, of course, find the source of the true and good in a personal God, whose goodness and truth are made manifest in the person of Jesus.

Most of us are familiar with the ways that emotions can cause right reasoning to go off the rails. Rage, jealousy, and envy are notorious for impeding right reason and sound judgment. Less frequently commented upon are the ways that our loves and desires aid and abet our efforts to win knowledge and other intellectual goods. (And wouldn't it be odd, given our integrated human nature, if the highest sorts of knowledge

---

[5]A. G. Sertillanges, *The Intellectual Life: Its Spirit, Conditions, Methods,* trans. Mary Ryan (Washington, DC: Catholic University of America Press, 1987), 19.

were as accessible to a scoundrel as to a saint?) To see what contributions our properly tutored affections make to excellent cognitive functioning, it will help to look more deeply into the valuational foundation of all intellectual virtues: the love of truth.

INTELLECTUAL VIRTUES IN PARTICULAR

An underlying motivation supporting our pursuit of intellectual virtue is the "love of knowledge." Aristotle asserts in the *Metaphysics* that human beings, by their very nature, want to know and understand the world around them. Even the smallest infants delight in sensory stimulation and, as they grow older, become more discriminating, seeking more complex knowledge, deepened understanding, and richer experiential acquaintance. But this natural appetite for knowledge, itself an expression of the will, needs to be refined and brought to mature completion. The apostle Paul points us toward this refinement: "Whatever is true, whatever is honorable, whatever is just, whatever is pure, whatever is lovely, whatever is commendable, if there is any excellence, if there is anything worthy of praise, think about these things" (Phil. 4:8).

Love of knowledge in the Christian tradition seeks knowledge that is significant, worthy, and relevant.[6] Significant knowledge interconnects with other things we believe, perhaps by entering into broader explanatory frameworks or serving as the basis or support of other beliefs, and thus contrasts with isolated facts of the sort stuffing trivia games. Worthy beliefs bear on matters of deep human concern, such as justice, friendship, and overall human well-being—matters that make up what Aristotle called *eudaimonia* (happiness or blessedness). This is not to say that worthy knowledge must be practical in having obvious application to human needs. Intellectual pursuits such as mapping the human genome or discovering how stars are born not only prove to be interesting in their own right but also spur the learner on to related knowledge, independently of practical relevance. Yet intellectually virtuous learners appreciate knowledge that is practical—i.e., knowledge directed to an intellectual agent's local concerns, the concerns of her society, and the intellectual practices she cultivates.

---

[6]See Augustine (*Confessions* 10.35) and Thomas Aquinas (*Summa Theologica* 2–2, Q 166, 167).

By contrast, intellectual agents who pursue knowledge from wrong motives use immoral means, seek trivial or immoral content, or apply knowledge in morally questionable ways. Imagine someone whose intellectual desires and energies were directed to memorizing pages of the phone book or calculating the number of grains of sand in a cubic meter of the Sahara. Such a person would, no doubt, acquire truths—lots of them—but they would be trivial in comparison to what the person could acquire. Vicious knowledge, and vicious means of acquiring and disseminating knowledge, abound: freak shows, plagiarism, gossip, corporate spying, and eavesdropping, to name a few. Not all knowledge is of equal value. The Christian tradition clearly teaches that persons with ability and opportunity have a responsibility to oversee their intellectual development. To ignore this responsibility, or to discharge it badly, can result in our forfeiting a share of important intellectual goods.

A refined and mature love of truth grounds many of the other intellectual virtues. Because of an overriding love of significant, worthy, and relevant knowledge, *intellectually humble* people set aside vanity and arrogance and willingly hear criticisms of their views. *Intellectually generous* people go to lengths to impart knowledge and to nurture it in others because they think it a great good that others should know the truth. For truth's sake, *intellectually courageous* people face into perceived harms that may accompany their seeking, testing, or sharing knowledge. And a love of knowledge motivates people who display the virtue of *intellectual tenacity* not to abandon their beliefs at the first whiff of criticism or to cling to beliefs, theories, research programs, or understandings if, after due consideration, they see that the balance of evidence weighs against them. The virtue of *intellectual autonomy* marks those who balance well the dual concern to honor received wisdom but also to think independently and to form judgments that may refine or even overturn tradition. We see, then, that intellectual virtues fit us to function well where intellectual goods are at stake: in shaping our intellectual appetites, in giving and receiving criticism, in changing our minds or sticking to our guns, in deferring to intellectual benefactors and forming independent opinions, in teaching and disseminating in various ways the knowledge one acquires, and more. These and other intellectual virtues all have their root in a love for knowledge that overrides ego, fear, overreliance on other people's judgments, and other impediments to truth.

INTELLECTUAL VIRTUES IN THE ACADEMY

Intellectual virtues, as mature perfections of our cognitive powers, must be nurtured in congenial environments and in the midst of specific intellectual practices that put our cognitive powers to determinate uses in order to achieve intellectual ends. Reading, teaching, debate, scientific research, and artistic creativity are just a few of the intellectual practices found in the academy that pursue intellectual goods. The interdisciplinary context of a liberal arts college provides ideal soil for cultivating intellectual virtues as it steeps students in multiple practices whose goals are understanding, experiential acquaintance, knowledge, and other intellectual goods. How do specific disciplines such as philosophy, the arts, and the sciences help students to foster particular intellectual virtues and avoid various intellectual vices?

Consider the discipline of philosophy. Philosophers prize, among other intellectual virtues, *dialectical proficiency*, the ability to articulate and defend one's beliefs orally and in writing. Through courses in logic and critical thinking, students become skilled at cutting through the fog of imprecision and vagueness to clarity and understanding. Sometimes, however, virtues distort into vices when the volume of our admirable traits has been turned up too high. In "Trying Out One's New Sword," Mary Midgley calls attention to the ancient samurai practice of testing the merits of a new blade by attempting to bisect innocent passersby in a single stroke.[7] Like logical samurai, some of my philosophy students have taken their newly acquired dialectical skills into their other classes with the aim of slicing through the ideas and opinions of their fellow students. Dialectical proficiency, untempered by charity, can breed intellectual arrogance, leading students to infer, falsely, that their logical acumen confers an entitlement to correct others in all contexts. Disagreement is inevitable in the academy. Yet Christian professors who model graciously how to make judgments in the midst of peer disagreement help students to speak in love what they take to be the truth.

---

[7]Mary Midgley, "Trying Out One's New Sword," in *Heart and Mind: The Varieties of Moral Experience* (London: Routledge Classics, 2003), 80–87.

Likewise, study in the visual and performing arts ideally fosters several virtues, especially a capacity to discern and appreciate beauty. If, as some philosophers claim, humans possess an aesthetic sense as part of their native cognitive equipment, and if virtues are the completion, maturation, or perfection of our faculties, then artists surely nurture this ability in a privileged and powerful way. Creativity, too, counts as an important intellectual virtue, along with *perspectival flexibility*: the ability to see something—a scene, an image, a photograph—from multiple points of view. Artists have a remarkable facility to visualize with elasticity, to see patterns, or to rearrange elements of some visual scene in novel ways. If you have ever been helped to see the two visual parts of a gestalt image, then you have some sense of what artists can do on a much grander scale. Perspectival flexibility, in turn, helps to combat a hardening of the visual categories that limits the way we see things except from a very limited point of view.

Visual flexibility facilitates a corresponding cognitive flexibility, which allows artists to see and appreciate alien perspectives. However, artists risk growing overly attached to some of their preferred ways of seeing and doing. Though trained to perspectival flexibility, artists can fall in love with their own novel ways of seeing, so that the very virtue they are ideally poised to promote gets stifled. For example, when the French Impressionists first came onto the art scene, the established Romantic painters barred their works from the Academic Salons and Royal Galleries because the Impressionists had the audacity to paint ordinary subjects, such as peasants and haystacks, forsaking the preferred subjects of mythological figures, sublime landscapes, and formal portraiture. The Romantics, once the innovators to the Neoclassicists that preceded them, had become hardened, resistant to Impressionist innovation. The intellectual virtue of perspectival flexibility allows one to appreciate new paradigms and helps us to avoid enshrining one paradigm to the exclusion of others.

Scientific study ideally promotes virtues such as intellectual firmness, intellectual perseverance, and intellectual generosity, as they are crucial for success in science. Today, scientific research is seldom a solo endeavor; it occurs collaboratively. This requires that scientists cooperate and defer to the expertise of others on complex projects, which requires intellectual generosity. The famous primatologist Jane Goodall mentored intellectual generosity by insisting that all the interns and PhD students working with her at the Gombe Reserve break with prevailing practice by sharing their data. Scientists adept at delving into the intricacies of nature frequently stimulate a corresponding sense of reverence and awe at its beauty. Yet science, too, is susceptible to its own disciplinary temptations to vice. Rather than reverence, some scientists operate as tough-minded technicians who poke and prod nature in order to subject it to human mastery. They operate by the mantra "If it can be done, it should and will be done." They risk adopting immoral methods and putting their knowledge to pernicious use—a Faustian bargain.

The twentieth century alone offers many case studies of knowledge gained at the expense of human lives and well-being, including the Tuskegee experiments in the United States and the infamous Nazi experiments in Germany. The famous physicist Robert Oppenheimer exclaimed after successfully detonating the first atomic bomb, "It worked!" Yet, after the atomic bomb was dropped on Hiroshima and Nagasaki, he regretted his experiments. He later confessed to President Truman, "I feel I have blood on my hands."[8] Science pursued within the Christian liberal arts context is ever mindful of the way scientific practice must be morally bounded.

Students who seriously pursue a liberal arts education should also seriously pursue intellectual virtues. By sampling widely from among various disciplines, students can begin to cultivate a range of intellectual virtues as well as become inoculated against characteristic intellectual vices. Surely this is one application of Paul's exhortation, "Do not be conformed to this world, but be transformed by the renewal of your mind, that by testing you may discern what is the will of God, what is good and acceptable and perfect" (Rom. 12:2).

---

[8]Kai Bird and Martin Sherwin, *American Prometheus: The Triumph and Tragedy of J. Robert Oppenheimer* (New York: Knopf, 2005), 332.

CHAPTER THIRTEEN

BEYOND BUILDING A RÉSUMÉ

Stephen B. Ivester

Our role . . . crossing into the Promised Land . . . is the
taking of the land by choosing to plant the soles of our
feet on the "given ground" to possess it.
—JULIE GORMAN, *COMMUNITY THAT IS CHRISTIAN*

The LORD makes firm the steps
    of the one who delights in him.
—PSALM 37:23 (NIV)

I vividly recall a day when I was eighteen years old. At the end of the
summer, I packed a footlocker and a duffle bag into the family car and
drove with my mother from a small town in New England to a Christian
college in the Midwest. My thoughts were focused on the many challenges ahead over the next four years, especially living in an academic
environment and developing my abilities as a clarinet performance
major. I was the product of a rural New Hampshire school system on
my way to a liberal arts institution halfway across the country, and I felt
preoccupied with one thing: the credentials I would gain by getting a
degree in music.

Upon arriving at my residence hall, it was uncanny how similar my
thoughts were to my peers' in terms of why we came to college and what
we intended to do. We talked about our high school experiences, regaled
one another with humorous and moving tales, compared the qualifications that got us accepted, and shared our dreams for an ideal job. Each
of us revealed our idealism. Few of us considered how college might
shape our character and our convictions for life.

Twenty years later, in reflecting on my interests as a college educator who now works in student development, I realize that the direction

that I ultimately took in life occurred largely because I had become unconsciously shaped by a liberal arts philosophy of education. I did not openly set out to pursue a job in higher education. I fully believed I was headed toward the life of a professional musician. However, in hindsight, I see that my choice of vocation resulted from the collective effect of several things: engaging the breadth of academic disciplines; getting involved outside the classroom; building friendships with Christian peers; listening to godly mentors; and deepening my faith in Christ. All of these powerful influences redefined the life that I had first expected when I was eighteen. In truth, my liberal arts education instigated a lifelong journey toward the discovery of who I am, who I was meant to be, and what God desires for my life. Being effective in my work today depends upon my ongoing commitment to Christian liberal learning.

To be a student represents a high calling. It is an extraordinary gift. The years you spend as an undergraduate will not be like any other period in your life. As a follower of Jesus, you have been chosen by God to serve in his kingdom—to serve the church and to meet needs in society. Your calling, while a student, fundamentally involves prep-aration—"to plant the soles of your feet on the ground"—just as God's people have always done, and to take full ownership, under the grace of God, of your total college experience. In following the example of the Israelites as they were called to establish God's kingdom on earth, you have the opportunity to see these years in college as an experience that prepares you for effective kingdom service.

Your calling, then, requires you to explore the landscape of a liberal arts education. The fullness of a Christian liberal arts education is not about building a résumé but about pursuing a calling to become fully human. While in college you have the opportunity to (1) discern how you can become all God has called you to become, (2) search for truth inside and outside the classroom, and (3) intentionally build Christ-centered friendships.

GREATER EXPECTATIONS

It is common to enter college with big dreams for becoming a mis-sionary doctor, an elementary school teacher, an elected official, or a professional musician. The temptation to think of college primarily as preparation for a job seems all too common, even expected. This should not surprise us, given that we live in such a secular world, where the idea of education for transformation gets little attention.

Viewing your liberal arts college experience as a calling, however, involves much more than getting a good job after you graduate. While career choices do matter, a liberal arts theory of education asserts that the person you are becoming matters more than the kind of job you will eventually get. It is about shifting your focus and energy from trying to *do* something to learning how to *be* someone. In *The Idea of a Christian College* Arthur Holmes gives this commendation: "The Christian's vocation is larger by far than any specific ministry or vocation he may enter; it reaches into everything a person is and can be or do."[1] The power of Holmes's statement can be made real by hearing how a student recently experienced this in her own life. Consider her words: "Before college, I understood education as a goal to reach, a title to be earned. But now I echo a favorite professor: 'We are what we know.' As I've seen in my years in college, the responsibility is very great."

If a Christian liberal arts education has to do with preparing you to become a better person, it must serve the larger purpose of producing Christian growth. Your Christian education, then, distinctly becomes the context for God's creative and redemptive work. It is a process of transformation, not mere job preparation. It is about what the apostle Paul says in 2 Corinthians 5:17: "If anyone is in Christ, he is a new creation. The old has passed away." Learning in a liberal arts setting takes on a whole new meaning when understood in this context.

PUTTING THINGS TOGETHER

At its core, college emphasizes the classroom. The courses you take, the books you read, the papers your write, and the exams you complete will require a significant investment of your time and energy. Embracing these activities with enthusiasm can result in incredible intellectual growth. It goes without saying that to become a genuine Christian student you have to make an intentional commitment to nurture your

---

[1] Arthur Holmes, *The Idea of a Christian College* (Grand Rapids, MI: Eerdmans, 1975), 18.

intellectual life. As Professor Holmes explains, "Your first priority must be the quest for unchanging truth."[2]

But there is a larger sense of learning in college; truth travels beyond the four walls of a classroom. Learning is comprehensive and multidimensional. It takes place 24/7. This quest for truth should permeate all of your college experience. Ultimately, learning involves seeing God's entire world as the classroom. Consider every person you meet as a potential teacher, and consider every experience as a teachable moment.

During the past two decades, numerous scholars have documented the importance of students engaging life beyond the classroom and the influence this has on growth and personal development. Outside of a formal learning context, students are more poised, reflective, and ready to engage. Consider former Duke University president Nannerl Keohane's claim:

> Some of the most formative moments in a liberal education occur outside the classroom. A residential campus provides multiple encounters with other students and faculty members in extracurricular activities, sports and volunteer service. Bringing together seekers of knowledge across the generations, the campus is a uniquely powerful setting for such structured yet serendipitous exploration.[3]

This "serendipitous exploration" throughout the entirety of the college experience is critical for shaping the curious student into a complete person. "Real-life" collaborative experiences—such as living in a residence hall, attending campus social events, participating in athletics, engaging in a special-interest club, or leading a student-run ministry—can provide a laboratory for growth, enhancing the kind of holistic development that genuine Christian liberal arts colleges seek to promote.

One young woman in student government reflected how she was grappling with becoming a more effective leader. What was she learning? Serving as a committee chair allowed her to use her experience as a practice field for understanding the theory she was studying in class: human relations, resources, and systems. According to this student's

---

[2]Ibid., 112.
[3]Nannerl O. Keohane, "The Liberal Arts and the Role of Elite Higher Education," in *In Defense of American Higher Education,* ed. Philip G. Altbach, Patricia J. Gumport, and D. Bruce Johnstone (Baltimore, MD: Johns Hopkins University Press, 2001), 185.

perspective, she was "putting things together." As she discovered, integrating learning with a life of faith requires that you examine all of your experiences and invigorate your discipleship by connecting classroom life with what you are doing outside the classroom. Learn to dialogue between these worlds. Apply the theory you are discussing in the classroom to your real-life experiences in the residence hall. This sort of liberal learning requires a thoughtful integration and analysis, a blending of experiences and concepts, and an intentional application of theoretical structures. All of your life as a student, then, becomes a constructive task—to integrate your faith, learning, and living.

Be intentional by making decisions to participate in experiences that will allow you to do integrative work. If you are involved in the college radio station, enroll in a public speaking course to gain additional communication skills. If you enjoy poetry, join the staff of a student-run literary magazine. If accounting motivates you, manage the finances of a student club. Likewise, a soccer team will help you become not only a better athlete but also a better collaborator. A racial reconciliation discussion group will teach you not only to appreciate differences but also to be a more effective advocate for social change. In addition to fostering coordinated discipline and skill, a music ensemble will instill the value of mutual dependence in order to accomplish a task. These kinds of cocurricular activities will help you to excel within your courses and begin to discover who God has called you to be.

But here is the rub: you can overextend yourself. Taking on too much will hinder rather than promote the goal of character development. It will diminish what you learn. Some students are up to their ears in activities outside of class. They join multiple clubs, play on several intramural teams, lead a Bible study small group, and meet one-on-one with friends for accountability. They literally jump from one activity to the next, never fully engaging any of them, falsely believing that they can "do it all." These overcommitted students rarely experience freedom. They are slaves to their schedules. Their hectic search for "the right thing" ends up deflating their spirit. These students are in danger of becoming something less, not something more.

Seeing all of your experiences as a classroom should be foundational to how you view life as a college student. There should be no gaps.

Christian college life should be dynamic and fluid, not static and compart-mentalized. It changes every semester—different classes, new friendships, fresh opportunities for service, exposure to bigger ideas and growth in your convictions. All of these changes will delight, inspire, and challenge you.

FACE-TO-FACE AND SIDE BY SIDE

Our lives are whole entities with intellectual, spiritual, physical, and social concerns wrapped into one interactive package. All the different facets of who we are as persons come together. Being able to focus on this package as a unified venture is one of the benefits of a liberal arts education. This can be a rich blessing not only individually but also communally. A liberal arts experience depends upon students commit-ting to a journey—living, studying, serving, exploring, playing, and learning in communion with God and in community with others. We are created to live and learn together.

In college, community involves friends, classes, teams, floormates, and prayer groups. "Community is not an organization," Henri Nouwen explains; "it is a way of living: you gather around people with whom you want to proclaim the truth that we are the beloved sons and daughters of God."[4] What you believe—about yourself, others, the world, God, and truth—is lived out all around you: on campus quads or in the classroom; in residence hallways and in lounges; on intramural fields and basketball courts; while playing late-night video games or folding laundry. Through these interactions, you can learn to see yourself through other people's lives. As your friends share about what they are learning, you likely will reflect on your own growth. Your values become shaped by these rela-tionships; in turn, your values shape others with whom you interact. In *Habits of the Heart: Individualism and Commitment in American Life,* Robert Bellah explains the influence of community: "We find ourselves not independently of other people and institutions but through them. We never get to the bottom of ourselves on our own. We discover who we are—and who we are meant to be—face to face and side by side with others in work, love and learning."[5] The principle here is not only practi-

---

[4]Henri Nouwen, "From Solitude to Community to Ministry," *Leadership Journal* 16 (1995): 83.
[5]Robert Bellah et al., *Habits of the Heart: Individualism and Commitment in American Life* (San Francisco: Perennial, 1985), 84.

cal but also biblical: Christ calls us to follow him in community, and in that community we find our true identity.

Decades of theoretical and empirical research demonstrate that your peers, in particular, are the single most potent source of influence in your life. This means that you—not just your faculty or other adult mentors—are a person of influence in the lives of those around you. So then, devote considerable attention not only to your own growth and development as a whole and effective Christian, but also to those around you. Take the time to consider who you are and how that impacts your relationships. Maybe you need to grow in being a humble servant and appreciating every person the way that God has commanded. Or perhaps you are prone to talk over other people, and listening doesn't come easily. Initiate conversations with brothers and sisters in Christ about your weaknesses so that they can speak truth into your life. Growth happens from the outside in, not primarily by how you see new things about yourself but by how others call things out in you.

Pray for the Holy Spirit to guide your heart so that you may seek after a better understanding of who you know yourself to be, especially in relation to others. Pray that the Lord himself will satisfy you with his pleasure as you seek to serve those around you. It will make your life so much more fulfilling, and so much more beneficial to others.

Take your growth in college seriously and let your learning coalesce with the convictions that are developing through your studies. Challenge these convictions in the presence of your peers, test them according to Scripture, and explore how they affect the way you interpret the world around you. Learning in community requires you to take initiative and marshal the intellectual strengths of others toward a deeper understanding of life.

Investing fully in others' lives means taking some risks, sharing openly, and asking difficult questions. You can do this by being mentored one-on-one by a faculty member, serving alongside a classmate as a tutor in the inner city, or offering leadership to a club or ministry on campus. This intentional approach to learning enables our growth, making us more human. Here is one student's perspective on what he learned through community:

rned so much about how I relate to others, and as competent as
believe I am, it's always important to ask for help and seek the
ᴗᴗᴗᴗ pleasure instead of the praises of man. These are good life lessons, and believe me when I say that I'll be learning these things my
whole life!

LOOKING AHEAD

A Christian liberal arts education encourages you to become fully human
in Christ by concentrating on what shapes you into the person God has
envisioned you to become. It encourages you to integrate your learning and to foster this growth by crossing the boundaries between the
classroom and life outside the classroom. It calls you to form intentional
relationships that will challenge and support you as you learn from others in a Christ-centered community. Ultimately, a Christian liberal arts
education encourages you to become all that you are meant to be—more
completely human for the sake of God's kingdom. Consider these words
from one Christian college graduate who now works in community
development:

> What did the liberal arts education help me do that I don't think a dif-
> ferent kind of education would have done for me? Well, there are a lot
> of problems that I face day to day in my work. Facing these challenges
> involves connecting the dots. Consider the topic of rebuilding the com-
> munity; we have to talk about clean energy, immigration reform, and a
> lot of other issues. We have to talk about these issues from a policy per-
> spective, an economic perspective, a moral perspective, and a spiritual
> perspective. All in all, I think my liberal arts education helped me see all
> of those interconnected pieces of the same big puzzle, and integrating
> that, of course, with my faith—a faith that doesn't just call me to think
> about things differently, but calls me to live my life out differently in
> light of what I believe and who I am becoming.

For this student the various facets of life and work are connected by the
glue of faith.

And here is the key: the calling of a Christian liberal arts student is
a lifetime commitment, not something you just hang on the wall. Begin
now, by using all of your experiences in college, and especially the
relationships around you, to stretch your vision for growing in wisdom
and discernment as you intentionally pursue growth in character. Learn

how to be more adaptive, creative, flexible, and sensitive. Grow in your understanding of your talents. As you discern your God-given talents, develop those talents, now and throughout your life. Lean into the practice of discernment more fully in your college years, opening possibilities that go beyond the job you might get after you graduate.

Being a student is a calling. "Plant the soles of your feet" on the ground and fully explore the landscape of learning that a liberal arts education offers. As you journey toward becoming fully human in Christ, concentrate on how your college experience might shape you into the person God has envisioned you to become. It will require that you see these college years as preparation—for all of life.

SECTION FOUR

DIVISIONAL AREAS OF STUDY

When students hear the term "liberal arts college," they are likely to think first of the various content areas that are taught at such a college: languages, philosophy, anthropology, and so forth. What we have tried to show in this book is that a liberal education promotes something much more important than merely the mastery of a body of knowledge distributed over a range of academic disciplines. A liberal education—especially in the Christian tradition—promotes the development of the total person. To that end, it sharpens the intellectual skills and shapes the intellectual virtues that are characteristic of a whole and effective human being. To put this another way, a liberal education is less concerned with what you know and more concerned with who you are becoming. For Christians, such an education offers comprehensive preparation for kingdom service in the home, the church, and the world.

Having considered the skills that a liberal education develops and the virtues that it cultivates, we now take a look at some of the content areas that typically are covered over the duration of a liberal arts education. During a four-year undergraduate program, most liberal arts students take courses in subjects such as history, biology, sociology, and music. What we present here is a general introduction to these and other academic subjects, not by individual departments but according to the broad disciplinary divisions of an undergraduate college (natural sciences, social sciences, humanities, and the arts).

From the outset, it needs to be acknowledged that dividing a college according to academic disciplines (from which each student will choose to declare a major) is something of a departure from the liberal arts ideal. In its purest form, a liberal education values an integration of the many disciplines over specialization in just one. A distinctively Christian education offers a healthy corrective to the intellectual fragmentation that characterizes much of higher education today. By learning to view everything from a consistently Christ-centered perspective, the Christian liberal arts student finds fundamental unity in the person and work of Jesus Christ.

The following essays are offered to orient your undergraduate experience in a liberal arts college or university by describing the unique contribution that each area of academic life makes to human knowledge. Each of the liberal arts and sciences gives us a different way of looking at the world and understanding the human condition, thus helping us to know our place as citizens of the kingdom of God. Each discipline has its own method of exploration, way of thinking, and perception of reality. Each area of academic life offers its own means of experiencing the world, giving the Christian student new opportunities to bring honor and glory to God. To that end, we will explore how to think Christianly about traditional divisions within a liberal arts education, seeing what difference it makes to view each area of study through the lens of a Christian worldview.

CHAPTER FOURTEEN

A WORLD OF DISCOVERY THROUGH THE NATURAL SCIENCES

Dorothy F. Chappell

So vast, without any question, is the Divine Handiwork of the Almighty Creator!
—COPERNICUS, *DE REVOLUTIONIBUS*

The heavens declare the glory of God;
    the skies proclaim the work of his hands.
Day after day they pour forth speech;
    night after night they reveal knowledge.
They have no speech, they use no words;
    no sound is heard from them.
Yet their voice goes out into all the earth,
    their words to the ends of the world.
—PSALM 19:1–4 (NIV)

The late afternoon breezes blowing through the tall ponderosa pines brought relief, following the cloudless hot morning. These light winds soon gave way to a swiftly advancing storm front crossing the Black Hills of South Dakota. Picturesque displays of lightning danced across the afternoon sky, giving rise to bursts of thunder, which rumbled repetitiously off canyon walls. The light blue sky transformed to a dark background, lit with dazzling displays of lightning—an improvisation of nonrhythmic, jagged motion.

AWE, LIGHT, AND PROMISE

Suddenly a bolt from the sky struck and exploded a ponderosa pine, igniting the highly volatile terpenes in the trunk. The flames of this hot torch were not quenched by the light rain. As the ground heated around the stump of the burning tree, rattlesnakes emerged from the rocky surfaces and migrated to cooler, more tolerable rock ledges.

The storm approached the geological uplift known as the Black Hills, which rises approximately 7,200 feet above sea level at its highest peak. This unique, pear-shaped formation, over 125 miles long and 65 miles wide, represents a terrestrial island surrounded by prairie. Beautiful flora and fauna from north, south, east, and west converge and hybridize in this splendid environment. Grand geological features reveal an abundance of minerals and rocks, denoting the relentless forces of nature. The brilliant skies, unencumbered by competing artificial lights, offer an immense theater for study of stars and planets. Biologists, geologists, and astronomers enjoy exploring this island in the sea of prairie. Scientists who study the Black Hills from the eyes of biblical faith generally attribute a deeper understanding of God's glory and his creativity to the revelations they comprehend while in this rich natural environment.

As this storm receded, the dark clouds became fainter in the distant northeast. Several scientists walked up a hill into a lovely damp, grassy meadow. Their conversation abated as they crested the hill, where they heard intermittent clapping. They saw over a dozen liberal arts students sitting on the hillside, applauding each lightning flash as the storm moved northeast. When the students were asked why they were clapping, they responded, "The work of the Lord—isn't the lightning beautiful against the dark blue sky?"

A rainbow provided a capstone to this experience, and as one might guess, the students sat in silent repose and wonder, reminded of God's promise associated with the colorful prism arc. As the rainbow faded, the students and faculty talked about the ultimate purposes of the universe and earth, why humans were created, and how humans should relate to their Creator and the rest of creation. These were delightful, profound moments of learning. Experiences like these, that lead to discussion about ultimate questions, are cherished, especially by natural science faculty and students who follow Christ. Such conversations and realizations can occur in spectacular field settings or in the laboratories, classrooms, and offices of science facilities.

The students who applauded the work of the Lord were celebrating something they deemed good and beautiful in God's creation! They were thinking Christianly, acknowledging that the Father delegated Christ as the author, perfector, and sustainer of creation; he reveals himself, in part, through nature. Christ created the natural order, and therefore "it is good," as Genesis reminds us. This inspiring way of thinking about the natural world demands the time and attention that Christians can give to it. The creation is meant to be contemplated, and, in so doing, its Creator is meant to be praised and worshiped for this marvelous gift to humankind.

The setting and the circumstances of study described here provided the haven for this contemplation. These students and faculty had taken off their shoes, and they experienced the wonder of creation, what the poet Elizabeth Barrett Browning attests to in the following verse:

> Earth's crammed with heaven,
> And every common bush afire with God;
> But only he who sees takes off his shoes.[1]

The student or teacher "who sees" the grandeur of God in a bush, an antelope, a star, or a hill must go barefoot, experiencing God's glory and power reflected in creation. The work of science, then, especially for one who believes in the triune God, involves engagement of one's complete being. As scientists study the creation, they engage many methods to gain a breadth of understanding about the natural world.

LIBERAL ARTS, CHRISTIAN WORLDVIEW, AND UNIFIED MEANING

A liberal arts education informed by a Christian worldview provides a comprehensive way of encompassing and intertwining mind, heart, and soul. Contextualizing the liberal arts within a Christian worldview brings rich insights from the biblical grand narrative, showing the relevance of the traditional academic disciplines, including those in the natural sciences. For Christians, two helpful approaches, among others, shed light on the eternal meaning brought to contemplation and response in developing knowledge, praise, worship, and service for Christ.

---

[1]Elizabeth Barrett Browning, "Aurora Leigh," in *The Complete Poetical Works of Elizabeth Barrett Browning*, ed. Harriet Waters Preston (Boston: Houghton Mifflin, 1900), n.p.

First, when Christians interact with the Creator and his creation, they enjoy the wonder and ecstasy of the beauty and mysteries of the natural world, worshiping and praising God more fully. The stunning regularity of matter and energy in the universe, and in the laws that apply to them, provides an immense realm for exploration. Apprehending the glory of God, revealed in his beautiful creation, is not limited to professional scientists. Casual observers, and all students serious about liberal arts learning, can see God's glory in their explorations of creation.

Second, since the Christian worldview is all-encompassing and applies to all human knowledge, affections, and activities, it should shape our habits and the formation of our virtues. Our virtues, in turn, affect our acts of reconciliation. Specifically, virtues formed by a love of God, a compassion for human beings, and a respect for the creation can inform us about how science should be conducted. Accountability among scientists also includes the initiation of interventions through the practice of science in the stewardship of resources, alleviation of suffering, and protection of the environment. Arthur Holmes captures this well when he prompts us to remember that *thinking Christianly* is creative and constructive: "By seeing everything in relation to the Creator-God incarnated in Jesus Christ, it gives unified meaning, direction and hope to all we do."[2] Christians who are scientists or nonscientists can use science to do good for the sake of Christ's kingdom. Scientific study in the contemporary world is an exciting and consummate Christian calling.

CONTEMPORARY SCIENCE

Scientists are intrigued with the wonder and ecstasy of discovery; the mysteries of the natural world perpetuate dynamic human curiosity. The frontiers of science provide opportunities for studies that employ the use of the latest technologies and the largest amassing of data known to humans. Genetic data, astronomical images, and weather data, for instance, require huge computer storage for subsequent analyses. Likewise, interdisciplinary approaches to science and collaboration among investigators in labs around the globe characterize pace-setting contemporary science. The

---

[2]Arthur Holmes, "Toward a Christian View of Things," in *The Making of a Christian Mind*, ed. Arthur Holmes (Downers Grove, IL: InterVarsity, 1985), 12.

growth of scientific ethics has accompanied unparalleled advances in science that require guidance for the appropriate manipulation of nature and the use of technology.

Science is the major tool through which the natural world is studied. God's revelations of truth can be affirmed in nature. However, science represents a particular theoretical approach to knowledge, manifest in various disciplines, with accepted standards and procedures that address natural phenomena and do not go beyond the natural realm for explanations. The hypotheses and theories generated in scientific study are based upon empirically measured phenomena, which generally use interdisciplinary approaches, like applications of biology and chemistry for problem solving in pharmaceutical research. Characteristically, science is constantly in a state of correction as new data are evaluated. Two well-known examples serve to make this point: first, the publication of *De revolutionibus*, by Copernicus, in which he first suggested that the sun and not the earth is the center of the universe; and, second, Lysenko's decades-long use of Lamarckian genetics, the transmission of environmentally acquired characteristics, in attempts to breed wheat. Science is dynamic and embraces change as new evidence arises.

The fields of study among natural sciences are replete with opportunities for study by Christians employing honest attempts to discern something of the universe within the scope of the competencies (what science can tell us) and the limitations (what science cannot tell us) of science.[3] Although science uses a naturalistic methodology (methods with empirically based boundaries), it neither implies metaphysical naturalism (that the material world is all there is) nor requires that Christians who are scientists hold the view that naturalistic factors can fully explain all phenomena. God's work in the world—his providence—includes his continuing preservation of creation for his intended purposes. The assurance that God is at work in his creation, preparing for the future, accounts for the regularity of the natural world and also for miracles, which may appear to defy the natural laws of the universe. Regardless of whether God's work in creation is supernatural and miraculous or

---

[3]Del Ratzsch, *Science and Its Limits* (Downers Grove, IL: InterVarsity, 2000), 73–99.

revealed in the regular activities of the natural world, his providence is evident in the guidance of his creation to fulfill his intended purposes. Consider the phenomena of miracles as a case in point. Doctors who pray for miracles also continue to look for and administer physical interventions such as drug therapy, diet changes, and other treatments to alleviate suffering. The Christian physician recognizes and respects that human health is sustained by God; thus, physicians can be used by God in the healing process.

Furthermore, many advances in contemporary science are dependent upon the inseparable relationships of natural science with mathematics. Mathematics is one way rationality is preserved in contemporary science.[4] Its methods and principles are essential to scientific analyses:

> Mathematicians view the creative God as the source of knowledge in their studies, and mathematics has developed differently from natural sciences in that mathematics may be developed abstractly apart from the observable world. The results in mathematics are verifiable by logical axiomatic arguments and are not subject to change unless the underlying axioms are modified. Mathematics is effective in modeling many physical and social phenomena.[5]

It is a high calling to respond to God, serving as a natural scientist or a mathematician in contemporary science culture, and to use one's gifts for the glory of God in studying his creation.

DISCOVERY, WORSHIP, AND SCHOLARSHIP

Natural scientists who are Christians often delight in the use of nature as their laboratory for study. The inspiration for, and the motivation of, Christians to contemplate and study creation is captured beautifully by the psalmist: "Great are the works of the LORD, studied by all who delight in them" (Ps. 111:2). The theologian John Calvin made a bold case for taking God's works seriously: "Let us not be ashamed to take pious delight in the works of God open and manifest in this most beautiful theatre. . . . Although it is not the chief evidence for faith, yet it is the first evidence in the order of nature, to be mindful that wherever we cast

---

[4] Del Ratzsch, *Philosophy of Science* (Downers Grove, IL: InterVarsity, 1986), 16.
[5] Personal correspondence with Dr. Robert Brabenec, professor of mathematics, Wheaton College.

our eyes, all things they meet are works of God, and at the same time to ponder with pious meditation to what end God created them."[6]

Scholarship in science has revealed aspects of the natural world that were unfathomable by other generations. We not only comprehend various aspects of the natural world, but we also construct technology to manipulate it, as we do with the creation of synthetic genomes and the development of a quantum machine. Whether the detection of exoplanets or the existence of water on Mars, such remarkable feats have only been accomplished with the advent of advanced technology.

Another type of legitimate scholarship for Christians is incorporating theology and philosophy into thinking about the natural world. Such philosophers and theologians of science address questions of purpose and meaning in creation. Christians should be enthusiastic about the process of discovery as scientific data affirm Christ's handiwork, eliciting praise and worship for the splendor of all creation. The heavens and creation declare the glory of God!

CREATED ORDER, CURIOUS MINDS, AND TECHNOLOGY INVITE DISCOVERY

A sound biblical theology provides a proper basis for scientific inquiry. The great drama of creation, fall, redemption, and the reconciliation of all things, properly understood, establishes the basis for studying God's creation. Christ, who has all knowledge and power, accepted the delegated authority of the Father to create and sustain the intricate and vast features of the natural order. Therefore, the creation is real, has intrinsic value, and is, to a large degree, comprehensible. It was created by God, whose image we bear. Yet, creation is not God. There is a distinction between the Creator and what he creates. Further, creation is fallen, though it still reveals the glory of God through its physical laws in all their simplicities and complexities.

The mysteries of creation can stimulate God-given human wonder and curiosity, challenge the rational mind, motivate sustained human investigations of nature, and inspire untold acts of compassion. Simple exploration and well-designed experiments, as well as

---

[6]John Calvin, *Calvin: Institutes of the Christian Religion*, ed. John T. McNeill, trans. Ford Lewis Battles (Philadelphia: Westminster Press, 1960), 1.14.20.

the serendipitous exploration of nature, yield new and complex data, concepts, and theories.

The curiosities and interests of individual scientists are tied to the development of technologies that push the boundaries of discovery for things like the prevention and cure of HIV infections, identification of the Higgs particle, disassembly of the *Anthrax* toxin, prediction of volcanic activity, elucidation of genetic diseases, illumination of mammalian pathogens, and determination of roles of Vitamin A in lung fibrosis, among many others. Explorations of the vast realm of nature lead to new discoveries, upon which other discoveries depend or hold promise for the good of humankind, the earth, and the universe.

Curiosity is an intellectual trait that often starts early and persists throughout scientists' lives. They develop reservoirs of complex questions worthy of exploration. Science addresses only questions about the natural order. Questions such as "Of what is the universe made?" are the types "that science is good at eventually answering," according to Owen Gingerich.[7] He goes on to say that questions dealing with *why* and *purpose* (e.g., "Why is there something rather than nothing?") should be left to philosophers and theologians. Investigations of very simple or complex phenomena and engagement in the process of discovery through observations, experimentation, and theory formation represent disciplined activities of scientists. They dedicate their God-given ingenuity, talent, energy, wisdom, and curiosity to the exploration of the frontiers of energy and matter on earth and throughout the universe. These intrepid explorers want to know more about the frontiers of the universe, and their studies encompass investigations from the center of the earth to the distant stars.

Simultaneous with, and essential to, the practice of science is the development of sophisticated technology used by scientists to observe and record data in their investigations. Scientific studies, from the bottom of the ocean to deep space, are dependent upon developments in technology. Some technologies are developed specifically to accumulate data and insights about the natural world, while other technologies are by-products from larger projects where practical uses are made available

---

[7]Owen Gingerich, *God's Universe* (Cambridge, MA: Belknap Press, 2006), 84–85.

for everyday benefits. Digital technology, for instance, was developed for a specific purpose and now has other applications throughout our daily lives. There are engineering and technological marvels that charm the general public and inspire scientists to learn more about the physical world. Bridges, communication systems, and diagnostic imaging equipment are a few of the astonishing engineering and technological feats we now take for granted. Physical chemist Peter Walhout writes that "because Christians are called to stewardship and holiness, they are also called to be thoughtful, careful users of modern technology."[8] He challenges Christians "to be at the forefront of society, asking the difficult questions regarding the ethical use and consumption of technology."[9]

For Christians who are scientists, facts discovered through analyses of large data inventories stored through the marvels of computer technology, or data generation from simple experimental protocols, overlap with the scientist's awe of God's creation. Natural scientists who affirm the Bible seek *knowledge for the sake of knowledge* and are intrigued with the sophisticated and intricate details of creation. In the words of one group of scientists, "Most of us can see the beauty of a sunset, but not many get the opportunity to marvel at the mechanism that produces the proteolytic cleavage of proteins. Science makes that knowledge possible."[10]

SCIENCE AS A MEANS OF GRACE TO HUMANKIND

Natural scientists engaged in applied scientific research are often concerned about care of the planet, its inhabitants and atmosphere. Chemists and environmental scientists, for instance, use sophisticated technologies to monitor air and water quality. Advances in technology influence the quality of food and its distribution as well as treatments for disease made by predictions about genes. Knowledge about light spectra has led to the development of many technologies in which visible and invisible light improve health and efficiencies in daily life, especially through the use of lasers. Large gene libraries are seeding the development of

---

[8]Peter Walhout, "How Are Technology and Engineering Related to Christianity?" in *Not Just Science*, ed. Dorothy F. Chappell and E. David Cook (Grand Rapids, MI: Zondervan, 2005), 244.
[9]Ibid., 245.
[10]"The Natural Sciences at Wheaton College: Understanding Their Significance in Light of Our Christian Educational Mission" (2003), 18.

new and wondrous cures for diseases and fueling the expansion of the development of useful plants and animals while also providing insights into life and the development of organisms. As people of God, part of our stewardship commitment is to use scientific knowledge as a means to serve humans, such as preventing and treating human diseases, ensuring clean air and water, or developing nutritious food for hungry people.

In addition to the delights of worship and praise found in the study of creation, devout scientists recognize expressions of common grace to creatures and to all people everywhere, regardless of whether they follow Christ. Wherever God's beauty, goodness, and truth are found, they derive from Christ, whether humans know it or not. Many scientists use science to help others in the plights of disease, impoverishment, and malnutrition, among many other works beneficial to humans and creation. These expressions of common grace, offered by Christians and non-Christians to all creatures and humankind, serve as tangible forms of God's provision, and can have mitigating effects on evil in creation. Humans can help people who lack food, clothing, or shelter and can apply science to produce and distribute food and other resources. It is a high calling and an application of common grace for Christian liberal arts students to develop excellent skills in science and then to unselfishly apply what they know to a needy world.

RECONCILIATION AS A VISION FOR CONDUCTING SCIENCE

Is it sufficient for scientists to practice natural science ad infinitum without concern for the stewardship of the earth and its inhabitants? Scientific discoveries have the potential for good or ill, and scientists who are Christians are concerned that scientific work not be isolated from other dimensions of life. When good things are developed, they should be shared with others. The requirements of justice must take precedence over the unlimited pursuit of knowledge, power, or possessions. God acts within his established law, and justice is his righteousness. For instance, the use of soft power through negotiation would be preferable over the use of hard power where weapons developed through scientific knowledge destroy life and property. The development of weapons in this fallen world, however, arguably serves as a deterrent in preventing some evil acts. In this sense, they can help preserve justice.

We are agents of God in carrying out justice, whether it is to deliver others from slavery itself or from the slavery of malnutrition, where food is not available to some people. Scientists' work to improve healthy foods, such as amino acid–rich corn for human consumption in order to sustain life, is an act of justice. One must recognize in this discussion that belief structures are very important, and so are ethical teachings based on moral principles and virtues. Christ had immense concern for righteousness and justice. The work of scientists can be used for promoting and sustaining such justice among God's people and in the world.

God is the author of all true reconciliation, and as we mature in Christ, we see several foci of reconciliation. The restoration of human relationships with God is the most crucial. As fallen humans we are in need of God's active work through Christ's atonement. Christ's death restores us to God, and we are justified by the shedding of his blood (Rom. 5:8–10). We also are responsible to be reconciled to others (Matt. 5:23–24). As a result of God's work of reconciliation with humans, we have a mandate to be reconciled with other humans and also with God's creation and to serve in reconciling roles defined by the prophet Micah, who asks, "And what does the LORD require of you? To act justly and to love mercy and to walk humbly with your God" (Mic. 6:8 NIV). Those acts of reconciliation have to do with economic, political, and other types of justice, and include providing moral goods the scientific world can address through feeding the hungry, treating the sick, and providing clean water and air.

Scientists who are Christians must share in the responsibility of stewardship and management of the earth and its atmosphere, and work against, not contribute to, the effects of evil in this world. For example, scientists who are Christians can work to prevent the pollution of waterways or prevent brown fields where toxic wastes seep into the environment and negatively affect the people who live there; they may also develop strategies for cleaning up pollution left by previous generations. Reconciliation here means that physicians use discretion in administering prescriptions and work toward health planning that includes diet and exercise with practical treatment of the whole individual. Reconciliation also means that scientists consider the effects of genetic transplants and evaluate forms of eugenics. The compassionate use of science to help people and repair God's creation follows personal reconciliation with God, and it is a noble and high calling for scientists who are Christians.

GLORIFYING GOD THROUGH NATURAL SCIENCE

In summary, a liberal arts education, contextualized with a Christian worldview, allows students to praise and worship the Lord through their study of natural science and to use science as a means of grace to human-kind, the earth, and its atmosphere. Conducting science as a method of exploring God's creation is a legitimate enterprise for Christians; they can have an enormous impact on the larger science academy because of their credible work, publications, and presentations in professional societies. Likewise, they can have a huge influence through their use of technologies and theories to provide for the betterment of humanity and the creation.

It is important to recall that "all truth is God's truth," as Arthur Holmes reminds us, wherever it may be found, and that God's revelations are trustworthy. God has not given his gifts only to Christians but to everyone, and we can learn from non-Christians. Only Christians, how-ever, will return the praise of those gifts to God. Nature and Scripture are not in conflict with each other—both disclose truth from God. Human interpretations of Scripture and nature may be flawed because humans and their interpretations are fallen, but God's revealed truths are trust-worthy and sure. The liberal arts tradition humbly brings philosophical, theological, biblical, and scientific views into holistic discourse, where truth can be perceived and assimilated. A secular scientist can discover the cure for AIDS, but it is still within God's providence and under his control, regardless of whether the scientist acknowledges it. The heavens and all of creation declare the glory of God, and since "earth is crammed with heaven, and every common bush afire with God," liberal arts stu-dents, whether scientists or not, should explore landscapes of lightning, listen to the thunder, observe the flowers, the stars, and the animals, and then applaud the Lord with friends, for what they see and hear.

CHAPTER FIFTEEN

EXPLORING A UNIVERSE OF RELATIONSHIPS THROUGH THE SOCIAL SCIENCES

Henry Allen

A new type of thinking is essential if mankind is to survive and move toward higher levels.
—ALBERT EINSTEIN, *EINSTEIN ON PEACE*

[In Messiah] are hidden all the treasures of wisdom and knowledge.
—COLOSSIANS 2:3

During the 1990s the Walt Disney Corporation released its most popular and prosperous animated adventure, *The Lion King*. In the opening scene, the audience witnesses the coronation and birthday celebration of the lion cub, Simba, who is destined to succeed his father Mufasa, the Great Lion King and wise leader of the kingdom. We listen as the chorus of African wildlife sings, "From the day we arrive on the planet and blinking step into the sun, there is more to be seen than can ever be seen, more to do than can ever be done." The rest of the movie is about how Simba learns to be king after the tragic death of Mufasa, despite the evil opposition of the usurper, Uncle Scar. One of the greatest lessons Simba must learn is the value of relationships.

As a young cub, Simba thinks that other beings are merely instrumental to his role as king. He has to learn the value of relationships, the deep meaning of friendships. He has to learn about his trusted network of friends. He has to learn loyalty to friends and humility before others, as well as to revere his father's legacy. He has to learn why and how his identity is unique but also connected to generations before him. He has to learn responsibility, how his reign will affect the social organization of the kingdom and its animal constituents. In short, Simba has to learn to appreciate and to negotiate the universe of relationships that constitutes his social world.

While it is an animated story based on fantasy, *The Lion King* captures the essence of what the social sciences collectively explore. Consider the following subjects in relation to the film. We see psychology in the probing of consciousness and the factors (internal as well as external) that shape its unfolding across the lifespan. We see economics through the investigation of how resources (land, labor, capital, and expertise) are produced and allocated throughout the kingdom, under the jurisdiction of market mechanisms and rational decision making. We see political science in the focus on how governments rule, from philosophical or ideological premises to tangible policies or consequences. We see anthropology through the examination of different cultures, tribal affiliations (social networks), and their artifacts. We see sociology, ultimately, in all these domains, in the presentation of social organization (what holds groups and societies together) and social disorganization (what keeps groups and societies apart). No single account from within the social sciences could ever capture the complexity of all these scientific fields combined.

Our aim in this chapter is to introduce the social sciences, seeing them as telescopic or microscopic lenses for studying relationships across multiple categories: individuals, groups, social networks, communities, organizations, markets, industries, and social systems. This process of search and discovery produces unmistakable joy! Social scientists explore social spaces and the collective or individual actors who move in them throughout time. Using empirical evidence as our set of clues, as *The Lion King* suggests, we investigate "more to see than can ever be seen, more to do than can ever be done." Our motivation within the Christian liberal arts is to pursue the truth about the realm of the true King of kings, and Lord of lords—our Messiah—and about the people who live together in the world that he has made.

For a Christian social scientist, exploring the universe of relationships is a sacred task. Recognizing that our triune God exists in relationships, and that he created humans as relational beings, we have the privilege of exploring how the reign and rule of God permeates the relational cosmos. At their best, social scientists explore how God operates his kingdom purposes within the human realm, across the spectrum of tragedies and triumphs. The kingdom of God is the reign and rule of the Lord of hosts in every realm of life, as indicated by the following key passages from the Bible: Psalms 2; 110; 1 Chronicles 29:10–13; and Hebrews 1:1–4. Our God even rules over those who reject him (such as Satan, in Job 1–2). Moreover, all the kingdoms of this world are subject to him (John 16:33; 1 John 4:4; 5:4). Christian social scientists study all empirical dimensions of God's sovereignty and his reign over humans.

COMMON THREADS IN THE SOCIAL SCIENCES

One common presupposition of all social sciences is that humans are inherently social creatures. We must have relationships with other humans to exist and dwell in our symbolic (cultural) galaxies. Inevitably, humans create symbols, such as language and signs, as well as gestures, to create cultural worlds populated by social groups. Hence, effective remedies for human problems must contain a social component, whatever their basis—theological or secular.

A second presupposition of the social sciences is that all conjectures about human relationships must be evaluated according to the scope and rigor of the tangible, empirical evidence that relates to them. In this sense, social scientists are like seasoned detectives or forensic scientists, who are not impressed by obvious schemes or statements; rather, they are skeptical of popular claims unless the evidence systematically supports them. Similarly, social scientists are not impressed with ethnocentric societal claims of goodness, justice, and virtue unless rigorous empirical evidence substantiates these postulations. We use various methodological techniques or schemas to sift the wheat from the chaff as we scrutinize ideas, interpretations, and associated evidence. Peer review (having peers in your field rigorously scrutinize your work to expose faulty ideas or evidence, biases, and imperfections) serves as our jury system, with the sanction of falsification (empirical results that invalidate our assumptions, evidence, and conclusions) acting as our judge across nations and generations. Scholarship in the social sciences is a global enterprise, refuting colonialism, racism, totalitarianism, imperialism, sexism, and other idolatries.

Let me emphatically state that the social sciences differ from the humanities in outlook. Whereas the humanities evaluate and interpret the cultural heritage of civilizations, the social sciences anchor themselves in scientific methods in order to explore present or future phenomena. Our frame of reference is not the past, although we are eager to mine the most precious gems or nuggets from previous eras. We are not satisfied with mere interpretations of documents or texts produced by past geniuses or plebeians, no matter how well written or popular. Interpretations matter in the social sciences as they do within the humanities, but not nearly as much as the evidence that supports them.

What are the origins of the social sciences? Why were they needed in the first place? What do they contribute to society and our world? We turn now to address these important questions. In short, the social sciences emerged as intellectual tools needed to deal with crises that lie beyond the frameworks of theology, philosophy, and the humanities. While the humanities offer important insights for life, they were unable sufficiently to address the explosive changes unleashed by the social forces of the Renaissance, the Reformation, and the Scientific Revolution, including urbanization, industrialization, capitalism, slavery, socialism, and international warfare.

From European antecedents to their recent forms, the social sciences have pursued clues about the nature of humans in societies via structures, processes, and outcomes of various kinds. *Structures* are the patterns we observe in social life. *Processes* refer to the ways these patterns are generated via human agency, by individuals or collectivities. *Outcomes* are the conditions produced by human structures and processes. For a vivid example from the history of the United States, the structure of a society (its constitution) generates norms and forms of action (such as voting, immigration, or taxation policies) that produce outcomes (forms of social inequality, like slavery, that result from those structures and processes).

Think of each social science as an intergenerational taskforce of detectives searching for clues about how the world operates. We use different lenses, some microscopic (individuals, small groups) and others macroscopic (organizations, industries). Discovering unrecognized facts about how the social world actually works is a dynamic and enjoyable experience. We assume that looks are often deceiving and that life is often counterintuitive, even unpredictable. Yet, we acknowledge that patterns occur when collectivities or groups surface. Every group has to have some pattern of organization, not unlike what students observe in intramural sports, concerts, and traffic. Collegiate athletics, academic classes, dating habits, spring break excursions, movies, social media, and careers all reflect aspects of social organization and disorganization.

As the detectives of human interactions, we realize that social life has multiple dimensions. One dimension is overt, public, and formal: things that can readily be seen or grasped locally. But the best social scientists know that it is the covert, informal, and private dimension that underlies what we see. What happens behind or underneath the public eye is more crucial to social outcomes than what we often witness. In cities, the vast majority of citizens do not scrutinize the informal alliances, negotiations, and secret decisions of civic and commercial leaders that shape the public policies broadcast by various media outlets. To cite another example, we do not see the hidden interests or private evidence politicians use to justify the invasion of another nation. Many of the most powerful social forces are not perceived until they erupt in a riot or war, akin to volcanic eruptions or earthquakes. Social scientists delight in revealing these subterranean shifts in social phenomena—whether they occur in voting patterns, consumer fads, or patriotic fervor. Like the Old Testament prophets, social scientists must challenge the inertia of the status quo in every society for the good of humanity. This does not always lead to popularity! In critiquing culture the most diligent social scientists—whatever their academic discipline—value integrity and accuracy.

SOCIAL SCIENCE AND REVELATION

Social scientists, as a whole, study a cosmos rooted in concrete relations and observations. Yet, we routinely use abstractions to communicate about the patterns we observe across different groups (or other units of analysis) and their social environments. Social scientists measure the impact of close versus distant and direct versus indirect relationships. We know that social life is often counterintuitive. Our telescopic or microscopic venues are rife with multilevel, multidimensional inferences between samples and populations, across various age cohorts. We recognize the contingent nature of society: there are always multiple options and multiple conditions. What one generation venerates, another generation may despise. Like the author of the Old Testament book of Ecclesiastes, we can observe wisdom and vanity, foolishness and heroism. We can detect the madness of unreflective, a-historical differentiation. Christian social scientists can see how the energy of negative social forces, especially ideas and institutional patterns, can be redirected to positive pursuits, as Romans 12:21 reveals.

A careful study of all the social sciences can yield a deep appreciation for human diversity, as well as awe about how God has endowed human beings with aspects of his image. Humans have the breath of life. We can exercise the power of choice, good and bad, wise and foolish. Humans can be cruel or creative, generous or miserly. Social scientists get to investigate all of this reality, directly or indirectly. In a direct sense, we participate in the social world we study by interacting with human beings in our sphere of influence. Indirectly, we can learn from the communications of past members of society or enter the virtual worlds of technological populations in the current era.

SOCIAL SCIENCE AND THE CHRISTIAN LIBERAL ARTS

The social sciences are rooted in the pursuit of knowledge. When combined with theology and other liberal arts disciplines, they can be instrumental to the best wisdom humans can access. Social sciences target human beings and their social relationships in their methods of research. We use historical methodologies to probe how the current social situation under our investigation occurred. We employ social surveys and statistical analyses to gauge public opinions about political matters and social problems. We use field research or participant observation to unearth the hidden dimensions of social groups and their emergent features—as is evident when we study deviant behavior within gangs or the covert dimensions of governmental and corporate corruption. We develop experiments to test how factors (independent variables) or treatments influence tests or other tangible outcomes. We create sophisticated mathematical and computational models to monitor industries, military strategies, and terrorist networks. All of these methods can be utilized to build the church and improve society by yielding the knowledge needed to make better diagnoses of social problems. Our unstated aim is to make the world a better place for human beings. For Christian social scientists, this is the fulfillment of the redemption mandate mentioned in John 10:10 and elsewhere: "The thief comes only to steal and kill and destroy. I came that they may have life and have it abundantly."

Social science can be a powerful tool for informed Christians. To use my own experience as one example of the work that social scientists can do for the public good, I have used the intellectual treasures of social science to help numerous nonprofit agencies grapple with diversity and organizational changes so that they could fulfill their missions with practical solutions. I have worked with economists to improve the welfare of union laborers, remembering the social issues identified in James 5. I have worked with psychologists in the FBI's Behavioral Science Unit to enhance the status of law enforcement officers worldwide. I have assisted political scientists in interpreting survey data about the voting behavior of church members, used social science to help school systems improve academic achievement, and worked with urban pastors to help churches and denominations meet the needs of urban neighborhoods. I have also integrated social scientific concepts and methods in pursuits as diverse as marriage counseling with young couples in my church, creating a civic association (the African American Leadership Roundtable), and promoting local activism (political protests).

Through social science, one obtains the ability to explore the image of God in persons of all types, to encourage the full dimensions of redemption (spirit, mind, emotions, relationships, and body), and to reduce toxic ideas or outcomes (evil). This exploration brings joy as intellectual good triumphs over ignorance, evil, oppression, and sin, at both individual and structural levels. When such professional activities in the social sciences fuel teaching, research, and service under the rubric of the Christian liberal arts, magnificent and enduring changes occur!

FINAL THOUGHTS ON SOCIAL SCIENCE AND LIBERAL ARTS

Some students trip over the many abstractions that characterize the social sciences, while others are discouraged by them. Students should remember that these abstractions refer to patterns of observations created by concrete social actors and designated or codified by social scientists to promote a common nomenclature for their work. Social scientists see a world that is generated by different arrangements (patterns) of social relations. Since these arrangements are created by humans, we say that they are socially constructed. As atoms are to the physical universe, so are the concepts we study to the social universe. Unlocking these secrets among global societies is an intellectual treasure hunt full of intrinsic rewards. Social science exposes the power and responsibility humans have as stewards of creation.

Truth liberates goodness. A Christian liberal arts education must prepare Christians to recognize the nature and implications of overt or covert social forces across generations. As Psalm 145 suggests, there is a moral imperative to pursue truth across all generations, as God reveals himself by the tested truths of common revelation. At its best, a Christian liberal arts education connects God's truth in the domains of special (biblical) and common (natural) revelation. Within the Christian liberal arts paradigm, the social sciences reveal the multidimensional parameters needed to love human beings in such a way as to encompass the full spectrum of their interpersonal and institutional diversity.

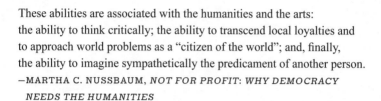

CHAPTER SIXTEEN

THE HUMANITIES AS INDULGENCE OR NECESSITY?

Jill Peláez Baumgaertner

These abilities are associated with the humanities and the arts:
the ability to think critically; the ability to transcend local loyalties and
to approach world problems as a "citizen of the world"; and, finally,
the ability to imagine sympathetically the predicament of another person.
—MARTHA C. NUSSBAUM, *NOT FOR PROFIT: WHY DEMOCRACY
NEEDS THE HUMANITIES*

Happy are those who find wisdom,
    and those who get understanding,
for her income is better than silver,
    and her revenue better than gold.
—PROVERBS 3:13–14 (NRSV)

When I was a sophomore at a college in Georgia, I first read William Faulkner. In a nonairconditioned dormitory room one summer, with crickets already going strong at eight a.m., I read *Absalom! Absalom!*, and the direction of my life was changed forever. The world I read about was magnetic, drawing me into it, forcing me to experience vicariously the struggles of a family over several generations and to grapple with issues I had never considered before. Up to that point literature had been merely diversion for me. However, with Faulkner I began to understand that fiction, well written by the hand of genius, asked the big questions about human nature and God and our place in the world; it also, not incidentally, gave me both place, in describing the South where I had serious roots, and vocation, by calling me to a life in literature. I switched majors from chemistry to English. My father had apoplexy.

My father's response occurred in 1966. Some fifty years later this kind of response remains typical from parents of undergraduates choosing to major in one of the disciplines in the humanities—and in fact it has increased exponentially. This is what I hear as dean, and you may hear it, too, as students. History is not enough, one parent recently complained to me about her daughter's choice of major, and the mother insisted that the daughter pick up a second major outside of the humanities. This time it was business, but other parents are pushing majors in the scientific and technological fields—all practical, they insist—because they will lead to jobs after college.

As faculty at liberal arts institutions, we certainly champion our science and business majors, who also participate in the liberal arts conversation. But parents of English majors or history majors or philosophy majors still ask: What can one *do* with these majors? We respond that because reading, thinking, and writing are at the core of these disciplines, students can go in multiple directions, from medicine to law to editing to public relations to myriad other professions. We cannot, of course, offer guarantees, and with the price of higher education at an all-time high, one understands parents' nervousness. "What if my philosophy-major son with outstanding educational loans ends up bagging groceries?" they worry.

On the other hand, there is the example of my friend whose two children took majors in criminal justice and in accounting. In both cases these students hit the job market, quickly found positions, and then within a couple of years discovered that they were not cut out for this kind of work. But because neither student had been sufficiently challenged within their disciplines in the areas of critical thinking or writing, and because their education had not prepared them for the flexibility they would need in a changing world, they were both caught in occupations for which, as it turned out, they had no passion. Their work fast became a form of drudgery, not a true vocation. This is the potential that the pressure for early specialization within technical and professional fields carries with it. Just how does a Christ-centered eighteen-year-old know what kind of kingdom service she wants to embrace for the rest of her life, especially if she has not yet been introduced in any substantial way to the great ideas that have formed civilizations and that still inform the human person?

THE HUMANITIES, THE UNIVERSITY, AND THE CURRENT CRISIS

The humanities were for centuries the core of the university. Identified closely with the liberal arts, they dealt with the education of the whole person who had the liberty and leisure to pursue knowledge and wisdom. During the early modern age, however, the sciences began their ascendency. Patrick J. Deneen writes:

> The crisis of the humanities in fact began . . . with the argument that a new science was needed to replace the "old science" of the liberal arts, a new science that no longer sought merely to *understand* the world and its creatures, but to *transform* them. This impulse gave rise first to a scientific revolution in theory, and eventually a scientific, industrial, and technological revolution in fact.[1]

It was at this point, and in response to the rise of the modern multiversity, that the humanities began to lose their place of centrality in a curriculum that hitherto had been devised for holistic education. Specialization in applied fields became the wave of the future and, in fact, is now the direction of most higher education.

We are even at a point that students are accused of being self-indulgent if they want to pursue studies in literature, languages, philosophy, or history. In an essay based on a lecture given to freshman students at Stanford University, William Deresiewicz writes the following:

> Think of what we've come to. It is one of the great testaments to the intellectual—and moral, and spiritual—poverty of American society that it makes its most intelligent young people feel like they're being self-indulgent if they pursue their curiosity. You are all told that you're supposed to go to college, but you're also told that you're being "self-indulgent" if you actually want to get an education. Or, even worse, give yourself one. As opposed to what? Going into consulting isn't self-indulgent? Going into finance isn't self-indulgent? Going into law, like most of the people who do, in order to make yourself rich, isn't self-indulgent? It's not OK to play music, or write essays, because what good does that really do anyone, but it is OK to work for a hedge fund.

---

[1]Patrick Deneen, "Science and the Decline of the Liberal Arts," *The New Atlantis*, no. 26 (2009/2010): 60–68 (http://www.thenewatlantis.com/publications/science-and-the-decline-of-the-liberal-arts).

It's selfish to pursue your passion, unless it's also going to make you a lot of money, in which case it's not selfish at all.[2]

The crisis in the humanities is reflective of a larger crisis in higher education. In our culture, college is no longer looked upon primarily as a place to ask the deep philosophical and theological questions. In the early years of the twentieth century, college presidents still taught courses in moral philosophy, which helped students shape their lives. That is no longer the case. The secular university is not, most students learn, a place to shape souls or to ask questions about the meaning of life.[3] Instead students are migrating away from the subjects that pursue these questions, leaving the humanities to explore other interests. Eight percent of all bachelor's degrees awarded are in the humanities. In the late 1960s it was eighteen percent. The implications of this drop for the humanities are dire.

WHAT THE HUMANITIES OFFER AND WHY THEY ARE IMPORTANT

In spite of these difficulties, the humanities continue to thrive at many Christian liberal arts colleges. This may be because in these places a strong recognition exists of what it means to be a truly educated person on the way to becoming a responsible world citizen. These are places where questions about the meaning of life are not denigrated; such life issues thrive because professors are not reluctant to tackle philosophical and spiritual issues and are deeply committed to the development of their students as whole persons. These are also places where the importance of science and technology is recognized, but the importance of studies in the humanities matters also: reading contemporary and classical litera-ture; learning to write well and to argue coherently; learning to speak a foreign language; studying world history; learning to think theologically and biblically; learning to speak clearly and convincingly; learning to think philosophically; and appreciating and assessing world cultures and world religions. Often such academic concerns are not only addressed in

---

[2]William Deresiewicz, "What Are You Going to Do With That?," *The Chronicle Review* (2010): B12.
[3]See Anthony T. Kronman, *Education's End: Why Our Colleges and Universities Have Given Up on the Meaning of Life* (New Haven: Yale University Press, 2007).

the curriculum of the various academic majors but also emphasized in the general education program of required courses for all students.

In the best programs these humanities courses are intentionally interconnected. They avoid the "disconnected series of courses" that Gerald Graff has identified as one of the liabilities of the contemporary university system; he also notes the poor quality of discussion that often takes place in classes, and he calls for improvement in this area.[4] In a culture saturated with opinion sharing in the form of shouted epithets, students must learn to argue coherently, carefully, and logically. For this reason, the kind of dynamic thinking and teaching one often finds in humanities classes is especially important.[5]

Two important qualities the humanities can engender are curiosity and a propensity to ask questions and pursue answers. Learning to ask the right questions is what philosophy, theology, literature, and history emphasize in their concentration on the thinking of great minds of the past. Similarly, learning to get to solid answers is a benefit that contributes to lifelong learning. Active learning, in which students are not mere passive recipients of information but rather are active partners in their own education, is also an emphasis in most humanities courses, especially those in which discussion predominates as a pedagogical approach. Students learn to question and to pursue answers to their questions by taking responsibility for their own education, another lifelong learning pattern that involvement in the humanities fosters. In fact, through discussion students learn more together than they could alone.

Perhaps the most important activity that the humanities encourage is growth of the imagination, without which life becomes dull and human potential is in danger of never being realized. The humanities encourage the student to experience vicariously that which opens new worlds, insights, and the capacity to empathize with others. Through the Socratic dialogues of Plato, one begins to see how a person of principle lived his life in ancient times, confronting issues not so different from those we confront daily. Mark Twain's *The Adventures of Huckleberry*

---

[4]Gerald Graff, *Clueless in Academe: How Schooling Obscures the Life of the Mind* (New Haven: Yale University Press, 2003), 27, 90.
[5]Martha Nussbaum, *Not for Profit: Why Democracy Needs the Humanities* (Princeton: Princeton University Press, 2010), 47–77, 93–94.

Finn presents nineteenth-century American life to the reader, who is forced to confront the issue of racism because of sympathies engendered by Huck and Jim as they make their way along the Mississippi River. Through the poetry of a novel like Ron Hansen's *Mariette in Ecstasy*, a reader begins to question our culture's interpretation of the clash between science and religion. Through the biography of Abraham Lincoln by David McDonald, a reader is surprised by deep parallels between politics in the mid-nineteenth century and that of our own day. Through Elie Wiesel's *Night*, we experience the horrors of the Nazi concentration camp, the hopelessness of the prisoners, and their questioning of God's silence. Our imaginations are stirred and broadened by such exposures. We begin to be able to see the world as others see it and, in Martha Nussbaum's words, to "cultivate sympathy."[6] At such moments of engagement with the concerns presented through great books and great thinkers in the humanities, we are closer to becoming whole human beings.

Nussbaum contrasts this kind of education to that which emphasizes the "technical and factual." She presents the example of John Stuart Mill, a nineteenth-century philosopher whose intensive education omitted the importance and growth of the imagination:

> As a young adult, he suffered a crippling depression. He credited his eventual recovery to the influence of Wordsworth's poetry, which educated his emotions and made it possible for him to look for emotion in others. In later life, Mill developed an account of what he called the "religion of humanity" based on the cultivation of sympathy he had found through his experience of poetry.[7]

Nussbaum points to poetry and the arts as a means to "wonder about the inner world" so we can gain a greater sense of ourselves—our depths. She writes further, "We do not automatically see another human being as spacious and deep, having thoughts, spiritual longings, and emotions. It is all too easy to see another person as just a body—which we might then think we can use for our ends, bad or good."[8] It is through these

---

[6]Ibid., 96.
[7]Ibid., 102.
[8]Ibid.

encounters, which the humanities provide, that students begin to acquire intellectual and spiritual dimensions. They begin to see themselves and others as full human beings, capable of good and evil, but infused with God's grace and, in their best moments, acting accordingly.

AN EXAMPLE OF WHAT ONE POEM CAN OFFER

One of my very favorite pieces of literature is a poem that I have always seen as an Advent poem, even though there is no mention of the Christ child or Mary or the fullness of time. In fact, it describes a bleak, terrifying landscape and series of events. The poem was published in 1960—about the time families were building individual bomb shelters in their backyards—and the stories of how and if we would survive a nuclear holocaust were rampant in our culture. It was in this environment of fear that Edwin Muir wrote his poem "The Horses."[9]

Muir describes a group of neighbors who are survivors of a cataclysmic world war that lasted one week. Unlike the story in the first chapter of Genesis, this week was one of uncreation. On the second day of that war, he says, the radios failed and there was no answer when they turned the knobs. On the third day, a warship passed them with dead bodies piled on the deck. On the sixth day, a plane plunged over them into the sea. Since then, the speaker of the poem reports, the radios have been silent. The tractors lie abandoned in the fields; at evening, he says, they look like dank sea monsters crouched and waiting. "We leave them where they are and let them rust," he says. "We have gone back . . . far past our fathers' land."

And then the surprise occurs. One evening, late in the summer, the strange horses arrive—at first only a distant drumming on the road, the sound finally becoming a hollow thunder. "We had sold our horses in our fathers' time to buy new tractors," the narrator says, too afraid now to go near the herd of strange beasts who have appeared out of nowhere. "Yet they waited," he explains, "stubborn and shy, as if they had been sent by an old command to find our whereabouts." Among them were six colts newly born in the wilderness of the broken world—"yet new," the narrator calls them, "as if they had come from their own Eden."

---

[9]Edwin Muir, *Selected Poems* (London: Faber & Faber, 1960), 246–47.

The horses give themselves to this small group of survivors. The poem concludes:

> Since then they have pulled our plows and borne our loads,
> But that free servitude still can pierce our hearts.
> Our life is changed; their coming our beginning.

The horses bring the gift of themselves to the brave group of humans who are left, who must now create the world anew. "Their coming our beginning," the survivors say.

As engaged readers, we are eager to find connections between the freely offered grace in this poem and God's grace we daily celebrate. Christ's coming our beginning, we say, a surprising gift of a servant king. And he, like the horses in this poem, chooses to be bound to us, his free servitude piercing our hearts and, in turn, giving us hope and freedom and life. We read this poem through the eyes of faith, integrating our knowledge of God the creator and redeemer with the images the author has chosen.

The reader of Muir's poem encounters history, theology, and politics, experiencing vicariously through the imagination a time of holocaust and apocalypse, of questions with no immediate answers, until God's grace appears. This is the kind of experience the humanities offer: intense intellectual, emotional, and spiritual engagement with the big questions of human nature and existence. As Anthony Kronman writes,

> The humanities study this nature. They represent it. They meditate on its meaning. They bring it into view and concentrate our attention on it. They invite—they compel—us to confront the truth about ourselves and help us to inhabit with greater understanding the disjointed condition of longing and defeat that defines the human condition. . . . Technology invites a forgetfulness of mortality that hides this subject away. Only the humanities, whose subject this has always been, can help us recover it.[10]

Our culture currently seems to value skills above wisdom. The kind of training in the humanities that is the most profound is that which begins long before the college years. The music children are exposed to,

---

[10]Kronman, *Education's End*, 239.

the art they find in their homes, the literature read to them as toddlers that they then pick up as older children, the theological, political, and philosophical discussions around the dinner table—all of this is part of the education of the well-rounded person. One's vocation, God's calling for one's life, is broader and more important than a career choice. As Frederick Buechner says, "The place God calls you to is the place where your deep gladness and the world's deep hunger meet."[11] You will begin to know that gladness and recognize that hunger through the worlds the humanities open to you.

---

[11]Frederick Buechner, *Wishful Thinking: A Seeker's ABC* (San Francisco: HarperOne, 1993), 119.

CHAPTER SEVENTEEN

SINGING GOD'S PRAISE

Michael Wilder

Music expresses that which cannot be said, and
on which it is impossible to be silent.
—VICTOR HUGO, *WILLIAM SHAKESPEARE*

Shout for joy to the Lord, all the earth,
    burst into jubilant song with music.
—PSALM 98:4 (niv)

At the most significant moments in our lives, whether we are suffering or celebrating, in the pit of despair or at the pinnacle of happiness,
we often reach to the arts and especially to music. Music serves as a
dynamic, personal, expressive vehicle for comfort, healing, and praise.
For liberal arts learners who follow Christ, we ought to examine the
place of music in our lives and the variety of ways that we are invited
into music making as a means of learning, listening, ministering, and
worshiping.

Our lives are filled with music. In fact, music has been discovered
in nearly every known culture.[1] In the West, we can hardly escape its
presence as it dominates the media of film, television, and advertising.
Not surprisingly, it also plays a vital role in the church, in ceremonies,
and in family gatherings.

As it wakes people in the mornings and puts them to sleep at night,
music encourages both motivation and relaxation as a nearly constant
companion. Music pervades the lives of people the world over, reflecting deep cultural and aesthetic values. It invites creativity and interaction in ways that nothing else can, and it serves as a reflection of the
hearts and minds of those who create it.

Humans are ideally suited to make and to receive music. The human

---

[1]See John Blacking, *Music, Culture, and Experience* (Chicago: University of Chicago Press, 1995).

body serves as an amazing mechanism for imagining, producing, hearing, and storing music. To study and analyze the inner workings of the voice, the ear, and the brain—especially as they relate to each other in the midst of the experience of music making and listening—is to explore a world of staggering capacity.

Music is a lifelong partner. Humans are able to hear and respond to music well before birth,[2] and musical propensity lingers for many people into the final days of life. As memory, speech, and mobility are developing in young children, and as these abilities wane in our final years, music is often actively present.

Our music making can be of our own creation. We sing, play musical instruments, clap, and participate alone or with others. The expanding set of listening devices, Internet resources, performance, and exhibition venues offers a world of music that is immediately accessible to us as listeners. We encounter music at every turn. As Jeremy Begbie aptly recounts, "A teenager said to a friend of mine recently: 'Music is the ocean we swim in.'"[3]

The Bible offers many examples of music making, including singing in celebration of the rebuilding of the wall of Jerusalem in Nehemiah, flutists participating in a funeral in Matthew, David celebrating the moving of the ark to the sound of trumpets in 2 Samuel, Asaph and others making music before the ark of the covenant in 1 Chronicles, and the Israelites singing, dancing, and playing instruments to celebrate David's victory over Goliath in 1 Samuel.

As it relates specifically to salvation, "the drama of redemption is and has to be a musical. From the morning stars singing together at creation, to Moses singing by the sea (Exodus 15), to the exiles returning with singing (Isaiah 55), to the Christmas carols in Luke, to the final triumph songs of Revelation, it is never sufficient merely to tell the story of our salvation; we must always sing God's praise."[4]

What then is the purpose of music? What are the limits of its

---

[2]"Researchers in Belfast have demonstrated that reactive listening begins at 16 weeks g. a. [gestational age]." "The Fetal Senses: A Classical View," David B. Chamberlain, Association for Prenatal and Perinatal Psychology and Health, last modified 1997 (http://www.birthpsychology.com/lifebefore/fetalsense.html).

[3]Jeremy S. Begbie, *Resounding Truth: Christian Wisdom in the World of Music* (Grand Rapids, MI: Baker, 2007), 15.

[4]Philip G. Ryken, letter to author, February 2, 2011.

potential? As Christians pursue liberal learning, what is God's musical invitation to them? What are his goals and purposes? Are the answers to these questions different from vocational and avocational perspectives? The Bible is generous in providing answers. God's invitation to each person involves listening, praise, communication, and ministry. And his intent appears to involve music making by each person in a variety of settings, as his praise is made glorious on earth and through eternity.

AN INVITATION TO LISTEN

By its definition, music involves sound—the making, receiving, and sharing of it. This sound might be audible: the voice of a singer, the sound of a musical instrument, or music produced through a set of head-phones. Our bodies themselves are unique musical instruments, ideally equipped to clap, stomp, sing, shout, snap, click, whistle, and more.

While often audible, music can also consist of nonaudible sounds hidden within the mind of the music maker. The amazing capacity of humans to imagine sound is yet another example of our being created as dynamic musical creatures. We are capable of hearing music "in our heads" and using this imagined sound to compose, improvise, and ana-lyze music. Labeled "audiation," this capacity is to music what thinking is to language.[5]

Audiation allowed Mozart and other composers of the past to com-pose within their minds before notating music. It allowed Beethoven to continue writing musical masterpieces after he became deaf. This ability permits the conceptualization of music mentally before the actual pro-duction of an improvised melody or harmony. Audiation allows for the preservation of music and for passing it on to others, even though the music may not have been written down or recorded.

Consider the typical amount of space in the mind, specifically the memory, that is filled with music. We each have had the experience of recalling a melody that we have not heard in years, only to find that it is still perfectly preserved. Maybe the tune comes to mind while driving the car or falling asleep.

Humans possess a powerful ability to interact with music as listeners

---

[5]Edwin Gordon, *Awakening Newborns, Children, and Adults to the World of Audiation* (Chicago: GIA Publications, 2007).

even though they themselves may not actually be producing the music. This kind of vicarious aesthetic sensibility allows people to engage actively and deeply with music and to borrow music of composers from generations past, to function as active participants in live music making, and to experience music on a very personal level as it is re-created again and again. Personal listening devices, online music libraries and vendors, home music systems, and music in film and television all speak to our immense love of music listening.

AN INVITATION TO PLAY

The Hebrew word *zamar*—often translated "to touch the strings" or "sing praises"—serves as an encouragement to make musical sound in response to a sense of adoration toward God. As God instructs us to express our most intense emotions (praise to our Creator) through the specific art form of music, we learn something about the value he assigns it, as well as its potential.

The terms "music" or "musician" appear over one hundred times in the Bible as we are encouraged to use music making for an important purpose, namely, the praise of God:

> Praise him with the sounding of the trumpet,
>   praise him with the harp and lyre,
> praise him with tambourine and dancing,
>   praise him with the strings and flute,
> praise him with the clash of cymbals,
>   praise him with resounding cymbals.
> Let everything that has breath praise the Lord.
>   Praise the Lord. (Ps. 150:3–6 NIV)

As the culmination, the grand finale, of the entire book of 150 psalms, the psalmist invites the use of musical instruments as useful and appropriate tools in praising God. Of the many ways that this monumental book of the Bible might have concluded, it does so by directing the reader toward praise through musical sound.

Having established music as a fitting and welcome vehicle for praise, the psalmist clarifies just who is invited to this activity: in fact, everyone is encouraged to make music as praise to God. Psalm 150 makes no distinction between those who are called to professional music making and those who are not. It further does not encourage the reader to make music as praise to God only when in the mood or only if she is good at it. While the Bible often encourages us toward excellence and quality of craftsmanship, this particular psalm does not comment directly on the quality or level of music making. It appears that music, as praise to God, is intended as a powerful tool of praise for all who would embrace it. God delights in the music making of his children. Here is how Harold Best summarizes the purpose of music in the life of the Christian: "Music is freely made, by faith, as an act of worship, in direct response to the overflowing grace of God in Christ Jesus."[6]

The word "praise" appears hundreds of times in the Bible. However, the emphasis in our culture is often not so much on music as praise as it is on music as performance and the resultant ticket revenue, stardom, and acclaim for performers. Consider that the word "perform," as it pertains to an artistic performance, is mentioned only once in the Bible. In Judges 16, Samson, now blinded from having his eyes gouged out, was brought from prison to perform. This was intended as a mockery of him and, of course, resulted in a cataclysmic event. On the other hand, there are 351 uses of the word "praise" in the Bible (176 in the psalms), many of them related to the arts. As Christians—both those who are highly trained as musicians and those with no training at all—we might be well advised to focus on praise instead of performance.

Francis Schaeffer imagines asking the psalmist, "'David, why do you sing? Just to amuse yourself? Only the little white-faced sheep will hear.' And David will reply, 'Not at all. I'm singing and the God of heaven and earth—he hears my song and that's what makes it so worthwhile.'"[7] A recent college graduate took a similar view as he reflected on his involvement in a music ensemble as an undergraduate nonmusic major: "Though I will never be a solo vocalist or on anyone's recording, I sing with confidence and joy instead of weakness and shyness. This is because I can praise God with my voice instead of worrying about what I sound like, and because I think God delights when we learn

---

[6]Harold M. Best, *Music through the Eyes of Faith* (New York: HarperCollins, 1993), 158.
[7]Francis A. Schaeffer, *Art and the Bible* (Downers Grove, IL: InterVarsity, 1973), 38.

to use each talent he has given us, regardless of how it seems, nearsightedly, impractical."[8]

That God has intended music primarily as a vehicle for praise is clear. This stance can serve as a critical guiding principle for all who are compelled to make music. But the Bible goes further in instructing those who serve as vocational, trained musicians. These instructions involve the admonition to make music with an eye toward excellence and high musical standards. Psalm 33 and 1 Chronicles 15 instruct musicians to play skillfully, and 1 Chronicles 25 refers to a number of musicians who are "trained and skilled in music for the LORD" (v. 7 NIV). Encouragement to make music with excellence, while offering this same music as praise, is an exciting combination of factors for vocational musicians. As one of the most influential composers in all of history and one of immense accomplishment, Johann Sebastian Bach modeled a musical life of unparalleled artistic excellence, humility, and deep Christian commitment. As an inscription in the scores of each of his cantatas, he wrote "SDG" (*soli Deo gloria,* "to the glory of God alone") as he attempted to "make his praise glorious" (Ps. 66:2 NIV).

Because music is often intensely resonant, it allows for the expression and exploration of the deepest emotions. In fact, Christians seek ways to express that which the Bible describes as inexpressible: "Though you have not seen him, you love him; and even though you do not see him now, you believe in him and are filled with an inexpressible and glorious joy" (1 Pet. 1:8–9 NIV). These verses present something of a special challenge for the Christian. While humans are deeply communicative and often possess a strong desire to share their emotions with others, the joy described in this verse, a strong impetus for our desire to make music as praise, is characterized as "inexpressible." How can we express that which is inexpressible? In this dilemma, music often comes to our aid: instrumental music, songs, family music, music of the church, songs from childhood. Each of these is capable of aiding us as we reach for a vehicle with which to express our inexpressible gratitude, anticipation, petition, and wonder as children of God.

Expressing what cannot be said in words rings true in the Christian

---

[8]E-mail to Dr. Mary Hopper, Wheaton College Men's Glee Club conductor, from Thomas Crum, 2004 English graduate, Wheaton College, dated October 30, 2010. Used with permission.

life. Even though expressing our praise through music may sometimes seem insufficient, we attempt it nonetheless. God has designed us this way. Just as he loves our attempts to be holy and to live purely for him, he welcomes our offerings of praise through music, in whatever form.

It appears that praise offerings will continue after our life on earth is over. By all indications, heaven will be filled with music. The book of Revelation offers numerous descriptions of this predicted musical outpouring. Revelation 5 refers to the music making of the largest choral groups ever assembled:

> Then I looked and heard the voice of many angels, numbering thousands upon thousands, and ten thousand times ten thousand. They encircled the throne and the living creatures and the elders. In a loud voice they sang. . . . Then I heard every creature in heaven and on earth and under the earth and on the sea, and all that is in them, singing. (Rev. 5:11–13 NIV 1984)

Try to imagine the sound of this music! It will be like nothing we have ever experienced, nothing ever created or heard before.

Not only does God surround himself with the most powerful music in existence, but it also appears that our Creator, himself, actively makes music. In the book of Zephaniah, we discover that Jehovah will express his affection toward us in song:

> The LORD your God is with you,
>> he is mighty to save.
> He will take great delight in you,
>> he will quiet you with his love,
>> he will rejoice over you with singing. (Zeph. 3:17 NIV 1984)

Further, in Psalm 32, the writer tells us that in times of difficulty, God will surround us with songs:

> You are my hiding place;
>> you will protect me from trouble
>> and surround me with songs of deliverance. (Ps. 32:7 NIV 1984)

In Hebrews, God the Son is described as singing not only over us but also with us: "I will proclaim your name to my brethren, in the midst of the congregation I will sing your praise" (Heb. 2:12 NASB).

It appears that music will be integral to our lives in heaven, that it will remain as a valuable aid in communicating praise. Furthermore, God will encourage us to actively continue in its production throughout eternity, and we will make music together with many others—yes, even with God himself.

AN INVITATION TO COMMUNICATE

Henry Wadsworth Longfellow, the popular American poet of the nineteenth century, once wrote, "Music is the universal language of mankind."[9] Many people think that his words ring true, that music serves as a universal language. However, though music is universally present on earth, it includes many unique and discrete vernaculars. Music is as personal and unique as any spoken language. There can be vast differences in music from one culture to another. For example, compare Han Chinese folk music to Hungarian Tánchaz folk music, and you will find that many of the differences between the two are not easily translated. Further, one need only play a recording of Indonesian Gamelan for those accustomed to polka, or recordings of the Inuit musical games for those who enjoy raga music of Southern India, and the nonuniversal nature of musical understanding will quickly become apparent

Because musical styles, inflection, interpretation, and preferences are culturally determined and individually held, music serves as an excellent vehicle for learning about the lives of others and for understanding differences and values. If a culture is to be explored and understood, then the music of that group is a rich invitation to such understanding.

To be sure, some of the most innovative and beautiful achievements of any culture can be found in its music, the result of individual insight and creativity and the product of the cumulative impact of multiple generations within a culture. Many of these musical expressions are available to us in written and recorded form, accessible for the enhancement of our lives and the understanding of the lives of others.

The nature of much musical performance rests on the re-creation

---

[9]Henry Wadsworth Longfellow, *Outre-Mer: A Pilgrimage Beyond the Sea* (New York: Harper & Brothers, 1835), 202.

of a composition, providing a direct link to the creativity and insight of the composer. Performance also offers a rich opportunity to create a unique interpretation of the work, combining the forces of the original composer with musicians producing the work anew. This strong musical thread, connecting past and present, allows us to explore the lives of countless people and their worlds and culminates in an ever-growing collection of music that communicates across generations and cultures, linking people and ideas.

AN INVITATION TO SERVE

Music can be a powerful tool of ministry, soothing those who are sick, comforting those who are dying, and enhancing a variety of therapeutic settings. Hospice treatment centers, drug and alcohol rehabilitation services, prisons, and many other ministry outreach programs have discovered the impressive ministerial potential of music. There are numerous accounts of hospital scenes and the last moments of a person's life when music was the ministerial balm that allowed poignant expressions of emotion, care, and ministry. In times of great tragedy and sorrow, music has been employed to comfort and heal. Where words are insufficient to communicate the deepest emotions, music provides a unique path for love and compassion that reaches powerfully into the lives of others.

As a window into individual lives and cultures, music is useful in better understanding a new friend, someone you have known for many years, a group of people, or an entire culture present or long past. As it offers insight into the hearts and minds of people and nations, music is capable of bridging chasms between various groups.

Members of the church and the academy, as influential patrons of music, can effectively facilitate the ministerial power of music making. This role includes teaching, nurturing, inspiring, and encouraging. Schools and churches that foster environments that are rich in music are able to unleash the extraordinary power of music to communicate and minister.

AN INVITATION TO GROW

As we each seize the invitation to explore music's role in our lives, and as we purposefully examine music's place in our individual liberal learning agendas, a few suggestions might be helpful.

Seize the invitation to make music. Each person should be encouraged to experience the thrill of creating music, whether making music alone or with others, all the while embracing the invitation to music making as a wonderful privilege. Care should be taken to avoid the trap of believing that only those with professional skills should make music. An *amateur* is defined as someone who has love for the activity at hand. Committed music making should not be reserved for those who receive a paycheck for it but ideally should be integral to the lives of all, amateur and professional alike.

Find your own voice if you have lost it. Harold Best observes, "The human voice is the only musical instrument that God has directly created. By doing so, he has provided equal access to music and singing for everybody."[10] For those who hesitate to engage their voices in singing, Best encourages, "Singing is not an option for the Christian; no one is excused. Vocal skill is not a criterion."[11]

Note a word of caution. In spite of its powerful attributes, music is a vehicle and not the primary subject itself. It is tempting to focus on the music, to elevate its importance, particularly when it is powerful, grand, or a cherished favorite. However, our Creator offers music to us as a tool for the purposes of praise, worship, communication, insight, and creative expression. The distinction between performance and praise might again be helpful in sorting this out.

Music is intensely personal, and, because of this, we are often quick to label and reject various musical styles. We are tempted to pigeonhole music, generalizing about style, venue, and instrumentation. Music within the church suffers in this regard because of our tendency toward labeling: "contemporary," "traditional," "classical," "modern," and equally limiting monikers. Isn't it possible that nearly all music might be used as praise, regardless of style, tempo, or instrumentation? Our embrace of music should be wide, generous, and marked by gratitude for the many ways that it reflects the multiple facets of the maker and the Maker.

---

[10]Harold M. Best, *Unceasing Worship: Biblical Perspectives on Worship and the Arts* (Downers Grove, IL: InterVarsity, 2003), 143–45.
[11]Ibid.

Learn of music's potential through careful listening and observation. Listen to the music of children in any land and use their sounds, faces, and approaches to music as a model for better understanding music's role and potential. Listen to the beauty of the voice of a young mother singing to her child, the rhythmic lure of drums from afar, the glorious sound of voices singing songs of praise. Inside and outside the church, bask in tradition while fanning the flame of creativity. Embrace all that is good, true, right, and beautiful in traditional forms of music and, at the same time, celebrate brand-new music that is being created today and music that will be created tomorrow and in the days to come.

Where will God lead in this musical journey? What is the proper place of music in your life? What will God's song sound like as it is revealed on the other side of glory? How will our voices sound as we join him in song? Begin answering these questions now. Follow Scripture's admonition in praising the Lord with music for your sake, for the edification of others, and for the pleasure of God himself.

CHAPTER EIGHTEEN

LEARNING TO PERCEIVE THROUGH VISUAL ART

E. John Walford

Art does not reproduce the visible; rather, it makes visible.
—PAUL KLEE, *CREATIVE CREDO*

Ever since the creation of the world his eternal power and
divine nature, invisible though they are, have been understood
and seen through the things he has made.
—ROMANS 1:20 (NRSV)

Many students, even at a liberal arts college, wonder why an introductory course in visual art should be required as part of their general education. What is the value of such study? This question perhaps seems natural, especially for those who have had limited exposure to the arts. If a student is to engage art with any sense of personal investment or worthwhile outcome, then the perceived value of such a requirement should be understood in a way that promotes positive learning. But with so many pressing spiritual and societal needs, why should a Christian even bother to pay any attention to the visual arts?

As far as we know, Jesus did not study art in any formal manner. For that matter, he did not take time to acquire a four-year college education (though he certainly studied in the temple, Luke 2:39–52), possess the means for personal transportation (Christ borrowed a donkey when he rode through the streets of Jerusalem, John 12:14–15), or own a house (he did not even have a place to lay his head, Luke 9:58). Neither did Jesus continue in the trade of his earthly father, as a carpenter, which would have been the normal thing to do in his day. Even though there is so much to learn from Jesus's example, his particular purpose and way of life are not intended to establish an exhaustive model for us to follow.

WHY VALUE THE VISUAL ARTS?

So then, from a Christian standpoint, what is the basis for valuing the visual arts? The creation mandate, set forth in the first two chapters of Genesis, calls for creative human stewardship of all earthly resources, and this applies to us just as much now as it did when it was first given. Made in God's image, we are to be like our Maker, making things of beauty and significance, and we are to value this process not only in ourselves but also in others. This biblical reality has never been revoked. Indeed, we were created to care for God's creation and to be co-creators; therefore, it holds true for *all* of us to heed this injunction and fulfill it with all our strength, will, vision, and imagination.

The visual arts can remind us that creative expression matters to God. Indeed, our Creator places a responsibility on us, not only regarding the natural environment and what we do with natural resources, but also regarding how we create and use the distinctly human-made environment of culture. Because we are all created in the image of our Creator, his way of putting the world together is a model for us as we consider cultural participation and expression—each according to the gifts given. As Leonardo da Vinci understood, the painter's mind is "a copy of the divine mind, since it operates freely in creating the many kinds of animals, plants, fruits, landscapes, countrysides, ruins, and awe-inspiring places."[1] For this very reason, da Vinci argued, and because of its enduring power, painting should be included as one of the liberal arts.[2]

God also made us for community, and as citizens, we share some of the responsibility for the environment we shape for one another. Artistic giftedness is but one manifestation of how humanity is endowed to carry forth the creation mandate, but it is unique in its potential to make the unrealized realm visible through art. As Paul Klee puts it, "Art does not reproduce the visible; rather, it makes visible."[3] Art also makes visible what is in the heart and mind of humanity, much as creation makes visible what is in the heart and mind of God. Like speech and writ-

---

[1]Bruce Cole and Adelheid M. Gealt, *Art of the Western World: From Ancient Greece to Post-Modernism* (New York: Simon & Schuster, 1991), 139.
[2]Frederick Hartt, *Art: A History of Painting, Sculpture, Architecture*, 4th ed. (New York: Harry N. Abrams, 1993), 668.
[3]Celeste Snowber, *Embodied Prayer: Toward Wholeness of Body, Mind, and Soul* (Kelona, BC: Northstone, 2004), 60.

ing, music and song, and theater and dance, visual art is a God-given medium through which we can both voice creation's praise and share with one another the breadth and depth of our human experience—its joys and its miseries. Visual art, then, functions, among other purposes, as a means of expression through which we live and share in community our sense of what it is to be human, dwelling in a world of inexhaustible complexity and curiosity. As a mode of exploration and discovery, art reports back our findings about existence.

Despite the richness and depth that come from this mode of human exploration and discovery, some Christians still raise the objection that the contemporary world of the visual arts seems void of God, excessively exclusive, and outside the mainstream experience of everyday life. Some Christians even ask, "Are we not therefore better off simply ignoring it?"

Evangelical Christians have historically answered this question with a bold "Yes, we are better off ignoring visual art." The problem with this response, however, is that the disregard of the few has become the ignorance of the many. Today, many Christians know nothing, do nothing, and have nothing to say or contribute to this area of human activity. The arts offer Christians a culture-shaping opportunity. Indeed, for almost fourteen hundred years the church was the prime patron of the visual arts, yet today the world of visual art lacks Christian involvement and support, let alone interest. Consequently, centuries of neglect of the arts has left a deeply regrettable legacy—one of God's richest gifts has been given over to the near-complete monopoly of secular, anti-religionists.

Fortunately, however, at present there are promising signs of change. An increasing number of churches are seeking to incorporate the visual arts in one manner or another into their corporate experience of worship. And an increasing number of Christians recognize the arts as having the potential to enrich the life of the faithful and bear witness to the truth of God's world.

As a result, in recent years, art departments at many Christian liberal arts colleges across the country have begun to flourish and expand. Along with this encouraging trend, organizations such as Christians in the Visual Arts (CIVA) and International Arts Movement (IAM) have grown from a handful of isolated artists and art professors into organizations with a national reach and a capacity to promote significant traveling exhibitions as well as various supporting publications.

THE CHRISTIAN NEGLECT OF A CULTURE-SHAPING MEDIUM

With historic neglect, Christians have also overlooked how visual modes of expression function as a powerful mediator of cultural forces and ideas, not least of which are those that pervade in today's media culture. Pause to consider the omnipresence of visual media—film, TV, advertising, and the Internet. Now, also, think about the museum and the gallery, where visual images abound. Next, think about the presence of photography in virtually every domain of contemporary human endeavor. All of these venues for visual media prove to be very powerful. Douglas Kellner, professor in the Graduate School of Education and Information Studies at UCLA, explains the importance of visual images today:

> Visual images have long been of utmost significance for human life and our ways of seeing. Indeed, how we interact with and interpret visual images is a basic component of human life. Today, however, we are living in one of the most artificial visual and image-saturated cultures in human history, which makes understanding the complex construction and multiple social functions of visual imagery more important than ever before.[4]

To deny the power of visual culture is to remain critically unaware of the influence it has upon our lives.

Regrettably, the perspective of the Christian has been almost totally dismissed from this arena of cultural discourse, limiting serious influence and value formation. However, Christians have not always been absent from influencing art. Long before New York's Madison Avenue advertising executives wised up to the power of the image, moving people to action for economic reasons, Pope Gregory the Great, in the sixth century, recognized the power of art to make visible and memorable the teachings of the church. He, like many other Christian leaders before and since, understood that visual art operates as a commanding cultural force. By its very nature, art is vivid to the imagination. Although we

---

[4]Douglas Kellner, "Critical Perspectives on Visual Imagery in Media and Cyberculture" (http://gseis.ucla. edu/faculty/kellner/ed270/VISUALLITcritical.htm).

tend to forget much of what we hear, we generally retain what we see. Thus art has the power to arouse emotions and to concentrate and move our will to constructive action.

By the same token, in contemporary culture, absent the presence and activity of Christians in this arena of human activity, visual art can serve to make visible and persuasive those human values, beliefs, and behaviors that run counter to any credible Christian social vision. Therefore, the question remains, "How can Christians engage the arena of visual art if they are not truly familiar with its discourse and actively involved, in some way or another, with its social impact?" If we do not participate in the arts arena with understanding and insight, we do not have any credibility to offer critique or even object to what we may perceive as its negative social impact and morally destructive influence within the mainstream of culture.

Scripture calls Christians to act as salt and light within the culture, entering and occupying all arenas of human endeavor. Within their realm of possibility, believers in Christ are to strive to act as a counterforce to godless, secularist influence, in whatever contexts believers choose to become involved. Few of us, as disciples of Christ, may find ourselves significantly gifted to practice the visual arts. But all of us are capable of at least becoming informed regarding the ideas and issues prominent in this realm of human expression, a realm that continues to shape our culture. Like it or not, the visual arts are a significant force in shaping and reinforcing human values and thereby influencing social behaviors—for good or ill. Therefore, we would do well to pay closer attention, and engage the issues as best we can.

Through a Christian liberal arts institution's general education curriculum, students have the opportunity to gain from a purposeful encounter with the visual arts, and thus they can begin to understand and appreciate their cultural impact. Indeed, the same opportunity is found at other sorts of colleges and universities across the nation but without the coherent biblical perspective that informs a theological and moral framework for making, interpreting, and critiquing art. Awareness of visual art represents one aspect of becoming a broadminded, thoughtful, and insightful citizen, ready to engage the world in all its fullness and complexity for Christ.

OBSTACLES AND OPPORTUNITIES TO ENGAGE MODERN AND CONTEMPORARY ART

Even with a generous measure of goodwill and open-mindedness toward exploring the visual arts, many Christians find themselves deeply perplexed by the arts, as practiced today and presented in galleries and museums of contemporary art. Such art seems to betray most, if not all, of the basic principles and conventions that previous generations have typically associated with art.

Thus a survey of contemporary art leaves many at a loss to know what to make of what they see. By the measure of traditional standards—which typically means an image constructed according to Renaissance or Romantic or Realist standards of perspective, space, harmony, and proportion—there seems to be a lack of ideal beauty. As commonly understood, there is an absence of verifiable technical skill: no attempt at lifelike representation, no elevating or inspiring subject matter, and no readily accessible meaning, as was patently the case in the past. An adventurous few may ask the question why this should be so, and what it might signify. But a more common response is to turn away in dismay, restricting one's attention to pre-twentieth-century art. Many want a museum tour of the famous pieces of art, not the ones that challenge our pre-established categories of appreciation.

This perplexed reaction is understandable, because all of us are easily confused and even threatened by what we do not understand. When we have the choice, we typically take the easier route of retreating from the unknown and uncomfortable to embrace what is better known, which feels safer to us. But is that how Christ and his disciples engaged the world? Did they choose the path of least resistance? Truth be told, they pursued the path that others tended to avoid, which required faith in God's provision as they met challenges head-on, engaging in dialogue with strangers and opponents for the sake of Christ.

In the visual arts arena, as in others, it is vital for us to do likewise as best we can. Therefore, especially for those of us with the requisite interests and sensibilities regarding art, we need to equip ourselves for the task of engagement, just as Christ and his disciples did. We need to know what is in the heart of our fellow mortals and engage them at the points where they are thinking and living. Christians need to lift the shade and open the window to the visual arts, looking onward with an informed and purposeful gaze and, at the same time, looking upward and beyond with a discerning mind and faithful heart.

Timothy Van Laar and Leonard Diepeveen observe that when we exclaim, "That's not art!," we are unconsciously presupposing that art has a fixed identity and purpose—one that we know and can approve. For example, we may possess the expectation that art should manifest particular skill, or ideal beauty, or lifelikeness, or subject matter.[5] As Van Laar and Diepeveen rightly observe, there is an inherent problem in the tendency to see all art-making in terms of "a monolithic social category" in which it is wrongly assumed that all artists are "engaged in the same general activity."[6]

In reality, artists assume diverse social roles and intend diverse functions for their art. Therefore, one needs to approach, understand, and debate the efficacy of art in terms of that diversity. Among the diverse goals that artists pursue, Van Laar and Diepeveen list the following, which, when used in the interpretive experience, can expand the understanding of liberal arts college students who are trying to make sense of the visual images before them. (I place these diverse goals in the form of questions.) First, do this artist and work explore the formal properties of art, namely, the potential of varied visual strategies, with the goal of extending the expressive range of art, and if so, how? Second, does the artist express humanity and the exploration of the subconscious, thus considering art as a form of self-expression, and if so, how? Third, do the artist and the art challenge established values and institutions via a socio-critical function, and if so, how? And, fourth, do the art and artist attempt to transform society by advocating for various social, political, and economic agendas, and if so, how?

Once a viewer has examined the underlying motivation for any given type of art, the social function of the work can be understood, as well as the formulation of the criteria for its evaluation. As Van Laar and Diepeveen further observe, much misunderstanding within and around

---

[5]Timothy Van Laar and Leonard Diepeveen, *Active Sights: Art as Social Interaction* (New York: McGraw-Hill, 1998), 1–21.
[6]Ibid., 6.

the art world stems from parties working from conflicting assumptions about the social functions of art and the assumed social roles adopted by artists. Indeed, once one becomes aware of this diversity in the social functions of art, all manner of hidden agendas that run throughout the spectrum of institutions of the art world become at once more evident, and the biases of various parties toward one type of function or another become equally apparent. Thus, to take a simple example, those who believe that the value of art lies in its power to advance, say, the agenda of gender politics will have little patience for formalist work, and vice versa. This consistent pattern of perspectival critique is found throughout all the institutions of contemporary art: art magazine reviews, museum curatorial decisions, grant allocations, and commercial gallery selections.[7] Value judgments are a part of the art experience, and they should be for liberal arts students as well. But, as in all aspects of life, knowledge and insight must precede judgment.

THE DIVERSITY OF OPPORTUNITY FOR CHRISTIAN ARTISTIC ENGAGEMENT

By this same token, within the diversity of social functions adopted by the contemporary art world, there lies open to the adventurous artist— or would-be artist—a wide spectrum of opportunity to exercise artistic gifts within society. These may not lie most evidently, or easily, within the traditional structures of the art world of the past but need to be reimagined in terms of the society in which we find ourselves. So long as God continues to forge human beings endowed by their creator with artistic gifts and sensibilities, he will have need of those who can make sense of art. While it remains true that the art world is an exceedingly difficult and challenging arena in which to find gainful employment and navigate one's way effectively and wisely, it is important to remember that God does not create people for redundancy—we are each called to a particular purpose to express unique gifts. It is therefore our challenge to nurture and shape the gifts we are given to the possibilities that exist for their expression in the world.

The artistically gifted may need to temper their grandiose ambitions

---

[7]Ibid., 7–13.

about becoming the next rising star in the art world and first think more moderately about where their gifts can fit and serve within their more immediate community. If they are gifted and have a particular sensitivity to the key concerns of their unique time and place, then perhaps their impact and repute will expand of its own accord. We are all called to do whatever it is that we are gifted to do, as God-pleasers, and to do it with all our might. That is a task big enough for a lifetime. Most of us find our Christian calling on a modest stage, content only that God sees, and that what truly counts, in the end, is that when we meet our Maker, he will say, "Well done, good and faithful servant." The servant is not above his master; the artist is not above the Creator. Christ himself reminds us that he came not to be served but to serve, not to receive accolades but a crown of sacrificial thorns. For the faithful artist, there is no difference.

By cultivating a discerning approach to art, Christian liberal arts students enhance their perception not only of each visual art form but also of details in everyday life, great and small. No one who has ever stood long before Rembrandt's *Return of the Prodigal Son* (Hermitage, St. Petersburg) can fail to grasp the wonder of undeserved forgiveness, just as anyone who has studied Jacob van Ruisdael's landscapes can never again look at wheat fields and ancient trees in the same way. Attentive viewing brings great rewards, like the mastery of any human skill. It also enhances daily engagement with people within various environments, whether natural or man-made. The eyes are great natural receptors; and just like motor skills in sports, we can learn to use them more deftly toward a better result—to observe carefully what is around us.

As students attend to the lines, colors, shapes, and textures that visual artists orchestrate, they discover the richness and nuance of what is given to the eyes. With practice, this skill can carry over into all aspects of life, influencing and enriching the art of living. As the eyes see things never seen before, life expands in its fullness and meaning. As students observe the varied dimensions of visual art, they learn to see the world and the other more completely, and in so doing they appreciate more completely the One beyond, who artistically made all beings and all possibilities.

CHAPTER NINETEEN

THEATER AS AN IMPERFECT MIRROR

Mark Lewis

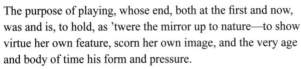

The purpose of playing, whose end, both at the first and now,
was and is, to hold, as 'twere the mirror up to nature—to show
virtue her own feature, scorn her own image, and the very age
and body of time his form and pressure.
—WILLIAM SHAKESPEARE, *HAMLET*

For if any be a hearer of the word, and not a doer, he is like unto a man
beholding his natural face in a glass: For he beholdeth himself, and
goeth his way, and straightway forgetteth what manner of man he was.
—JAMES 1:23–24 (KJV)

We have not traveled a significant distance from the director's notes for the
players at Elsinore, the castle in Shakespeare's *Hamlet.* When we attend
the theater, we go to see and to hear the stories of our own human existence embodied—to see ourselves reflected. The mirror of theater is not a
perfect one, and the glimpses we catch are not simple, either to measure
or to understand. Nevertheless, the purpose of a play, if we are to believe
Shakespeare, is to powerfully reflect something truthful and memorable
about life—about your life, and mine, in a kind of conversation.

Immersion in liberal learning has likewise been likened to a conversation, one in which we deeply entertain the ideas of another—not
because we will always agree with those ideas, but because in the process of considering them we become educated. In this kind of conversation, the philosopher Hans-Georg Gadamer says, "One learns to look
beyond what is close at hand—not in order to look away from it but to
see it better, within a larger whole and in truer proportion."[1] Looking
into theater's imperfect mirror, we are given the opportunity to consider

---

[1]Hans-Georg Gadamer, *Truth and Method* (London: Sheed & Ward, 1979), 143.

a horizon beyond our own and in doing so to recognize our own life's experience in the experience of another.

Think about the last good play you saw—one that powerfully moved or challenged you. The lights went down. You were presented, across a divide, with an actor (or actors) *pretending*. After a few minutes, you began to let down your guard a little and to relax for a time into what Samuel Taylor Coleridge called the "willing suspension of disbelief."[2] The actors moved in their story, and as it unfolded, your imagination moved as well. By engaging the play in the process that Coleridge describes, you entered another world.

How did this movement of your imagination occur? Unlike the experience of watching a film, where the eye is directed, you looked where you wanted to look in the lighted space presented to you. Sometimes this was at the actor who was speaking, so you could understand the story being told. Sometimes it was at the actor being spoken to, or at the peripheral character who reminded you somehow of your grandmother. Maybe you started thinking about the last time you saw your grandmother and tried to remember when you had last called her. After a breath or two, you began to entertain the story once more. If the play was an especially good one, you were not distracted by the passage of time as the events presented to you moved forward.

Finally, when the play came to an end, the lights of the pretend world were shut off. The actors took their bows (both to remind you that you had been watching a play and to give you a chance to say thanks) and the house lights came up, illuminating your way back to the lobby. You may have felt as though you were waking up from a nap in which you had dreamed a vivid dream. As with most dreams, many of the play's images faded quickly, gone forever. But a few lingered with you—some perhaps indelibly. I can describe to you in detail specific images from plays I saw more than thirty years ago. The mirror was held up, and I was caught in it.

THE LAST CAMPFIRE

How, exactly, had I been caught? How does theater work, when it is working well? We might acknowledge at this point that many of us

---

[2]Samuel Taylor Coleridge, *Biographia Literaria* (London: J. M. Dent, 1906), 161.

have never had the experience of catching our reflection in a piece of live theater. Most of us have spent a great deal more time watching movies than seeing plays. Perhaps you have felt something similar to the experience described above while exiting the theater after seeing a movie that affected you deeply. Does the experience of being caught by a play's mirror differ appreciably from the experience one might have seeing a film?

I think it does. A key difference is in the act of co-creation. At a play, the actors and the audience become bound together in the work of making a story. Without the active participation of both groups at once, sharing a single space, theater cannot happen. It is this work *together*, a conversation of sorts between the audience and the actor, that creates a mirrored moment in a play and allows the play itself, finally, to succeed. The playwright Terrence McNally once referred to theatergoers as "kids around the campfire."[3] Theater is a place where our stories are told in community and where, in the words of Linda Loman, from *Death of a Salesman*, "attention must be paid."[4] For a play to happen well, we must truly *spend* time *paying* attention.

Theater demands that we incline to the events before us. In our twenty-first-century life, with its emphasis upon individuality and technology, we are far more accustomed to stories that we can experience in a receiving posture. This is certainly our experience of watching a movie at our local multiplex. Semi-recumbent, we allow a story to wash over us, our extra-large soda never far from our fingertips, the digitized soundscape thrilling our ears. Everything is being done for us technologically. We experience a privatized reality, totally filled in for us by the medium.

One could argue for other environments where communal connection might take place, including church, but increasingly these environments have come to resemble more closely our screen life—in which experiences are created for us, with an individual viewer in mind. As we lose familiarity with the practice of making stories together, it is natural that the practice becomes less attainable—and maybe less attractive as well. Our "screen stories" are much more conveniently and efficiently shared.

But human beings have always had a great need to be reflected in

[3]Terrence McNally, *It's Only a Play* (New York: Dramatists Play Service, 1986; rev. 1992), 62.
[4]Arthur Miller, *Death of a Salesman* (New York: Viking Penguin, 1949), 56.

live stories as well, and theater has been an important part of every great civilization for precisely this reason. It can provide the opportunity to see and hear—in the kind of mirrored conversation I have begun to describe—a piece of our common human experience. What are some of the qualities of these mirrored conversations? How do they occur?

TWO STORIES

I drove recently to a neighboring town to speak to an adult Sunday school class on the subject of live theater. On the way, I experienced a familiar unease. Discussion of theater among Christians is most often concerned, it seems, with broad questions of evaluation—of what is useful and edifying, what is worthy, and what should not be pursued. Certainly these kinds of discussions are necessary, and, in my experience, occasionally fruitful. But what is rarely discussed, and not very simple to discuss, is how theater actually operates—how it works.

The Sunday school class was composed of a group of people that ranged in age from teenager to octogenarian. Several colleagues were there, as well as a couple of my students. I spoke for a few moments to introduce our topic and myself, and then presented the circle with a prop and a challenge.

The prop was an old baseball, one that had been given to me, already well used, in 1979. The challenge was simple. As the baseball was passed from person to person around the circle, the individuals were asked to provide an introduction—not by giving their own name but by identifying themselves as the son or daughter of one of their parents. They were to say aloud to the group the full name (first, middle, and last) of the chosen parent, his or her birthplace (as precisely as possible), and the day in history on which the parent had been born.

The results of the exercise, which lasted perhaps a half an hour, were revealing. Most of the individuals in the circle participated, although some simply passed the ball along without speaking. Those who spoke employed a number of different acting *techniques* (and I am choosing that term purposefully) to manage the moment's task. Some looked only at the baseball, seemingly lost in thought as they uttered the name of their mother or father. Others connected more directly with the people of the circle. Some combined both strategies. Facial expressions varied, sometimes from moment to moment. There was blushing. Tears surprised some, and others forgot what they were trying to say.

When the game concluded, I asked for brief feedback and then made only one point—a simple but crucial one in understanding the mechanics of theater. Theater makers are always responsible for two stories, which are told simultaneously. The first is the playwright's story, communicated through the play itself and the imagined lives of the characters. The second story is that of the embodied human being before us, the actor. The actor uses his body as an instrument and his life experience as a bridge to connect the audience to the playwright's story. Both stories are necessary for a play to occur powerfully.

Capable actors learn to hold the two stories in tension. They spend their lives looking for the connections from their own experience that will allow them to tell universal stories well. Sound acting technique teaches that all of us have in our lives the raw material, the experience, to tell these stories.

In the words of Shakespeare teacher and scholar Eloise Watt, we learn both to "mind the text, and to *mine* the text."[5] Serious theater makers are involved in an excavation of personal experience, elusively housed in memory, that will allow them to embody a character, and to make their character's experience clear—first to themselves, then to others in rehearsal, and finally to an audience. The ability to tell *both* stories well is vital to the success of any play.

A COMMON MOMENT

During a performance of *August Osage County*, at the Steppenwolf Theater in Chicago, a teaching colleague from another discipline was struck by a different kind of "two-story" moment, which she later described. In the performance, the actor playing the matriarch of the family was descending a long and steep flight of stairs when she miscalculated a tread and slipped, coming very close to falling a great distance. What happened in that instant, and in the moments following, commanded my colleague's attention as well as her further reflection.

The actor quickly caught and worked to steady herself, successfully

---

[5]Eloise Watt, "Shakespeare in Performance" (New York: Public Lecture, Michael Howard Studios, March 17, 2001), emphasis original.

avoiding a terrible fall. (This action, of course, had very little to do with the character or the story; it was simply a person trying not to fall down a flight of stairs.) But in the next moment the actor wordlessly acknowledged the slip to the audience, before incorporating it into the life of her character and continuing the play. What impacted my colleague so profoundly was the feeling in the room. She described it as utterly exciting but could not describe why.

I believe that what happened in that audience at Steppenwolf involved a sort of collaboration of consciousness: actor and audience—present with one another—caught in a common moment. The audience, already imaginatively focused on the actor and the story, suddenly found their focus interrupted by an incident outside the world of a play. And because the actor was deft, she knew how to strike a balance between two stories. For an instant she was just like us—a human being trying not to fall. In the next moment she worked to recover the thread of the character's life—the story she was telling. The audience scrambled with her.

Everyone in the room shared a brief journey together and, in a way that might surprise some, the bond between actor and audience had not been diminished. In fact, it had been deepened, strengthened by the actor's acknowledgment that she was alive both in the story of the play and in the same room as her audience. Solid acting technique demands a responsibility to be "alive" in both realms at once.

We have a good deal of experience witnessing actors (as well as other public figures) engage in something like the opposite of this. I once saw, on Manhattan's Lower East Side, a production of *Romeo and Juliet* that took place in a venue that had been wittily advertised as "Shakespeare in the Parking Lot." The performance's setting was just that—an urban parking lot, minimally adorned. In this production, I witnessed an example of two young actors working feverishly to maintain one story while completely denying the second. The play had been proceeding largely without incident. Then, in the middle of a pivotal moment in the lives of the characters, a garbage truck wheeled around a corner, entered the parking lot, backed up to a dumpster a few feet away from the action, hoisted and relieved the dumpster of its load, and then returned it with great clamor to the pavement before driving away.

The actors, meanwhile, worked with astounding commitment to completely block out something that was for their audience an undeniable reality. Refusal to acknowledge something so admittedly distant from the world of Shakespeare's Verona might have seemed like the right thing to do. But cocreation demands not only that we balance two stories within ourselves; it asks that we acknowledge being physically present with those who are cooperating with us in the creation of the story—that we include them in everything we do.

I am not suggesting that the actors should have completely stopped their work on the scene to affirm the beeping garbage truck. That would not have balanced the moment either. But neither was it an effective choice to completely deny it. It existed for them, the actors. It existed for us, the audience. What the actor going down the stairs at Steppenwolf Theater somehow knew and the young actors in the New York parking lot failed to acknowledge is that the act of theater depends absolutely on our desire to experience moments communally. In a shared space, an individual or a group of actors asserts, "We will pretend a story for you." And a second person or a group of people respond, "We will do the work of believing you." This is the fragile contract that allows plays to be created. It is why human beings have always made and attended theater.

THE GREATEST CONVERSATION

Are these basic theater-making practices useful for students and educators considering Christian liberal arts education? I believe they are.

In our life together, each of us is called to balance two stories consistently. One is what we have called the "first story," the story at hand, any narrative that is pertinent to our immediate situation. This story might simply be practical. It might have an educational purpose or a moral one. On another level, one reason to pursue a liberal education at a Christian college is the belief that faith in Christ is best described in a story, and that these years in education should be spent in learning to tell it more fully. Why not, then, simply concentrate on that story and its telling?

The reason is that telling any significant *first* story well demands that we acknowledge and investigate the *second* story, the personal one. The part of any story that we are qualified best to tell is the one that has been witnessed from a very particular vantage point. Any person (or audience) will experience a story more fully when they sense that the teller has searched both stories rigorously and that they are sharing generously and authentically. It is through the process of searching out and seeking to balance these stories that the most authentic and powerful Christian witness springs.

Michael Howard, one of America's important teachers of acting, encourages professional actors in his class by reminding them that it is *their* imperfect voice, *their* connection to the character, that provides the audience its best chance to receive and connect to the play. Similarly, Professor Jim Young once described characters in a script as "trapped on a page," freed only by the self-sacrificial work of actors willing to reveal their own stories in an act of service to another, greater story.

In the process of this kind of education, our ability to listen and to empathize will grow as we become accustomed to seeing and hearing moments of our own lives mirrored back to us in the stories of others whose horizon of experience is beyond our own—even those stories that on the surface seem distant and strange. Of course, theologically, we know that all human stories are deeply connected in this way. In the words of Dr. Timothy Keller, founder and pastor of New York's Redeemer Presbyterian Church, "The Christian gospel is that I am so flawed that Jesus had to die for me, yet I am so loved and valued that Jesus was glad to die for me."[6] Our personal story, along with everyone else's, is a tension-filled one.

In our human communities, we will learn to receive the stories of others with humility only to the extent that we are able to recognize their connection to our own. Likewise, we must acknowledge that no human voice can serve adequately to represent the thundering narrative of God's intervention into human history—specifically, the drama of the Son of God entering our story to make the sacrifice that enables us to become part of his story. In order to witness faithfully and courageously, we must learn to *mind* the text and *mine* the text. Along the way, we will be encouraged when we are reminded that there is no wholly sufficient storyteller or perfectly represented narrative. There is only the imperfect actor, proceeding forward in an act of faith.

---

[6]Timothy Keller, *The Reason for God: Belief in an Age of Skepticism* (New York: Dutton, 2008), 181.

THE END OF CHRISTIAN LIBERAL ARTS

A Christian liberal arts education is something to savor, not to squander. Liberal arts students who make the most of their time in college—especially students who believe that all truth finds its ultimate reality in Jesus Christ—are well prepared to live life to the full and to make a maximal difference for the kingdom of God.

Such expansive vision runs counter to prevailing trends in higher education. Colleges today are predominantly secular, not sacred. Their curricula tend to be narrowly vocational, not liberally educational. There is a widespread sense that students are not getting what they need or pay for. Many may be able to sympathize with Zooey's complaint in one of J. D. Salinger's novellas: "You never even hear any *hints* dropped on a campus that wisdom is *supposed* to be the *goal* of knowledge. You hardly even hear the word 'wisdom' mentioned."[1]

In this section we consider the end of Christian liberal arts education, using the word *end* in several different senses. First, we consider the possibility that we are witnessing the end of liberal arts education as we know it. This is not simply because authentically liberal education is becoming an increasingly rare commodity but also because the contemporary media environment discourages deeply reflective thought. As a percentage of the college-going population, the number of liberal arts students is relatively small. And even programs that are advertised as "liberal arts" may bear little resemblance to liberal education in the goals and practices of its classical tradition.

Then there are the massive cultural trends that work against the goals of the liberal arts. In our desire not to "miss anything," we constantly monitor our electronic devices. But this is a distraction from the kind of human presence, heightened attentiveness, careful observation,

---

[1] J. D. Salinger, *Zooey* (New York: Little, Brown, 1961).

thoughtful reflection, and creative imagination that produce the best academic work and are most satisfying to the soul.

We also revisit the purpose of Christian liberal arts education, exploring its *end* in the sense of goal or purpose. What is a liberal education for? This is the question that concerns Anthony Kronman in his widely reviewed book *Education's End: Why Our Colleges and Universities Have Given Up on the Meaning of Life*.[2] The question of meaning is even more pressing for Christians, who believe that all of life is for the glory of God. For us, education is not exclusively or even primarily about information; rather, it is about transformation—the formation of a whole person into the beauty of Jesus Christ. Going to college is more than merely job preparation to earn an income. Thus, Christian liberal arts education does not take place from the neck up but from the head down and the heart out. It gives us what Kenneth Burke described as "equipment for living."[3]

Finally, we use the word *end* in its most ultimate sense, its eschatological sense, as referring to the destiny of all things. Are the liberal arts only for a certain time and place, or are they for all times and all places, including the life to come?

We believe that the vital tradition of Christian liberal arts education—a tradition that began with the ancient Greeks and Romans before it was adopted and sanctified by the church—has an important contribution to make to the world. By cultivating the life of the mind, liberal arts education can help Christians everywhere to serve as faithful citizens of the kingdom of God—all through life and then forever afterwards.

If this is true, then the student's calling has heavenly significance. As Arthur Holmes has written, "Christian liberal arts education has an eternity in view."[4] By pursuing the liberal arts in all their beauty and variety, we participate in the glories of the coming age, when "the kingdom of the world" will become "the kingdom of our Lord and of his Christ" (Rev. 11:15), and when all the children of God will rise up to praise their loving creator.

---

[2] Anthony T. Kronman, *Education's End: Why Our Colleges and Universities Have Given Up on the Meaning of Life* (New Haven, CT: Yale University Press, 2007).
[3] Kenneth Burke, quoted in Marilyn Chandler McEntyre, "Gleaning as We Go," *Books and Culture* (March/April, 2011): 3.
[4] Arthur F. Holmes, *The Idea of a Christian College* (Grand Rapids, MI: Eerdmans, 1975), 45.

CHAPTER TWENTY

SOCIAL MEDIA AND THE LOSS OF EMBODIED COMMUNICATION

Read Mercer Schuchardt

If we understand the revolutionary transformations caused by new media, we can anticipate and control them; but if we continue in our self-induced subliminal trance, we will be their slaves.
—MARSHALL MCLUHAN, INTERVIEW

Those who make them will be like them,
    and so will all who trust in them.
—PSALM 115:8 (NIV)

It is a strange fact of the human condition that one organ only—the mouth—serves two completely separate functions. Weirder still is that one of these functions is physiological, while the other one is psychological. The ear only hears, the eye only sees, the nose only smells, but the mouth of the human is the strangest of strange organs, for it is both a consumer and a producer: it is an input mechanism for food and also an output mechanism for words. The tongue is that odd multitasking organ that both tastes your food and flavors your speech.

Jesus himself seems to have noticed this dichotomy when he pointed out that "it is not what goes into the mouth that defiles a person, but what comes out of the mouth; this defiles a person" (Matt. 15:11). Eating is bestial and necessary; speech is angelic and sacred, one reason why so much of wisdom consists in biting your tongue. And this bestial/angelic dichotomy is perhaps why it is always considered rude to talk with your mouth full—you can hardly sound like a saint when you are chewing your cud like a cow; under these conditions your words most often come out like the grunts of an ape.

Since receiving our original God-given medium of speech, we have altered our speech by altering the medium through which we communicate our humanity in specific historical instances. The media prophet Marshall McLuhan lays out these shifts in human communication as distinct ages. Since our beginnings in the Oral Age (when speech was the only form of communication and required the immediate physical presence of two people), we have moved through the Writing Age (in which we added the ability to communicate meaning to those not physically present), and the Print Age (in which the printing press provided mechanical reproduction of our ideas), through the Electronic Age (in which electricity accelerated the rate at which this process happened), to the present moment, when we find ourselves in the Digital Age (in which digital natives inhabit an increasingly virtual world and behold eight to twelve hours per day of electronic mass media). We fondly use the term *technological progress* to describe these changes. But if the kingdom of God is not food and drink (Rom. 14:17), and if out of the abundance of the heart the mouth speaks (Matt. 12:34), then Christian liberal arts students should be wary of the common media diet, lest they become what they behold (Ps. 115:8). As Mom used to say, "You are what you eat"; this axiom seems equally applicable to the nonedible things that we daily ingest.

VICES OF THE VIRTUAL LIFE

So if you accept the metaphor that the new media, in its form (and in most of its content, though not all), is a type of fastfood for the soul, then the danger of the Digital Age is a sort of spiritual malnutrition that both weakens our own vitality and dilutes the beauty of what we offer to an undernourished world. In other words, consuming a supersaturated media diet while simultaneously attempting to articulate a gospel that claims timeless veracity to this present age may make us sound to the host culture like we are talking with our mouths full. And if time is the currency of love, then our daily investment in media consumption may be the best indicator of the peculiar shape of our love in this age, raising essential questions about whether our choices feed in us the truest self—the image of the living Word—or simply fatten the false things that distort true incarnation.

As the first generation to be born into the Digital Age, college students today face a particular constellation of challenges that stem from spending more time in the virtual world than in the real world. In the face of these real dangers, learning to grapple consciously with spiritual and intellectual effects of mass media and crafting a response that protects and nourishes embodied life in a world suffering from its absence become the most serious and vital work young Christians can engage in. The function of liberal arts has always been to promote and celebrate the growth of what is truly human, and this endeavor is now more important than ever. Being in—but not of—the virtual world is, at the most basic level, the difference between life and death. There are at least seven observable vices of the virtual life that we should vigilantly watch for in ourselves, our friends, and our loved ones.

WHATEVER

Probably the most easily diagnosed media effect, and the one that the average student feels intuitively, is passivity. It is the feeling you describe with the response "Whatever." If the average American spends at least half of all waking hours passively consuming culture rather than actively producing it, it isn't hard to understand why passivity is growing into a universally shared experience. The American TV habit of thirty-five hours per week is almost equivalent to a second full-time job. Even the alleged blessing of two-way new media—such as blogging, Facebook, Twitter, and other outlets—usually consists of regurgitating other people's content rather than any real artistic or intellectual originality.

Exposure to chosen media streams can give us a false perception of being permanently in the present tense, depriving us of the sober sense of time passing and creating a feeling that our options are perpetually open, when in fact time is passing us by the minute. There is a sense in which the very fact that physical activity requires us to consciously move our bodies through space and time creates a healthy awareness of the passing of time, while the physical inactivity of virtual life allows us to inhabit a place where the rules of time seem simply not to apply. The effect of this is that we spend time without consciously reckoning with the cost and value of what is slipping through our fingers. Thus, wasting time seems more effortless than ever. Cultural engagement, civic participation, voter turnout, and other markers all show signs of decreasing interest.

Over time, passivity can lead to a chronic lack of goal setting. Mark Edmundson calls people who get caught in the hyperactive passivity of going nowhere fast "possibility junkies."[1] They are among those who suffer the sort of regression found in thirty-five-year-olds who still live at home, indulging in Mom's cooking and laundry service. If Christians are to be salt and light or yeast in the world, we need to get out there and agitate things. We ought to afflict the comfortable and comfort the afflicted. One way to do this is to get off the couch, get off the web, get off the phone, and go do something worthwhile, preferably in the company of other living, breathing human beings.

I'M NOT FEELING IT

A close cousin to passivity, desensitization, began to manifest itself at the end of the Electronic Age. In 1964 Bertram Gross coined the term *information overload*, which was a communication technology version of the 1950s term *sensory overload*. Inherent in this term is the underlying idea that the human organism is capable of processing a limited amount of information before it shuts down in order to survive. In the Oral Age, when the only medium of receiving information was in embodied conversation, what we were required to absorb came to us on a human scale at a rate that allowed us to fully integrate the information we were given. For example, the only bad news we received was that of the immediate community, so sorrow came to us in a manageable, human shape. The current generation, by contrast, was born within a few years of the first use of the phrase *apocalypse fatigue* (1992), a term that attempts to describe what happens when digital conditions require human beings to shoulder the knowledge of horror on a global scale. We were created to handle the stories and sorrows of the tribe we were born into, and a profound exhaustion sets in when we are enabled through mass media to take on a godlike omnipresence in terms of what

---

[1]Mark Edmundson, "Dwelling in Possibilities," *Chronicle of Higher Education*, March 14, 2008 (http://chronicle.com/article/Dwelling-in-Possibilities/7083).

is known, without the accompanying omnipotence that would allow us to do anything about it.

This is the kind of psychic overstimulation that exhausts our ability to remain fully present to the sufferings of those around us. As Marshall McLuhan puts it, if the price of liberty is eternal vigilance, then "the price of eternal vigilance is indifference."[2] So if the pop singer Roger Waters had become "comfortably numb" by 1979, then it's little wonder that the Kaiser Chiefs were singing "It's cool to know nothin" by 2008. With so much to care about, one of the primary frustrations of students today is that adults keep telling them that they need to stop being apathetic and care more. This is a profound misdiagnosis of the problem. It is not that digital natives lack concern; it is that they *can't* care more—it is simply impossible for one person to care about every single issue and remain sane.

Scripture tells us that with more knowledge comes more sorrow (Eccles. 1:18), and digital media is nothing if not a knowledge multiplier. How to care at all when there's too much to care about is most likely going to be one of the great struggles of your entire life. The ability to empathize needs to be consciously sheltered; this is the first step toward healing the losses of desensitization. Thoughtful evaluation of the nature and amount of information that we ingest is absolutely essential. The second step is choosing the small way of love. As Mother Teresa said, "We can do no great things, only small things with great love," and it is in the daily discipline of finding quiet ways of rooting our love in the flesh and blood of our immediate community that will ultimately heal us. Overwhelmed with the paralysis of everything, we often choose nothing. Choosing something over nothing in the face of everything is the task of careful discernment, and it is one reason why the razor's edge has gotten sharper under digital conditions.

WILL THEY KNOW WE ARE CHRISTIANS BY . . . ?

Another media effect is narcissism. This term is often bandied about as simply being a heightened version of vanity or egotism, but in fact it is something more significant. Narcissism borders on solipsism, the

---

[2]Marshall McLuhan, *Understanding Media: The Extensions of Man* (New York: McGraw-Hill, 1964), 30.

condition of inhabiting a virtual world in which the individual self increasingly becomes the only self, and other selves become more and more shadowy. We live in a world of choices that revolves around our egos, from YouTube, MySpace, and iPods to my.college.edu, my.bank.com, and my.healthcare.com. But the bigger evidence of a more perilous narcissism is the way in which the online self is a created second self, a carefully crafted, grandiose false self that covers and protects the true self from wounding.

If you are just a regular kid in day-to-day life but a god on Façebook or World of Warcraft, then your second self may be bigger than your first, and your second self may indeed meet the qualifications of a false self erected to protect your true self from perceived threats or weakness. If you have taken more than one photograph of yourself for your Facebook profile to capture just the right you in just the right light from just the right angle, then you have already experienced the phenomenon.

Christians are to take no thought for tomorrow, for what we will eat or wear (Matt. 6:25). How can we reconcile this command with our obsession about how we look in our second life? Christians are to be known by their love—charitable altruism in sacrificing self for others whom we esteem as more important than ourselves (Phil. 2:3). They will not know that we are Christians by our digital avatar.

WHO DO YOU WANT TO BE TODAY?

While narcissism may appear to be an aggrandizing of the self, it is, ironically, evidence of a profound loss of identity. In the Oral Age there was a seamlessness between our essential selves and the words we spoke. We lived in an integrated acoustic-visual world and had not learned the fragmentation that lets us trade an ear for an eye. In other words, there was no physical or virtual distance between our physical presence and the words that we spoke. We had one clear, visible, physical self that did the communicating. In the digital world, when our words are spoken, written, typed, texted, and tweeted, they are no longer anchored to a nonnegotiable physical reality; they may refer to any number of our multiple selves, causing us and others to wonder which is the true self.

Since the invention of the first mass medium in 1450—the

book—human beings have been at threat of losing a singular identity in the presence of mediated alternatives. "Schizophrenia may be a necessary consequence of literacy," as Marshall McLuhan argued back in 1962.[3] Indeed, the term *doppelganger*—the legend of the shadowy double self—goes back to the late eighteenth-century literature of Germany, the same culture that invented the printing press. Since then, the options for bifurcating the self under digital conditions have multiplied to the point where we now look at multiple personality disorder not as a disease but as a form of entertainment, from Lady Gaga's accelerated costume changes in her videos, to the TV show *The United States of Tara*, which is about a mother with dissociative identity disorder (in season 3, two new personalities complemented the existing four personalities of the main character).

This should give us pause: it is Satan who is legion and Christ who is singular and brings all things into unity, including our fractured selves. If we are to have our identity in one and only one source, our Creator, then the new media present us with the danger of accepting disordered, disintegrating, multiplying selves as acceptable and normative. We are to be all things to all people, so as to witness to the one who does not change. Being all things to all people means, on the individual level, being one thing to one person, while bearing witness to the one who does not change. So the principle of unity does not change, as we are called neither to be all things to one person nor one thing to all persons. (The former would be psychotic; the latter would be boring, monotonous, predictable, and dull—the chief of cultural sins under digital conditions.) Even Einstein's theory of relativity only works if all things are relative in relation to the constant of the speed of light.

IT'S COOL TO KNOW NOTHING

The unfortunate irony about all these knowledge products is that they are making us demonstrably dumber than ever before. Students under digital conditions know less and less about more and more, such that they know something about almost everything, but in fact, all they really know is "I've heard of that." This growing stupidity is exhaustively documented

---

[3]Marshall McLuhan, *The Gutenberg Galaxy: The Making of Typographic Man* (Toronto: University of Toronto Press, 1962), 22.

in several recent books, from Mark Bauerlein's *The Dumbest Generation* to Charles P. Pierce's *Idiot America*, to Rick Shenkman's *Just How Stupid Are We?* The evidence shows that while technology may multiply knowledge, it is no longer inserting that knowledge into our skulls. The problem with an unconscious acceptance of unlimited information collection is that much of what we gather is splintered and unconnected to any real way of making meaning—it fills us but doesn't satisfy. As Neil Postman writes, "We have transformed information into a form of garbage and ourselves into garbage collectors."[4]

Almost all measures of intelligence, from fluid to crystallized intelligence, from long- to short-term memory, from reading to writing skills, are dependent on the functioning of mind, memory, and language. When the contents of mind, memory, and language can be externalized in a medium like "the cloud" and portable media devices give us the illusion of portable omniscience, we are really shifting the contents of our brains from an internal to an external hard drive, and our brains are getting softer in the process. This also helps explain why students nationwide resent assessments that test their hard command of facts and, more than ever, fail to understand why plagiarism is an issue.

The word *idiot* comes from the Greek *idiotes*, which essentially refers to a person so taken up with personal matters that he is unable to participate in civic life. This is precisely the kind of idiocy that we are manifesting—highly individualized people who have a very private knowledge set that may not be shared or valued by anyone else in the culture. In the pre-digital world there were a hundred musical bands with a million fans each; in today's world there are a million bands with a hundred fans each. Taken to its logical conclusion, everyone will end up listening to himself play his own music on GarageBand. The granularity of each niche audience is reducible to one in the digital age, which by definition creates a nation of idiots. It's not that the village idiot can't have a meaningful conversation; it's that his conversation is only

---

[4]Quoted on a display wall of the Bern Communication Museum, June 2011, and most likely a modification of the quote from Postman's essay "Science and the Story That We Need," *First Things*, January 1997, (http://www.firstthings.com/article/2007/12/003-science-and-the-story-that-we-need-44), which reads in full as follows: "Where information was once an essential resource in helping us to gain control over our physical and symbolic worlds, our technological ingenuity transformed information into a form of garbage, and ourselves into garbage collectors."

meaningful to himself and the few others who are reading his blog about his minutiae. Taken together, the result of digitally induced idiocy is a culture that values the individual over the group; however, the history of civilized cultures tells a fairly consistent story of a balance between the good of the group (the greater good) and the good of the individual. If the root meaning of *communication* is "community," then idiocy and community are clearly at odds.

LIGHT-SPEED EXPECTATIONS

In a digitally accelerated point-and-click media world, you are going to want things faster, sooner, now. Instant gratification is the blessing of most digital technology; it is also its collective curse. If you have ever complained about your school's Internet connection speed, or if you bought the iPad 2 just to get the 3-second faster startup time over the first iPad, then you know the feeling. There is a sense in which digital media so caters to instant gratification that people now feel the right to get angry when they don't get things as fast as they could get them under ideal technical conditions. It is a kind of mass infantilization that has some ugly manifestations. For example, road rage is the potentially violent frustration a driver feels when unable to instantly control the behavior of other drivers on the road. It is something that happens only when there is an expectation that results should be immediate. The problem is that literacy, character, and civilization itself are all built upon the assumptions of pleasures that are not immediately realized. Deferred gratification is the patient willingness to build slowly and incrementally towards an eventual outcome, possibly one that will not occur in your lifetime.

The difference is between medieval people, who built abbeys that are lovely even in ruins, and modern people, who now build tract housing that won't outlast a lifespan. With the rise of instant-gratification media forms, we see the loss of the old arts that necessitated deferred gratification, including letter writing, calligraphy, representational art, model building, and book reading. Pyramids and cathedrals are all built on the foundation of deferred gratification, and deferred gratification, in its purest form, is a movement away from immediate self-absorption toward the kind of humility that is willing to be a novice for a very long time. Indeed, heaven itself and the Christian faith can be seen as one long exercise in deferred gratification, "a long obedience in the same direction," to use Eugene Peterson's phrase.[5] The best antidote to the hazards of instant gratification is to cultivate a skill or a hobby that you cannot master within one year. Then do it again, several times throughout your life.

DISEMBODIED

At the end of the day, the first six media effects reach their cumulative and pernicious fulfillment in disembodiment, which is essentially our unconscious participation in the destruction of our ability to remain fully present—physically and spiritually—to the other real humans in our lives. This problem really matters. For a people called to imitate an incarnate Lord, this unwitting loss of the ability to fully inhabit the present tense, in our flesh and blood, is simply and tragically the loss of our greatest birthright. In the end, if the only thing that really matters is faith expressing itself in love (Gal. 5:6), we cannot forget that love happens in only one place, here, and at only one time, now. And that is where we have to choose to live. But instead—on the phone, on the web, on TV—we are simultaneously everywhere and nowhere. Never before has it been possible in this way to be physically present and spiritually absent.

We see this play itself out with endless variation: friends walking side by side but talking to other friends on cell phones; a husband sitting physically next to his wife, so close that their flesh is touching but lost in cyberspace so that his consciousness is completely removed; students physically present in the classroom but simultaneously surfing the web on a laptop. In this way, we become consciously detached from physical reality, as though the body doesn't matter—the physical manifestation of gnosticism. This creates a mind-body separation that both mimics death and parodies angels, removing us from the requirements of natural law and allowing us to become pure "information." Indeed, the growing struggle among students with pornography, masturbation, cutting, and body image may simply be an attempt by the human organism to get back in touch with its disembodied self as a means of verifying or

---

[5]Peterson's book *A Long Obedience in the Same Direction: Discipleship in an Instant Society* was published by InterVarsity, Downers Grove, IL, in 1980, the year Marshall McLuhan died.

proving one's physical existence. "I achieve self-stimulated orgasm, therefore I am," and, "I feel self-stimulated pain, therefore I am" may be this generation's way of proving to itself that it has not ceased to exist.

Disembodiment through digital media also results in an isolation and absence from the group. Sherry Turkle's book *Alone Together* documents this quite well. But if you have ever pondered why so-called "social media" preemptively requires you to engage in antisocial behavior by being alone at your computer, then you are already conscious of the paradox. And for the Christian whose identity consists in imitating the incarnated Christ, this represents a grave danger. Because our entire religion rests on the fantastical claim of the virtual made real, the idea of an invisible God actually and literally embodying himself in the physical presence of one historically real human being, Jesus Christ, then Christ really is the antibody to the virus of mass disincarnation. This is what the incarnation teaches us and why the sacrament of taking Communion into our physical bodies is both necessary and healing. It is also why the Christian faith offers the crucial road to sanity in a digital world.

THE REAL MADE MYTH

Taken collectively, these seven vices are really unintended consequences of otherwise marvelous technologies. But when you add them all up, they really can produce an absurd species, inhabiting an absurd culture, intent on what Neil Postman described as "amusing ourselves to death."[6] Digitally deprived of our autonomy, maturity, and identity, we can become a childish culture, motivated by the newest media stimuli that produce physiologically or psychologically forced responses. It sounds pretty bleak. But McLuhan explained that "nothing is inevitable provided we are prepared to pay attention."[7] Similarly, Jacques Ellul stated that the purpose of his writing on technology was "a call to the sleeper to awake."[8] We need to start asking of every technology, "Is this a technology in the service of true relationship, or does this remove me from myself, my body, and therefore from those that I love?" If we can move from a place of passively accepting the disincarnating effects of

---

[6]See Neil Postman's 1985 book, *Amusing Ourselves to Death: Public Discourse in the Age of Show Business*, but be sure to get the twentieth-anniversary edition with the foreword by Andrew Postman, Neil's son.
[7]*McLuhan's Wake*, directed by Kevin McMahon, 2002 (Disinformation Studios, 2007).
[8]Jacques Ellul, *The Technological Society* (New York: Vintage, 1964), *xxxiii*.

the virtual life to a conscious evaluation of the effects of the new media that we have uncritically embraced, there is every chance to wake from the somnambulistic trance that modern mass media creates.

This is why waking up is the truest picture of what we need to do. We are sleepwalking, and we need to become conscious of pitfalls ahead. If it was for freedom that Christ set us free, then it is crucial to consider that the medium of Christ's message was embodied communication, and that this may indeed be the only salvation from an otherwise technologically determined enslavement. It may also be the key to understanding why the founding fathers of media ecology—McLuhan, Ong, Ellul—were all devout Christians. Outside of the freedom found in Christ, they did not have any hope beyond a technologically determined (i.e., enslaved) future.

We do not necessarily sin when we create or participate in mass media or technological progress. But we do need to remember that Jesus is the Word. In a sense, the foundational work that underlies everything else we do in Christian academia is to answer T. S. Eliot's questions: "Where shall the word be found / Where will the word resound?"[9] and "Where is the wisdom we have lost in knowledge / Where is the knowledge we have lost in information?"[10] Perhaps the healthiest media diet is really simple: to walk, talk, and act in our embodied selves as Christ did among the poor, the sick, and the outcast. We need to quiet ourselves long enough to hear the whisper that will tell us what food will nourish us deeply and what food will only stuff our mouths and make it impossible to really say anything worth speaking.

[9]T. S. Eliot, "Ash Wednesday," in *The Complete Poems and Plays, 1909–1950* (New York: Houghton Mifflin Harcourt, 1971), 65.
[10]T. S. Eliot, "Choruses from 'The Rock,'" in *The Complete Poems and Plays,* 96.

CHAPTER TWENTY-ONE

LEARNING TO LIVE REDEMPTIVELY IN YOUR OWN BODY

Peter Walters

The Christian way is not the middle way between extremes,
but the narrow way between precipices.
—DONALD G. BLOESCH, *THEOLOGICAL NOTEBOOK I*

Don't you realize that your body is the temple of the Holy Spirit, who lives
in you and was given to you by God? You do not belong to yourself,
for God bought you with a high price. So you must honor God with your body.
—1 CORINTHIANS 6:19–20 (NLT)

To be a Christian college student who takes seriously the liberal arts orientation of becoming all that you can be—mind, body, and spirit—you must also take seriously the care and sustenance of the physical part of your being. However, numerous surveys reveal a disturbing picture of what most college students think about their bodies. Consider just one aspect of body image—body weight. According to Gallup surveys beginning in the 1950s, there has been a 100 percent increase in the number of women and men of the general population who are dissatisfied with their weight.[1] And body-weight dissatisfaction among college students may be even more dramatic. In one university study, two out of every five women and one out of every five men said they would trade three to five years of life to achieve their body weight goals.[2] In a larger 2008 study, 21 percent of women said they would go even further and trade a decade of their lives to reach their ideal

---

[1]Gallup Poll, "Close to 6 in 10 Americans lose weight" (2006).
[2]"Shocking Statistics," University of Colorado Wardenburg Health Center (http://www.colorado.edu/studentgroups/wellness/NewSite/BdyImgShockingStats.html), accessed November 15, 2010.

weight.[3] As alarming as these statistics are, perhaps the most disturbing results came from a group of young teenagers who said that they were more afraid of becoming fat than they were of nuclear war, cancer, or even losing their parents.[4]

How can college students who follow Christ, in particular, find a sense of physical contentment? Why do chest circumference, dress size, and skin texture matter so much in gauging a sense of happiness? When will the obsession with outward appearance cease to have so much power over us? A comprehensive response to these difficult questions goes beyond the scope of a brief chapter; however, an introduction to how to think Christianly about our bodies within the context of a liberal arts education is a realistic objective for this section.

One of the many advantages of a Christian liberal arts education is that problems are investigated from a multifaceted approach, informed by biblical values. Modern medicine has learned the importance of bringing multiple perspectives to the diagnostic table. Historically, health has been simply defined as the absence of disease. Disease was the enemy, and medicine was the solution. While this one-dimensional model was helpful in treating specific viral and bacterial infections, modern medicine has advanced to incorporate other disciplines in a more holistic treatment of disease. Virtually all medical experts now recommend a multidimensional model of health care, the biopsychosocial model, which examines health from at least three perspectives (biological, psychological, and social). These additional perspectives lead to a fuller understanding of the underlying issues that need to be addressed. Such an approach is consistent with a robust liberal arts perspective on learning, emphasizing multiple viewpoints that present a more complete and coherent orientation to reality and living. Rarely will sufficient enlightenment occur through the understanding of one discipline alone. From a Christian standpoint, God is the creator of all knowledge, and therefore we should consider all facets of creation as we make sense of ourselves—including our bodies—in order to live well.

---

[3] Nanci Hellmich, "Would you trade 10 years of your life to be an ideal weight?," *USA Today*, January 6, 2008 (http://www.usatoday.com/news/health/weightloss/2008-01-06-diet-confessions_N.htm).
[4] "Shocking Statistics."

IDENTIFYING THE TWO EXTREMES

Where do we begin when considering the significance of the human body? One approach is to consider worldviews that lie at opposite ends of the body image continuum: physical degradation and physical veneration.

A degraded view of the body emerged from an ancient group of Christians known as the Gnostics. Ancient Gnosticism emphasized a clear distinction between body and spirit, and went even further to say that the physical body is evil. Gnostic teacher Julius Cassianus captured the spirit of Gnosticism in his description of what he called our "sexual parts":

> Let no one say that, since we have these parts so that the female body is arranged this way and the male that way, the one to receive, the other to implant, sexual intercourse is allowed by God. For if this equipment was from the God toward whom we hasten, he would not have said that eunuchs are blessed.

He went on to say that Jesus had come to "reform us and free us from error and from the intercourse of these shameful parts."[5]

The Gnostic message is clear: at best, our erogenous zones need reformation, and at worst, they are a disgrace that needs to be eliminated. But it was not just our sexual parts that were believed to be shameful; rather, the body as a whole was considered base, carnal, and in need of purging. The Gnostic idea of the body's corruption led to the practice of "mortifying the flesh," which literally means to put the flesh to death. The process ranged from abstinence from certain pleasures (meat, alcohol, sex, marriage, and material possessions) to the infliction of pain (beatings, piercings, and cuttings).

Sadly, vestiges of this perspective still proliferate today. Well-meaning Christians argue that the body is nothing more than an exterior shell that holds our real treasure, the soul. Because our bodies came from dust and will return to dust (Eccles. 3:20), individuals concerned with temporal issues such as sleep, diet, and exercise are sometimes deemed less spiritual. Gnostics argue that the soul (defined as nonmaterial) is the only eternal aspect of humanity, so physical concerns are insignificant.

---

[5]Clement of Alexandria, *Miscellanies*.

My grandfather was one of the first Christians I knew who fully embraced the habit of regular physical activity, valuing the body along with the soul. He loved to play tennis and did so with great regularity. In addition, he was senior pastor of a large church in Phoenix, Arizona. My grandfather was surprised that some of the criticism he received during his pastoral tenure came from parishioners who were upset because he attended to his physical fitness when, according to them, "people were dying and going to a godless eternity." Statements such as these reveal an ideological dichotomy about the body and soul that is not supported by the Bible, one in which the physical self gets the proverbial leftovers.

Christian colleges and universities are not immune from the subtleties of elevating spiritual and intellectual virtues at the expense of the body. Take for example the growing trend of several liberal arts institutions to eliminate required physical education courses for their students. It seems ironic that in a time of unprecedented teen obesity and sedentary living, academic institutions are reducing any curricular requirement for physical education during the college years. Students can get caught up in a sort of academic gnosticism, allowing little or no time for physical activity, sleep, or Sabbath renewal. This runs contrary to truly liberating learning that takes the body seriously as a gift from God to be cared for and cultivated.

At the opposite end of the body image continuum is body veneration, which seeks to glorify physical appeal. Linda Wells, editor of *Allure* magazine, captures the clout that physical attractiveness has within American culture:

> There's no question [that] beauty is powerful. We know from scientific studies that beautiful children are given more attention in school. Beautiful babies are touched more than babies who aren't beautiful. Attractive women are hired more often, given higher raises, paid more than unattractive women. They're given more promotions. . . . They're believed to be more spiritual. They're believed to be nicer. And, of course, none of those things are true.[6]

Little wonder that women spend enormous amounts of time and energy

---

[6]*Beauty in a Jar*, directed by Lisa Ades and Lesli Klainberg, A&E, 2003.

focused on their bodies. According to the A&E documentary *Beauty in a Jar*, American women collectively spend a staggering seven billion dollars on cosmetics each year.[7] In 2008, 355,000 women spent an average of $6,500 for breast augmentation. That same year, 341,000 women spent an average of $8,000 per liposuction procedure.[8] These alarming numbers only begin to reveal the average American woman's obsession with physical attractiveness.

Although the majority of research on body image has a gender bias toward women, recent studies suggest that a growing number of men are fixated on physical appearance as well. In one developmental study, boys beginning at eight years of age expressed concerns about obtaining the desired "V" shape that comes from wide muscular shoulders and a narrow waist.[9] Some experts have suggested that during the most recent decades, the physical standards of what is appealing have changed more for men than women. As a cultural signifier of this phenomenon, consider what happened when investigators examined the anthropometric changes in action figure heroes. In the 1960s, G. I. Joe had a relative height of 5 feet, 10 inches, a chest width of 44 inches, and an upper arm measurement of 12 inches. Three generations later, Joe's height remained the same, but 3 inches had been added to his arms and a whopping 11 inches to his chest.[10] Apparently Joe spent quite a bit of time in the weight room during this thirty-year period, mirroring the preoccupation of the male culture at large.

Lest you think this fixation on body image is only an issue for secular males, think again. At one prominent Christian college in the United States, the desire among male freshman students for increased muscular size is three times greater than that of men in the general population.[11] Although this comparison is not a fair assessment of exact differences because of the age disparities of the two populations, it is significant to note that one in every four first-year men at this college reported wanting to increase his muscular size. So it seems that the shape and tone

---

[7]Ibid.

[8]Michelle Healy and Sam Ward, "Top Cosmetic Surgeries in 2008," *USA Today*, April 24, 2009.

[9]Sarah Grogan, *Understanding Body Dissatisfaction in Men, Women and Children* (New York: Routledge Press, 2008).

[10]Harrison G. Pope Jr., Katharine A. Phillips, and Roberto Olivardia, *The Adonis Complex: The Secret Crisis of Male Body Obsession* (New York: Free Press, 2000).

[11]P. H. Walters, "Desires concerning Body Weight" (http://collegewellness.org), accessed October 2, 2010.

of one's body has become a preoccupation for men also, making them susceptible to discontent. This data suggests an inordinate focus on the body that reaches beyond secular culture into the lives of students who claim to live in the freedom that the gospel brings through Christian liberal arts learning.

Avoiding excesses is a common thread that runs through many liberal arts institutions, and this can be traced back to classical Greek philosophers. Plato is credited with eloquently expressing, in books 2 and 3 of *The Republic*, the need for a balanced education, including music and gymnastics, in order to create harmony.

Seldom do individuals identify with extremist positions. While there are times individuals admittedly lean toward particular ideological positions, the average person views him- or herself as balanced and stable, at least in terms of beliefs held to be true. Although often unbalanced in behavior, humans frequently see moderation as the ideal solution. Yet is moderation the call of our baptismal faith as Christians? Even a cursory reading of Scripture calls Christian followers to something far different. Consider the greatest command in all of Scripture: love the Lord your God with *all* your heart, soul, mind, and strength. This is hardly a temperate injunction!

So how are we to apply Scripture, which contains a call both to moderation and to radical discipleship? Although the calls seem mutually exclusive, they don't necessarily have to be. The writer of Ecclesiastes describes well the realities of living with opposing circumstances, such as birth and death, destruction and construction, lament and cheer (Eccles. 3:1–8). Consider that biblical Wisdom Literature calls us to seek neither poverty nor riches (Prov. 30:8–9). As followers of Jesus, we are to ask God for our daily bread, and yet we are not to be enslaved by over-consumption of that bread (Matt. 6:11; Prov. 23:21). Christians are encouraged to work with all their might, yet rest is included in the Ten Commandments (Eccles. 9:10; Ex. 20:8–11). The call of our faith is one of both extreme devotion and moderated living.

The path of total commitment and balanced living is narrow and difficult. But this is exactly how noted evangelical theologian Dr. Donald Bloesch describes the Christian journey: "The Christian way is not the middle way between extremes, but the narrow way between precipices."[12] The remainder of this chapter will consider biblical ways of understanding our bodies as sacred gifts and then surrendering them to the service of God. We will focus on walking the ground between the precipices—the narrow way.

SACRED

"You are not special. You are not a beautiful or unique snowflake. You are the same decaying matter as everyone else, and we are all part of the same compost pile."[13] The attitude embodied in this quotation, from the book *Fight Club*, by Chuck Palahniuk, may seem extreme, but the general tone of current cultural conversations regarding the uniqueness and sacredness of human life confirms its accurate summation of how our society has come to view humanity.

The description of mankind in the biblical narrative offers a stark contrast to this worldview. God created an earth 24,860 miles in circumference, an ocean filled with 366 trillion gallons of water, and a sun 1.3 million times larger than earth, and called it "good." Only after God had created man do we read that everything God had made was "very good" (Gen. 2:31). Mankind alone enjoyed direct communication with God. Mankind alone was given dominion over all created things. Mankind alone was given a choice to obey or disobey God. James summarizes God's view of mankind: "We, out of all creation, became his prized possession" (James 1:18 NLT). From these Scriptures, it appears that mankind holds a special place in God's creation; but are humans sacred? This question is answered at the beginning of the Bible, when the Scripture says, "So God created human beings in his own image. In the image of God he created them; male and female he created them" (Gen. 1:27 NLT).

John of Kronstadt, a nineteenth-century Russian Orthodox priest who spent much of his life caring for homeless alcoholics, used to say, "This is beneath your dignity. You were meant to house the fullness of God."[14] Though fallen from our original design, we were created to "house the fullness of God." The scriptural narrative is primarily about

---

[12]Donald Bloesch, "Theological Notebook I," *Christianity Today*, April 24, 1995.
[13]Chuck Palahniuk, *Fight Club* (New York: Norton, 1996), 208.
[14]James Bryan Smith, *The Good and Beautiful God: Falling in Love with the God Jesus Knows* (Downers Grove, IL: InterVarsity, 2009).

the redemptive story of God bringing men and women back to their sacred calling.

At least part of God's "prized possession" includes our bodies, since that is an inseparable part of who we are. Some Christians believe that only the soul is sacred. When God created Adam, he formed him from "dust from the ground and breathed into his nostrils the breath of life, and the man became a living creature" (Gen. 2:7). But Stan Jones helps us interpret this passage with a proper awareness of God's purpose toward wholeness:

> Living creature literally means "soul," so this verse means that when God breathed life into the early body of Adam, the whole person of Adam, including his body, became a soul. Adam's body was an indispensably good part of who he was. God did not just intend for us to have bodies—we are bodies.[15]

For reasons only God knows, humans were not designed to be invisible ethereal spirits. Rather, an indispensable part of what it means to be human is to have a body. God created us as embodied souls, and, according to Scripture, we will still enjoy embodied existence in the resurrection (1 Cor. 15:35–53). So, whether on earth or in heaven, God has chosen to clothe mankind with a body.

So, what does it look like to embrace the sacredness of our bodies? Here are some possibilities: be filled with awe at the beauty of human form; wonder at the complexity of your physiology; give thanks for the breath of life; celebrate your anatomical parts; practice disciplines of fasting, healthy eating, physical activity, leisure, and rest; consider your body as a living sacrifice, consecrated to the Giver of life.

SURRENDERED

Arguably, few things are more our own than our bodies. The border of one's body is often referred to as "personal space." In the United States, personal turf is sensitively guarded. Medical patients have the right to keep their records private and to choose the method and limits of their treatment. Recently, there was an uproar among air travelers over the

---

[15]Stan Jones and Brenna Jones, *How and When to Tell Your Kids about Sex: A Lifelong Approach to Shaping Your Child's Sexual Character* (Colorado Springs, CO: NavPress, 2007).

use of enhanced body scanners for security purposes. We live in a society that voraciously guards infringement on personal rights—especially when our bodies are involved. Anyone who carelessly trespasses someone else's space without full consent most likely will soon be in need of legal counsel.

Given our cultural context, it is little wonder that Paul's words to the Corinthians strike a sensitive nerve: "You are not your own. . . . For you were bought at a price; therefore glorify God in your body and in your spirit, which are God's" (1 Cor. 6:19–20 NKJV). The complete surrender of mind, body, and soul to the rule of God is a theme that begins in Genesis and runs through Revelation. Generally speaking, most Americans do not mind if someone has a "little religion" as long as it does not interfere with their political, vocational, or social life. Religious faith is tolerable as long as it is personal and private. Yet the call of Christian discipleship is total, including the physical and social aspects of who we are.

Often, Christians relegate discipleship to the realms of the mind and the heart; however, the body also must be submitted to Christ, since it is with our bodies that we live out God's call on our lives. The body is a gift that is "very good," and our bodies belong to God as a result of being purchased by Christ. Our response to this generous gift should be loving surrender.

In a culture that selfishly defends personal turf, men and women of Christian faith are called to surrender not only their bodies but also their minds and hearts to God. This is not a call for the fainthearted, nor is it a broad road that many choose to follow. So what does physical surrender look like? View human beauty beyond hips, lips, waist, and chest to include the totality of human form. Deny the lips all forms of pretense, lies, gossip, and criticism so that the mouth can instead speak truth, justice, and love. Refuse visual space for media that deforms the image of Christ so that our eyes are free to embrace the majesty of God displayed in art, music, and on the movie screen.

This is only the beginning. We may also surrender the vain hope of unblemished skin, an abdominal six-pack, and bulging biceps to embrace such functional wonders as how the skin protects and cools the body, how the gastrointestinal tract digests and absorbs more than forty essential nutrients from a host of food varieties, and how the 614 muscles of our bodies work in concert to create movement.

SERVICE

Carnival goers take delight in placing their faces above the headless figure of a famous person, a clown, a muscle man, or a bathing beauty. They get their picture taken and laugh. What makes the scene so humorous is that the body does not fit the head. Our connection to Christ as the head of the body may also appear absurd at times, but loving service to others is perhaps the best way our bodies can "fit" with our divine head. Another way to look at this is to ask, "If the mind of Christ were my head, what would my body look like and what would it be doing?" While we do not have any description of what Jesus's body looked like, we have a great deal of information about what he did with his body: he welcomed children onto his lap; he walked toward people in pain; he sat with tax collectors and sinners; he touched blind eyes and made them see; he washed his disciples' feet; and he allowed others to beat his back, crush his head with thorns, and nail his hands and feet to a cross.

One of the most beautiful elements of the life of Jesus is that his words and actions were in perfect symmetry. In other words, his head matched his body. He said he had come to seek and to save the lost and then traveled from town to town searching for lost sheep. He preached, "Blessed are you who are poor, for yours is the kingdom of God"; then he lived with material scarcity (Luke 6:20). He taught his disciples to seek and pray for forgiveness, then he forgave those who crucified him. His life was a perfect mixture of "show and tell."

Service is largely about using our bodies to express love toward God and others. It is an outward manifestation of an inward reality. The hard truth is that what we do (typically, with our bodies) reflects what we really believe, regardless of what we tell others. With the possible exception of John, the Gospel authors wrote more about what Jesus did than what he said. Nor did any of the Gospel writers ever describe Jesus directly telling others that he loved them. But did he ever demonstrate his love by what he did!

Many students feel frustrated by their inability to serve the needs of others. They see pain and suffering in the world and want to do something about it. Earl Palmer, in his book *The Enormous Exception*, tells how one student chose to serve his pre-med classmate at the University of California, Berkeley. The pre-med student was a non-Christian with lots of questions and doubts about spiritual faith. Much to his dismay, he was hit with a severe case of the flu that kept him from attending ten days of an extremely challenging organic chemistry course. During his absence, a Christian classmate took copious notes and collected all of his sick friend's missed assignments. He then took time from his own studies to help his classmate catch up. Years later, the non-Christian pre-med student, who had eventually become a believer, told Palmer about what his compassionate classmate did for him: "You know that this just isn't done, but he gave that help to me without any fanfare or complaints. I wanted to know what made this friend of mine act the way he did."[16]

It was Dietrich Bonhoeffer, the theologian who actively participated in the German resistance against Adolf Hitler, who wrote, "One act of obedience is better than one hundred sermons."[17] We have all heard it before, but it remains true that our actions speak so loudly, it hardly matters what we say. Service, typically insignificant in terms of personal notoriety, powerfully portrays the goodness and glory of God to those inside and outside the family of faith. It is the physical expression of a body surrendered to the lordship of Jesus Christ.

So how do we use our bodies to serve those inside and outside the community of faith? Here are some possibilities. Touch others in an affirming and loving manner. Extend a helping hand to lighten the load of others. Sit, walk, and stand with others in pain. Bow before God in worship. And be willing to have your body bruised for the sake of others.

Christian college students are no less subject to the distorted views of the body that are common in today's culture. It is human nature to place the body on a level of value that significantly strays from the path of wisdom. A liberal arts education can help students understand the deficiencies of dualistic extremism.

Viewing our bodies within a biblical framework sets us free from

---

[16]Earl Palmer, *The Enormous Exception: Meeting Christ in the Sermon on the Mount* (Virginia Beach, VA: Regent College Press, 2001), n.p.
[17]"Dietrich Bonhoeffer Quotes," accessed April 11, 2011 (http://thinkexist.com/quotation/one_act_of_obedience_is_better_than_one_hundred/170306.html).

this discontent. By fully embracing our physical sacredness, we are filled with wonder and thanksgiving. By surrendering our bodies to the purposes of God, our gaze is drawn away from cultural norms of beauty and humanity to life-giving service: service that expresses our connection with the divine. The call to embrace our sacredness, to surrender to the rule of God, and to live a life of service helps to define the narrow path that Christ followers are called to travel, body and soul.

CHAPTER TWENTY-TWO

PERSONAL FORMATION AND THE UNDERSTANDING HEART

James Wilhoit

Many of you have done well in College. You have demonstrated
academic skills . . . [but] you may have not accepted the Word of God as
normative for your life. In the quiet dimensions of your soul, you are saying,
"I can make it on my own." . . . May God grant you an understanding heart.
—HUDSON ARMERDING, *THE UNDERSTANDING HEART*

Therefore I urge you, brethren, by the mercies of God, to present your bodies
a living and holy sacrifice, acceptable to God, which is your spiritual service
of worship. And do not be conformed to this world, but be transformed by
the renewing of your mind, so that you may prove what the will of God is,
that which is good and acceptable and perfect.
—ROMANS 12:1–2 (NASB)

Spiritual formation describes a slow but sure process of change.
Similarly, at a Christian liberal arts college you have the opportunity to
adopt a way of life that will make your experience more formative, that
will maximize the richness of liberal arts learning for your growth in
Christ. The work of spiritual formation comes through an indirect process. Instead of seeking to change yourself through willpower, spiritual
formation involves choosing a life path, and by following that path you
open yourself to the way of indirect change through the Holy Spirit.

WHAT IS SPIRITUAL FORMATION?

What does following this path look like? Imagine that you have a literature assignment on the short story "The Death of Ivan Ilyich," by
Tolstoy, and it invites you to look at how, as a judge and a lawyer, the
main character constructed a false public persona. After you have done
your reading, the formational response is to pray over the assignment
and ask yourself, "What am I to learn from this picture of a failed life?"

One of the principles of spiritual formation is appraisal. Everything has potential for formation. Even the most ordinary and boring moments in our lives are charged with God's formative potential. It is easy in college to be so future-oriented that you miss the importance of the present moment, which looks so ordinary. To help step back from this obsession with the future, take time to reflect. This is not a call for introspection on the big events of your life. Look at ordinary events, such as an ongoing conflict, and ask, "How can I steward this conflict with my roommate for my growth?" Living with the desire to develop an understanding heart means that we realize formation comes through our response to thousands of ordinary events. As Dallas Willard reminds us, "We must accept the circumstances we constantly find ourselves in as the place of God's kingdom and blessing. God has yet to bless anyone except where they actually are."[1] If we faithlessly overlook the significance of the ordinary situations we find ourselves in—such as the tough biology course or the demanding writing course or the irritating person on our ministry team—we will not be open to developing an understanding heart, for these are the circumstances of formation.

Our hearts are shaped to guide us toward particular ends. In the imagery of Scripture, the outcomes are either a heart that is softened and open to God or one that is hardened and closed to its Creator. The term *heart* is used to describe our interior state. For the biblical writers and ancient Christians, it is the seat of the mind, the will, and the emotions—the control center of our lives. Perhaps the closest equivalent to capturing this directional sense is to say that the heart contains our motives; in other words, the heart moves us toward what we love. It may relate to character, to core personality, and to motivational structures.[2] So when we speak of heart formation, we describe a spiritual shaping that affects our minds, our wills, and our emotions, making a lasting effect on our very being. Formation results not through direct

---

[1]Dallas Willard, *The Divine Conspiracy: Rediscovering Our Hidden Life in God* (San Francisco: HarperOne, 1998), 348–49.
[2]Tremper Longman, *Proverbs* (Grand Rapids, MI: Baker Academic, 2006), 153–54; Bruce Waltke, *The Book of Proverbs: Chapters 1–15* (Grand Rapids, MI: Eerdmans, 2004), 91–92; Timothy Keller, "Preaching to the Heart," address, Gordon-Conwell Theological Seminary, South Hamilton, MA, Ockenga Lectures on Preaching, April 5, 2006.

effort alone but through grace. None of us has the power to reach inside and mold our own heart—that is the formative work of grace, through the Holy Spirit.

The philosopher Dallas Willard reminds us that heart formation occurs to all sorts of people—whether intentionally or unintentionally: "Terrorists as well as saints are the outcome of spiritual formation. Their spirits or hearts have been formed."[3] Willard asserts that all people experience some sort of spiritual formation. Here I intend to focus on intentional spiritual formation, the kind we plan and carefully implement. We understand spiritual formation in Christ as an intentional communal process, one that involves growing in our relationship with God and becoming conformed to Christ through the power of the Holy Spirit, ultimately for the sake of serving others. In the words of Eugene Peterson, spiritual formation is "a long obedience in the same direction."[4] This process—which is advanced through Christian liberal arts education—aims at our becoming like Jesus, in the inner person, resulting in a deeper obedience to him.

HUMILITY AND THE FORMING OF AN UNDERSTANDING HEART

Saint Benedict was a sixth-century monastic reformer whose wise rule for monastic life continues to be followed fifteen hundred years after his death. He conceived of his monasteries as "schools of conversion" and placed the nurture of humility at the center of his formation plan.

With Benedict in mind, you might consider making humility part of your calling as a college student. Unfortunately, humility does not get a lot of good press these days. Consider how the respected *Oxford English Dictionary* virtually equates humility with low self-esteem: "The quality of being humble or having a lowly opinion of oneself; meekness, lowliness, humbleness: the opposite of pride or haughtiness."[5] June Price Tangney, a psychologist who writes on the virtue of humility, observes that "the 'low self-esteem' conception of humility is very prevalent not only in dictionaries, but also among many psychologists and the 'aver-

---

[3]Dallas Willard, *Renovation of the Heart: Putting on the Character of Christ* (Colorado Springs, CO: NavPress, 2002), 19.
[4]Eugene Peterson, *A Long Obedience in the Same Direction: Discipleship in an Instant Society* (Downers Grove, IL: InterVarsity, 2000).
[5]*The Oxford English Dictionary*, 2nd ed., s.v. "humility."

age person on the streets.'"[6] Humility is portrayed as an overdeveloped niceness and an inability to advocate for oneself, but humility is actually a character strength for the thinking Christian.

The historical Christian understanding is that humility involves seeing reality: we see our dependence on God for what it is, we assess our gifts correctly, and we acknowledge the contributions of others. So the humble person would not understate her gifts but would give as accurate an assessment of them as would her supervisor. A humble student would willingly volunteer for a coveted position because he believes he has the abilities the job requires. One fruit of higher education should be a deep humility, which comes from seeing the complexity of the world and the limitations of our knowledge. We become committed lifelong learners, who want to see reality clearer, and thereby grow in humility. We can say, with C. S. Lewis, that "perfect humility dispenses with modesty. If God is satisfied with the work, the work may be satisfied with itself."[7]

Humility carries with it many traits that are honored in colleges and universities, such as open-mindedness, a willingness to admit mistakes and seek advice, and a desire to learn. In seeking to live humbly, the following characteristics are essential: an accurate assessment of one's abilities and achievements; a willingness to acknowledge one's mistakes, imperfections, gaps in knowledge, and limitations (for Christians this would include confession of sins before God); an openness to new ideas, contradictory information, and advice; an abiding effort to keep one's abilities and accomplishments in perspective, "forgetting one's self" by developing a relatively low self-focus; and an attitude of gratitude for what one has received, with an appreciation of the many different ways that people can contribute to our world.[8] In the apt phrase of William Temple, "Humility does not mean thinking less of yourself than of other people, nor does it mean having a low opinion of your own gifts. It means freedom from thinking about yourself one way or the other at all."[9]

---

[6]June Price Tangney, "Humility: Theoretical Perspectives, Empirical Findings and Directions for Future Research," *Journal of Social and Clinical Psychology* 19 (March 2000): 71.
[7]C. S. Lewis, *The Weight of Glory: And Other Addresses* (Grand Rapids, MI: Eerdmans, 1949), 9.
[8]Tangney, "Humility," 73–74.
[9]William Temple, *Christ in His Church: A Charge Delivered by the Rt. Rev. William, Lord Bishop of Manchester, at His Primary Visitation*, 1924 (London: MacMillan, 1925), 145.

There are many opportunities to grow in humility, but two practices are particularly relevant in a college liberal arts setting. The first is to step back from justifying and excusing your actions. Allow God to be your vindicator. What does this mean? Try an experiment for a week: do not volunteer excuses for your actions. You arrive late for a meal, apologize and leave it at that. Constantly giving excuses can indicate an unhealthy focus on how you are being perceived by others, whereas humility requires no need of self-justification, even a measure of self-forgetfulness. The second step is to seek to learn from those with whom you disagree. This is not a call to surrender your convictions but to honor the personhood of those who hold opposing views to your own. In your next dorm discussion, when you see yourself getting a bit upset, try restating your opponent's argument as clearly and objectively as you can. Ask if you got it right. By seeking to clearly understand his perspective, you honor him and have the opportunity to learn, especially as you strive to see the texture and perspective of his argument. As you read, make it a practice to understand and to describe another person's perspective before you make an evaluation of it.

Relationships represent an essential part of college life, and the Bible places a great emphasis on our living well in relationships. In fact, the Old Testament understands justice primarily in terms of carrying out our relational responsibilities. As we Christians study Scripture, we will find multiple instructions to practice truth with one another in relationships. We learn humility as we seek to follow the guidance of Scripture concerning relationships rather than our own agendas and strategies. Scripture requires that we do the following: "Submit to one another" (Eph. 5:21 NIV); "Be kind to one another, tenderhearted, forgiving one another" (Eph. 4:32); "Bear with each other and forgive one another if any of you has a grievance against someone" (Col. 3:13 NIV); "Be devoted to one another in brotherly love. Honor one another above yourselves" (Rom. 12:10 NIV); "Be completely humble and gentle; be patient, bearing with one another in love" (Eph. 4:2 NIV); "Love one another" (John 13:34); "Welcome one another" (Rom. 15:7); "Agree with one another" (1 Cor. 1:10 NIV); "Teach and admonish one another with all wisdom" (Col. 3:16 NIV); and "Encourage one another and build each other up" (1 Thess. 5:11 NIV). The pervasive New Testament teaching on "one anothering" in the body of Christ calls every believer to a life of humble service to others.

ORDERING OUR LOVES, STANDING AGAINST THE WORLD

Our formation experience involves what Augustine called our *ordo amoris* (order of love): "It is a brief, but true definition of virtue to say, it is the order of love."[10] According to Augustine, the things we love make us into the people we become. He uses an analogy, drawn from ancient physics, in which objects were thought to contain weights that drew them back to their sources. So rocks fall because their weight draws them to the earth, and sparks rise because their weight wants to return them to the stars. Augustine explains, "My love is my weight." Our loves carry us along as surely as the wind drives a sloop. In this light, Steven Garber rightly states that the important questions to ask about your ongoing spiritual formation are the following: "What do you love?" and "What are you learning to love?"[11] The liberal arts have long been understood as an education that is liberating, and part of that liberation is coming to love the ideas, people, art, virtues, and intellectual skills that will help us reshape our loves.

In the Bible, the social forces that affect spirituality and provide its context are viewed as either supportive or negative. The general label applied to forces that stand against God's reign is "the world." In the Synoptic Gospels, "the world" can be understood as a temporary reality, in contrast to the enduring reality of God's kingdom. According to Paul's writings, the present age is evil (Gal. 1:4), also described as "enslaved to the elemental principles of the world" (Gal. 4:3; Col. 2:8, 20), "the rulers of this age" (1 Cor. 2:6), and "the god of this age" (2 Cor. 4:4 NIV). This age consists of those demonic forces, social practices, and governmental structures that oppose God's righteous rule. Paul admonished Christians, "Don't let the world around you squeeze you into its own mould" (Rom. 12:2 PHILLIPS). Worldly influences must be resisted, but this cannot be done by merely human effort, for, as Paul reminds us, we must "put on the full armor of God. . . . For our struggle is not against

---

[10]Augustine, *The City of God*, trans. Marcus Dods (New York: Modern Library, 1950), 15.22.
[11]Steven Garber, "Learning to Love What God Loves," Leadership University, July 13, 2002, (http://www.leaderu.com/common/garber-learning.html), accessed November 1, 2010.

flesh and blood, but against the rulers, against the powers, against the world forces of this darkness, against the spiritual forces of wickedness in the heavenly places" (Eph. 6:11–12 NASB).

When considering the evil forces of the world, we can learn an important lesson from the horrors of the twentieth century—the bloodiest of all centuries of recorded history—namely, that much of the societal evil came as a result of complacency—people conforming to ungodly standards. The courage to go against the grain, to be a dissenter, is part of what it means to have an understanding heart.

CHOICES SHAPED BY OUR COMMUNITY

In Christian spirituality there should be a dynamic between the believer's personal relationship with Christ and participation in the body of Christ. For example, Paul can affirm the reality of the personal relationship with Christ when he writes, "I have been crucified with Christ; and it is no longer I who live, but Christ lives in me" (Gal. 2:20 NASB). Still, later in this book he places an emphasis on the collective when he states, "My children, with whom I am again in labor until Christ is formed in you [plural]" (Gal. 4:19 NASB). Not respecting both commitments often leads to an individualistic piety that depreciates the value of community and tends to ignore the wisdom available from Christians in other traditions; either that, or it leads to a cultural Christianity or civil religion, where personal responsibility and the relational dimension of spirituality become diminished.

When considering the imitation of Christ relative to the formation of the heart, we must affirm that Jesus developed as a human being (Luke 2:52) through means that are accessible to all of us. He has modeled for us the best way of growing up into the fullness of the Father's love and grace. In stating this, we do not denigrate Christ's unique divine nature, nor do we presume that we can literally live with the same power and love as Christ; however, we can truly become "imitators of God" (Eph. 5:1), "partakers of the divine nature" (2 Pet. 1:4). The actions Jesus did, which are appropriate for imitation, were both corporate and individual.

Suffice it to say that some Christian traditions have privileged individual acts—such as solitude, personal prayer, and meditation—over corporate disciplines. Yet a first-century observer of Jesus would have seen him as a pious member of the Jewish community. His observed spirituality was deeply rooted in his community, and he was well studied in its practices and beliefs. He actively participated in corporate worship at the synagogues of Galilee. The synagogue was a place where he regularly taught and preached as a welcome guest. Both his birth and the beginning of his public ministry are tied to corporate religious events. The Gospel of Luke places great importance on the temple. Its birth narratives record that his parents brought him there to present him before God, at which time his role as Messiah was acknowledged by Simeon (Luke 2:21–35). He was baptized by John in the Jordan, and in this public event of baptism and the anointing by the Holy Spirit came the clear declaration of Jesus's sonship.

Jesus lived and traveled with his disciples. Together Jesus's followers shared meals, walked dusty roads, traveled by boat, observed his miracles, listened to his teaching, witnessed conflicts with his opponents, tried to involve him in rivalries with one another, and pondered the events surrounding his death and resurrection. In his ministry, Jesus and his disciples were also accompanied by supporters, both men and women, and had frequent contact with the crowds. Jesus readily took part in friendship, spent time with sinners, and attended various celebrations. In the feeding of the five thousand (Matt. 14:13–21) and the four thousand (Matt. 15:32–39), he hosted the common people of Galilee and provided a living picture of the kingdom's divine offer of forgiveness, welcoming sinners excluded from the religion of his day. Jesus was known as "a friend of tax collectors and sinners" (Matt. 11:19), which was a reputation that earned him the scorn of those who maintained rigid standards of religious purity. At the tomb of a dear friend, he was filled with grief and wept (John 11:35). To summarize, in his life and ministry Jesus modeled active community involvement and full participation in collective spiritual practices, including pilgrimage, celebration, simplicity, submission, service, guidance, and worship. He robustly participated in these practices in order to be a part of community life, not simply because they benefited his individual spiritual life.

Christ did have a life ordered by solitude: "Jesus Himself would often slip away to the wilderness and pray" (Luke 5:16 NASB). However, he also had a spirituality that was rooted in community: "As was His custom, He entered the synagogue on the Sabbath" (Luke 4:16 NASB). There has been a tendency in some recent writings on spiritual formation to privilege the personal devotional acts of Jesus when presenting him as a model to imitate. This is unfortunate, because it was the profoundly corporate practices of his religious tradition that fundamentally shaped his life before God.

So what does this consideration of Jesus's life mean for you as a student? Your college experience is going to form you. Realize that you have a role to play in your spiritual formation. Know that the kind of formation Paul wrote about—"be transformed by the renewing of your mind" (Rom. 12:1 NIV)—is not something you can bring about merely by trying to act spiritual. Adopt Paul's call to "pray continually" (1 Thess. 5:17 NIV) by reading your textbooks prayerfully and praying over your assignments. Accept that these are not ordinary days—these are the days that God is at work on your soul. Be open. There is no ordinary roommate conflict, no ordinary academic test, no ordinary temptation to cheat—these are all formational moments. Use them as a way of guarding your heart so that it grows in understanding. "Above all else, guard your heart, for it is the wellspring of life" (Prov. 4:23 NIV). We can acquire an understanding heart not by trying to look good but by the grace-filled, indirect means of imitating Jesus's life and seeking to walk in his humility.

CHAPTER TWENTY-THREE

LEARNING FOR A LIFETIME

John H. Augustine

For what you see and hear depends a good deal on where
you are standing: it also depends on what sort of person you are.
—C. S. LEWIS, *THE MAGICIAN'S NEPHEW*

Thus you will recognize them by their fruits.
—MATTHEW 7:20

The bright morning sun caught my eyes and woke me. A fresh snow from the night before enveloped Hidden House on a frigid Sunday morning in 1979. Due to record snow that winter, we had to dig a series of pathways and channels that allowed us access to the rest of the campus. We dug through eight-foot-high drifts—a group of five men in their senior year of college living together in a modest, college-owned dwelling. Our group included Kep, a spirited, purposeful, and action-oriented son of missionary parents from South America who majored in Bible; Bill, a strong yet kind, thoughtful leader from Illinois who majored in Christian education; Mark, a cerebral, intellectually curious, lover of climbing and the outdoors from Ohio who majored in biology; Paul, an outgoing and upbeat encourager and natural counselor from Kansas who majored in psychology; and me, a thoughtful, earnest, and approachable scholar from Minnesota who majored in English literature.

Our purpose for living together was to learn from each other through our different majors, our participation in sports (we competed on intramural football and basketball teams), and our diverse interests. As a group, we had to bid against other students in a lottery for the lease to our house, and eventually we got it: a slightly quixotic faux chalet with a two-story front—the most delightful feature was a large fireplace—linked to a converted garage in the back with two more bedrooms. We felt quite fortunate to obtain our lodgings, which somehow added to our sense of destiny at the time. The commitment that we made to each other was to spend time together and to be involved in each other's lives, and the discussions that followed were further stimulated by others who entered our circle. I can see now that our senior year was the beginning phase of preparation for our initiation into social and spiritual adulthood. I realize that, for each of us, our liberal arts education prepared and instructed us for challenges we could not have foreseen—and it equipped us for a lifetime of learning.

In the spring preceding our senior year, Paul wrote all of us a letter, audaciously requesting that we make our relationships within the house our top priority during the next year. He went on to say: "We see the opportunity to live together as preparation to develop our lifestyles with reference to family life, that the people we live with now are priority so our families will be later. So, we'd like to work on sharing, ministering, worshiping, working together, etc. I'm *really* excited about it."[1] We bought into his challenge and began our association of that year with a self-conscious goal. Seizing our chance to learn from each other about emotional and spiritual growth, we proposed to form a dialectical relationship utilizing the intellectual stimulation we were receiving from college.

What occurred then shaped all of us profoundly. In the context of our studies and spurred on by our college's ideal of excellence, we spoke often and earnestly about ideas. But what developed from it later—especially in the ten years of group correspondence that we maintained after graduation—was remarkable, because our individual paths reflected a fundamental viewpoint that we gained not only from each other but also from our liberal arts education. This essay offers one example of the outworking of life development among a group of friends in college. Of course, the college experience would be different for every class, every group, every year—but the fundamentals remain for anyone who pursues the life of the mind in the context of a Christian community. We left college well prepared, drawing on a rich curriculum in art, music, mathematics, history, drama, literature, chemistry, physics, and the life sciences, as well as on the conversations and debates during our life together at the Hidden House.

---

[1]Paul White, letter to author, May 1, 1979.

ENGAGING IN MEANINGFUL EXPERIENCES

A core activity for our house was to invite faculty or staff members on Sunday evening for casual seminars or conversations about their research interests and current events. Each house member invited a classmate or two to join us for these evenings of dinner and dialogue. I vividly recall one snowy Sunday night in January when our guest was Professor Clyde Kilby, the renowned J. R. R. Tolkien and C. S. Lewis scholar, who was, moreover, our good friend and neighbor. He merely had to cross the snow-encrusted street and make his way along our pathway to the front door. Our seminar that evening touched upon one of his favorite themes: passion for reading. In reading literature, as Lewis states, we "seek an enlargement of our being. We want to be more than ourselves. . . . We want to see with other eyes, to imagine with other imaginations, to feel with other hearts, as well as with our own."[2] Like Lewis, Kilby's neighborly advice that evening, and throughout our senior year, was to read deeply with our imaginations in order to shape our own capacities to live more fully.

Our goal as college students was to create a crucible for learning or, as was expressed so cogently by Leland Ryken, our job was "to prepare."[3] Harvard's Drew Gilpin Faust has said that an education is "designed to prepare us for life without a script—for a life with any script. Since you cannot know what you need to be ready for, we have tried to get you ready for anything."[4] We sensed we were doing just that—embracing our goal not only with genuine fervor, but also with passionate curiosity about a multiplicity of ideas and approaches. Our collaboration produced, in effect, an ideal synthesis for a liberal arts education. Many extraordinary scholars across the curriculum generously gave us their time and attention, particularly on those Sunday nights.

In addition to developing an intentional community and to cultivating our evening seminars, three of us had participated in a profound learning program, an intensive wilderness stress experience called Vanguards. The Vanguards program offered a strenuously physical version of the

---

[2]C. S. Lewis, *An Experiment in Criticism* (Cambridge UK: Cambridge University Press, 1961), 140–41.
[3]Leland Ryken, "The Student's Calling," chapel address, Wheaton College, 1984, and pp. 15–22 of this volume.
[4]Drew Gilpin Faust, "Commencement 2010: What Makes Learning Possible," *Harvard Magazine*, July/August 2010, 52.

concept of a liberal education as broadening and exploratory. For three weeks we took in as much character building as we could manage while navigating the forests of northern Wisconsin with a compass, climbing and rappelling rock faces, making group decisions under pressure, and spending three days solo (without food) in the wilderness. We were required to swim one mile, run 17.4 miles in 2.5 hours, and hike with a backpack for over 130 miles.

The principles of this kind of encounter are the same as those developed by Kurt Hahn for Outward Bound: to create a "process involving the acceptance of responsibility, of facing formidable challenges, of spending time in contemplation and reflection, of experiencing deprivation, of examining values, of developing compassion for others, of testing one's faith and character. In essence it is a process which enhances the maturation of an individual."[5] The motto of the Vanguards program was "To prepare by instruction, to know by experience." This is as good a definition of education as any I know. What we learned through instruction became known through experience. All three of us recognized Vanguards as a benchmark, referring to it with pride for years to come as something that instilled genuine leadership skills.

OBSTACLES ALONG THE JOURNEY

After graduation the five of us went forward into life equipped with everything that our education, our friendships, and our personal faith could offer. I will not say that we were naïve or overly idealistic, but it is true that not one of us had anticipated just how challenging the journey after college would be—a journey that can only be described as a quest. Our responses to the initiation experiences that awaited us after college bear witness to the education that we received. As Arthur Holmes had told us one Sunday night in Hidden House, a liberal arts education provides "an open invitation to join the human race and become more fully human,"[6] but nobody accepts the invitation in exactly the same way. The words of Richard Levin also proved prophetic for our quest: "The discovery of one's true calling may come early. More often it comes late,

---

[5]Bud Williams, "What Is Wilderness Learning?," unpublished paper, Wheaton College Honey Rock Camp Library, February 1975, 1.
[6]Arthur F. Holmes, *The Idea of a Christian College* (Grand Rapids, MI: Eerdmans, 1975), 43.

and it may come more than once in a lifetime."[7] But it came to each of us, and our Christian faith tradition provided us with a sense of noble, special purpose associated with our various callings. The ideals of a liberal arts education were reflected in our personal lives because we were indeed living without a script.

Our interesting moments, as with all literary quests from the *Odyssey* to *The Magician's Nephew*, were the difficult, challenging, and puzzling times. For some ten years after we parted company, we wrote group letters to each other, charting our progress, expressing our faith, defining our obstacles, and facing our frustrations. Our liberal arts education and our constant friendship shaped our responses to challenges we faced in our respective journeys after college. We all embraced aspirations that called for further education—and a fair amount of patience on the part of our families: Paul earned a PhD and became a psychologist; Mark attended Yale Medical School and became a psychiatrist; Bill became a lieutenant colonel in the US Army; Kep became a church planter in La Paz, Bolivia; and I became a teacher of English at Yale before becoming an investment banker.

One of our first responses upon entering our professional lives was feeling overwhelmed. We had prepared as well as we could, but, as in all classic initiation stories—whether the Bible's story of Joseph, *The Odyssey*'s Telemachos, or *Huckleberry Finn*'s title character, countless obstacles and trials lay in our paths. "Work continues to make large demands on my time and energy," wrote Mark, adding that he was facing "hard choices."[8] Paul reported, "I am burnt." Phrases such as "chronically exhausted" and even "killing ourselves as parents" popped up continually in our letters to each other, along with the complaint, "Work is consuming me." Even so, shirking our responsibilities or giving up was never an option. As Paul phrased it, "I'm still learning how to carry the load." These feelings exemplify what I now consider a necessary part of

---

[7]Richard Levin, "The Graduate's Role of Learning," in *The Work of the University* (New Haven, CT: Yale University Press, 2003), 120.

[8]All the quotations that follow come from the private letters that we sent to each other and are quoted with the permission of the following: Kep James, MA, missionary pastor, Bolivia; Bill Jones, MA, retired lieutenant colonel, US Army, and pastor, Colorado; Mark Servis, MD, associate dean for curriculum and competency development and professor and vice chair for education, Department of Psychiatry and Behavioral Science, UC Davis School of Medicine, California; Paul White, PhD, president, Family Business Resources, Inc., and director of family coaching and personal development, Navitas, Ltd., Kansas.

the initiation into post-college life itself—sharing your struggles. When we discussed our difficulties with each other, our perspectives changed. We knew that we were not alone—that each of us was experiencing similar shocks and realizations.

A specific turn, or change, in the middle of these busy times came when each of us began to comprehend our particular roles, vocations, and duties in life. Paul expressed this succinctly, writing that he had always been "future-oriented about life," but in relation to his sons, he realized that "it's now or never." Thus the importance of what we were involved with as spouses, parents, workers, sons, friends, coaches, volunteers, church members, leaders, and citizens in our communities, in a more or less frantic pace of life, started to dawn on us. Kep saw his role more in terms of calling (and this echoes Richard Levin's assurance that we each receive a call, as well as, of course, the weighty words of the apostle Paul). He still expressed his purpose in terms of struggle, particularly in the face of the decision to return to Bolivia at a point when a family member was critically ill. But the sense of divine call ran underneath it all as he spoke of "the tension we feel between knowing missions is what God has called us to do and the hardship of being away from a parent at a time when we frustratingly may not have time to spend with her."

Hardships came to us in unexpected versions. Even so, we held on tenaciously to the ideals of the balanced, meaningful life that we had committed ourselves to earlier, though we often wrestled to understand how to apply these ideals. In the throes of medical school, Mark saw it as a battle: "I am jealously guarding the rest of my experimental holistic lifestyle from the pincer grip of medicine." Likewise, when I found it nearly impossible, at times, to find a balance in life, particularly in my early years as a fledgling investment banker, my Hidden House friends encouraged me to hold on to my ideals, even when I could not make them my reality.

Occasionally, a flash of insight broke through, as we began to perceive a sense of purpose. Kep wrote about the stress of transitioning "from the simplicity of college life to marriage, three kids, living in Bolivia with all its interesting differences and hardships, involved in things I've always dreamed about being involved in. . . . There are many areas where I've experienced growth." Kep also confessed, "[I] never felt more fulfilled and useful in my life."

None of us felt that life after college was a steady, upward progression, by any means. At times, we felt utterly disheartened. And yet our communications with each other allowed us to work out our individual perspectives in community with our contemporaries. "I was indeed young . . . now I am old," Mark observed, contrasting college life with professional life. "I was a student—now I am a doctor. I was single—now I am married. I was isolated—now I am intimate. I was from Wheaton—now I 'went to Yale.' I was evangelical—now I am Christian. I was dogmatic—now I listen. I was nearing perfection—now I am unsalvageable. I was harsh—now I am gentle and accepting." Being of an academic bent, he qualified this with wry humor: "Of course, such dichotomies are false, in that all these adjectives simultaneously coexist within me—a kind of coinherence, strange and impossible." Yet Mark's reflections demonstrate a kind of inheritance that came from our liberal arts education: an ability to question honestly, to change authentically, and to grow purposefully.

I still find it difficult to maintain a steady balance in my life, especially with an active work schedule as an investment banker. Yet ideas continue to energize me, and I read loads of books. A passion for learning and the liberal arts shows up at home, too, particularly on weekends, in conversations with my family about this or that article in the *New York Times*, a Bible passage, or a new website.

We still stay in touch as Hidden House friends, though, ironically, our use of short e-mails has replaced sustained writings to each other. Like many college roommates, I think we will always be bonded together. And our enduring friendship continues to shape our capacities as we learn from each other.

PROGRESS ON THE JOURNEY OF INITIATION

In the midst of our post-college life experiences, we continued to learn, finding that the rewards of lifelong learning bring their own exhilaration. I wrote of my increasing "capacity for reflection" that developed during the time I studied at Merton College, Oxford. Mark's graduation from medical school stirred in him "excitement akin to the final mile of the Vanguards marathon." Bill reported that the army continued "to be a learning and maturing process for me" and that he could literally feel the "rough edges being knocked off." We wrote to each other about our continuing quest for a balanced life—one not consumed by our professional commitments. Sometimes we joked about it with bravado. "Don't let your environment control you, control your environment," enjoined Mark. And yet, through it all, we remained committed to our respective callings, as when Bill described his decision to stay in the army as being motivated by "[viewing] ourselves as Christians in a very needy place."

Nor did we forget the benefits of our liberal arts education. As Mark expressed comically during his sojourn through Yale Medical School, "What I lack in brilliance—I make up in broadness—liberal arts all the way." And another benefit that we derived from our training was the ability to question our perspectives. Again, Mark wrestled with this ongoing "quest for a dream," which resulted, instead, in a "loss of idealism and intensity in the face of academic redundancy and medical depersonalization and cynicism." Nevertheless, he acknowledged "attempts to recover or refine that state [of the ideal] through spiritual, physical, and relational health (or the 'balanced life'—yes, I think they are all connected for me)." The journey continues, however: "But perhaps I need to pioneer—or convert to—a new perspective rather than just recover the old one." Above all, we saw our lives as a quest, a "spiritual odyssey," as Mark termed it. Once he asked us, "[Has] your present spiritual status, personal relationship with Christ, changed?" This question led to a rich series of exchanges in which we reflected on our faith, though with the added benefit of adult life experience, representing our diverse paths since college. Our liberal arts framework assisted us in understanding our experiences.

THE TRUE END OF LEARNING

We continued to strive to learn and to put into practice what we discovered. Paul commented on "the relationship between knowledge and spirituality, that learning is not purely a cerebral event, but it expands who we are as persons." He was further "reminded that it was not the facts I learned but the experiences which accompanied my learning and thus changed my perceptions and world views—that is what education is all about." As Bill summed it up succinctly: "It is only through our 'deeds' that we will ever really understand the meaning of our 'words.'"

This brings me back to our commitment—shared by all of us—to experience learning by living it. My own favorite expression of this comes from Milton's *Paradise Lost*, where the angel Raphael counsels Adam and Eve:

> Deeds to thy knowledge answerable; add Faith,
> Add Virtue, Patience, Temperance; add love,
> By name to come called Charity, the soul
> Of all the rest: then wilt thou not be loath
> To leave this Paradise; but shalt possess
> A paradise within thee, happier far.[9]

We did not yet understand the full meaning of what we had learned—in an academic sense—until we lived it. If it is not too much to say, all five of us feel that we have come close to the ideal described by Paul Holmer in his definition of a true liberal arts education and its impact on students: "It surely is not that they know a great deal, though that may obtain; but it is also that they take pleasure in being alive, they stay curious and avid and perhaps evince a richer quality of responses. They may, for example, grieve more profoundly, laugh with heartiness, understand more tellingly, and manifest a wider variety of passions and interest."[10] At the least, we feel that we owe a debt of gratitude to our professors, especially those who joined us during our Sunday evening discussions at Hidden House and helped to set us on the path to learning for a lifetime.

---

[9]John Milton, *Paradise Lost,* ed. Merritt Y. Hughes (Indianapolis: Odyssey Press, 1957), 582–87.
[10]Paul Holmer, "Two Kinds of Learning," unpublished paper, Yale University Divinity School Library, New Haven, CT, 1.

CHAPTER TWENTY-FOUR

THE GOSPEL, LIBERAL ARTS, AND GLOBAL ENGAGEMENT

Tamara Townsend

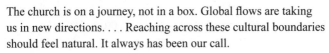

The church is on a journey, not in a box. Global flows are taking
us in new directions. . . . Reaching across these cultural boundaries
should feel natural. It always has been our call.
— MIRIAM ADENEY, *KINGDOM WITHOUT BORDERS*

After this I looked, and behold, a great multitude that no one could number,
from every nation, from all tribes and peoples and languages, standing before
the throne and before the Lamb.
—REVELATION 7:9

College students today find themselves in an increasingly interconnected world. Without leaving her dorm room, a North American student in Chicago can pull on a Real Madrid jersey, have a conversation
via Skype with a friend on a mission project in Senegal, drink Costa
Rican coffee with her Korean suitemate, and read *Le Monde* online to
prepare for a French exam. Globalization affects economics, technology, politics, culture, medicine, and just about every realm of human
activity. As Donald J. Boudreaux broadly defines it, "Globalization is
the advance of human cooperation across national boundaries."[1] A liberal arts education uniquely prepares students for life in this globalized
world, where international engagement continues to evolve. Liberal
learning that includes study of other languages and cultures challenges
students to reach beyond the borders they have previously known, both
the figurative limits of their knowledge as well as literal geographic and
cultural boundaries.

Even in this global context, some may question the need for learning
another language. Perhaps this makes sense for someone preparing to be

---

[1]Donald J. Boudreaux, *Globalization* (Westport, CT: Greenwood, 2008), 1.

a missionary, diplomat, or business executive in another country, but for everyone else, why bother? Indeed, much cross-cultural interaction in the United States, and even overseas, can be successfully achieved in English. For example, non-English-speaking immigrants to this country are generally expected to learn English to communicate with their neighbors. Many international corporations use English as a *lingua franca*. North Americans who travel abroad as tourists increasingly find that employees in the hospitality industry are well trained in English to meet their needs. Even groups traveling for the purpose of short-term missions or service find that they can meet their ministry goals with the aid of a translator. With all these opportunities and advantages accessible to English speakers, should students really expend valuable time and energy to study other languages and cultures?

Naturally, foreign language professors respond with an enthusiastic yes. In attempting to explain why, language teachers and textbook authors sometimes try to convince their students of the utility of learning another language by citing some of the things that a bilingual person can do and enjoy. A person conversant in a second language and culture can get a better job, appreciate more fully another country's beautiful historical artifacts and unique regional products, and have an influence in other cultural settings to a greater extent than a monolingual and monocultural person. However, there may be a problem with these frequently cited rationales, especially for language students who claim to follow Christ, because they mainly promise benefits for the good of the language learner alone.

Christian language professors David I. Smith and Barbara Carvill have observed that these sorts of reasons, while not without merit, prove ultimately inadequate because they derive from motives of profit, pleasure, and power.[2] Instead, an education in languages and cultures should involve learning about and from other people, as well as entering into their system of speech, action, and thought; yet ironically students sometimes can lose sight of the people, even as they study their ways. Certainly language fluency can help a student to appreciate the goods another culture has to offer or to build a stronger job résumé. However,

---

[2]David I. Smith and Barbara Carvill, *The Gift of the Stranger: Faith, Hospitality, and Foreign Language Learning* (Grand Rapids, MI: Eerdmans, 2000), 121–22.

a Christian student's calling is to look beyond these motivations and see language competency as a means to building bridges between people and cultures, an outcome that may have eternal implications.

THE IMPORTANCE OF HUMILITY IN LEARNING

The goals of liberal arts education can be instructive as we consider the question of proper cross-cultural engagement. Liberal arts does not consist of accumulating interesting experiences for their own sake, but rather its purpose is to educate the whole person, cultivating attitudes and habits that prepare a student for life and for responsible citizenship in the world. A student of the liberal arts learns to ask good questions and to listen. Furthermore, Christian liberal arts education serves to train students to become more Christlike and to recognize God's sovereignty over all of creation, including human culture, in all its diversity.

A key character trait for a Christian student to cultivate in order to achieve these goals, and in order to approach a new language and culture appropriately, is humility. Humility is actually the first step to genuine learning. In order to learn, I must recognize that I do not already have all the answers and accept that someone else has something to teach me. This is especially true in learning about other languages and cultures, because often we are unaware how dearly we cherish our own cultural values and beliefs. Before studying another language and culture, I might not even realize that other people do all sorts of ordinary things differently than I do, and I might not be aware of the extent to which my cultural background shapes the way I think about the world. For example, as a North American, I value punctuality. I like to show up on time, and I believe that other people should do the same. If someone arrives late without a legitimate excuse, I usually interpret this tardiness as a lack of respect. However, other cultures, such as many Hispanic cultures, take a different attitude toward time. For people in such cultures, forcing events to begin and end on schedule strongly suggests being in a hurry, with an unwillingness to let conversations and relationships develop at their own speed.

If I remain safely insulated in my own culture group, it is easy to feel that I am normal, that my habits, customs, beliefs, and ways of doing things are the right way. However, if I engage in a relationship with people from another cultural framework, this engagement forces me to confront our cultural differences, and my eyes may be opened to my tendency to prioritize work efficiency over interpersonal connections. A humble attitude allows me to recognize my own culture's shortcomings, that my beliefs and practices may need correcting, and that I may find value in the culture of the other.

When we think of the study of language and culture in the Christian context, we may conclude that its main value is to enable Christians to preach the gospel to other people. Clearly Christians should share the message of Christ's love with everyone, but communication (in any language) is a two-way street. Liberal arts education is about learning to ask good questions, not necessarily having all the answers. The humble attitude promoted by liberal arts learning should first and foremost enable learners of other cultures and languages to become good listeners, to seek to understand the experience of others before offering solutions.

Sometimes we struggle to really listen and feel frustrated by not having all the answers. For example, I once showed a movie in Spanish class about two Latin American refugees who migrated to California. The story depicted the struggles of their journey and their hardships in the United States. After we watched the tragic ending, a puzzled student asked me, "What message is this movie trying to convey? Is it pro- or anti-immigration? And what response does the movie propose?" These were good questions. I could understand the student's desire for some definite answers in response, but I could only conclude that the film raised more questions than it answered by portraying the complexities of the struggling immigrants' experiences. The film's ending may have seemed more satisfying if it had proposed a solution to the problems. Yet, it left students with a heightened awareness—a necessary starting point for those who are preparing to be responsible citizens of the world.

When we are not in the habit of listening to people who are different from us, we naturally think of ourselves and the people who share our culture as "insiders" and everyone else as "outsiders." This is especially true when we come from a dominant culture like the United States, which has a history of influencing other cultures, sometimes with adverse effects. However, a look into Scripture provides a corrective to the tendency of cultural superiority. If Christ is to be our example, we should take special note of his humility: our leader boldly approached the outsiders, drawing criticism for associating and eating with sinners. We could consider Jesus as the ultimate insider, being one with God the Father, yet he was willing to descend and enter into our humanity and to serve. In Philippians 2, Paul urges believers to imitate Jesus,

> who, though he was in the form of God, did not count equality with God a thing to be grasped, but emptied himself, by taking the form of a servant, being born in the likeness of men. And being found in human form, he humbled himself by becoming obedient to the point of death, even death on a cross. (Phil. 2:6–8)

All people stand outside of Christ's glory, not just the socially marginalized, yet Jesus reached out to us in humility in order to serve us and save us in obedience to the Father. As Christians who imitate Christ, we must also humbly serve and love others.

CROSSING CULTURAL BORDERS

The good news of the gospel tells us that God's love breaks down barriers. As Philippians 3 indicates, the greatest barrier that Jesus crossed was the one separating God from humanity. Jesus reaches across the divide, and this sets the example for us: no geographical, linguistic, or cultural barrier is insurmountable. Theologian Daniel Groody writes, "In migrating to the human race God enters into a place of 'otherness,' the very migration that human beings fear and find so difficult to make. . . . For God there are no borders that cannot be crossed, neither within himself nor in the created world."[3]

During his life and ministry, Jesus constantly challenged his followers' notions of who was "in" and who was "out" of the kingdom of God. Contrary to common belief, the religious leaders were much further from the kingdom than the tax collectors and sinners. Equally surprisingly, citizenship in God's kingdom no longer depended on Jewish ancestry. Paul reminded the Ephesians that Jesus "preached peace to you who were far off and peace to those who were near. For through him we both have access in one Spirit to the Father. So then you are no

---

[3]Daniel G. Groody, "Crossing the Divide: Foundations of a Theology of Migration and Refugees," *Theological Studies* 70 (2009): 650.

longer strangers and aliens, but you are fellow citizens with the saints and members of the household of God" (Eph. 2:17–19). Within God's family there are no borders; in Christ we are all members of one body. This means that cross-cultural engagement is especially important with our Christian brothers and sisters of other backgrounds.

Similarly, believers should reach out across borders and model Christ's love to those who do not profess Christian faith. Throughout Scripture, God directs promises toward all people, regardless of their cultural origin. Genesis 1:27 declares that humans were made in the image of God, and this creates a framework for seeing equal value in all people from all cultures. In Genesis 12, God's first call to Abraham includes the promise that all families or all peoples on earth would be blessed through him. In the books of the law, even as God showed special favor to his chosen people, specific provisions and protections are mentioned for foreigners living among the Israelites: "When a stranger sojourns with you in your land, you shall not do him wrong. You shall treat the stranger who sojourns with you as the native among you, and you shall love him as yourself, for you were strangers in the land of Egypt: I am the LORD" (Lev. 19:33–34). Notice that the justification for the command to love the foreigner as oneself is that the Israelites "were strangers in the land of Egypt" and thus can remember what it feels like to be an outsider. In the same way, all Christians today should empathize and identify with outsiders, since without Christ we would be outsiders to God's love. Furthermore, students struggling to learn a foreign language or living abroad with a host family have unique opportunities to discover what it feels like to be an outsider as they face obstacles to communication. The humbling experience of negotiating a language or cultural barrier can remind us to show compassion toward all kinds of outsiders.

The New Testament further stresses the inclusion of foreigners and outsiders, portraying God's kingdom as a global kingdom. Jesus demonstrated love for others, regardless of their spiritual, social, or cultural category, when he reached out to sinners and tax collectors, and he crossed multiple cultural borders by reaching out to a Samaritan woman of ill repute (John 4). Christ's twofold summary of the Great Commandment includes the charge to love our neighbors as ourselves, and in response to the question "Who is my neighbor?" Jesus taught the parable of the good Samaritan (Luke 10:25–37). David I. Smith notes that the parable is told in such a way that the Samaritan is not presented as the needy neighbor to whom we must reach out and serve but, rather, provides the example of what a good neighbor looks like.[4] Outsiders, then, are not merely lost people who exhibit visible needs; sometimes they are the ones who exemplify godly compassion.

Expanding on the twofold command to love God and love our neighbor, Jesus leaves his disciples with the Great Commission, a call to share the gospel across any and all borders. It is remarkable that soon afterwards the Holy Spirit's presence at Pentecost is manifested in the ability of the believers to speak in different languages. Smith summarizes the meaning of this event: "The power that is given at Pentecost is not the power to conquer foreigners, but the power to speak to others in the way that they hear, the power to hear anew across lines of difference, the power to love one's neighbor as oneself."[5] This episode shows the importance of inclusiveness in the community of Christ's followers, so it should likewise be a priority for believers to look beyond their own small community of insiders to see where the Spirit is at work. John's vision in Revelation of the future kingdom includes a multitude of believers "from every nation, from all tribes and peoples and languages" worshiping the Lamb (Rev. 7:9). If heaven is an intercultural and multilingual community, we can and should begin to practice and celebrate this diversity now, on earth.

HEARING THE VOICE OF THE OTHER

I return to the question I posed earlier, "Why should an English-speaking student bother to learn another language?" Most of us who speak English have the luxury of not needing a foreign language to survive. However, cross-cultural interactions are all but inevitable for today's graduates, and as Smith points out, when these exchanges are limited to English, we can hear the voices of only the "cosmopolitan" and "elite" members of other cultures, the educated people with the means to study our own

---

[4]David I. Smith, *Learning from the Stranger: Christian Faith and Cultural Diversity* (Grand Rapids, MI: Eerdmans, 2009), 74.
[5]Ibid., 136.

language.[6] Instead, Smith suggests looking at the Golden Rule, Jesus's command that "whatever you wish that others would do to you, do also to them" (Matt. 7:12), as a justification for studying other languages and cultures. He summarizes, "You want others to make life easier by learning your language? *Learn theirs.* You want others to understand you? *Work to understand them.* You want others to hear what you have to say? *Be attentive to them.*"[7]

Today's Christian college graduates will engage an increasingly diverse and interconnected world. What will be their motivation for cross-cultural engagement? What will be the outcome? Christian liberal arts education uniquely positions students to challenge the accepted notions that education in other languages and cultures should primarily enrich and empower the learner. Instead, the Christian scholar is called to cultivate a Christlike humility, living out the gospel by listening well and reaching across borders in love.

---

[6]Ibid., 94–95.
[7]Ibid., 71.

CHAPTER TWENTY-FIVE

LIBERAL ARTS IN THE NEW JERUSALEM

Philip G. Ryken

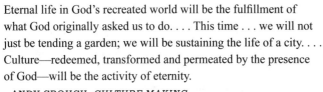

Eternal life in God's recreated world will be the fulfillment of
what God originally asked us to do. . . . This time . . . we will not
just be tending a garden; we will be sustaining the life of a city. . . .
Culture—redeemed, transformed and permeated by the presence
of God—will be the activity of eternity.
—ANDY CROUCH, *CULTURE MAKING*

And I saw the holy city, new Jerusalem, coming down out of heaven from God,
prepared as a bride adorned for her husband.
—REVELATION 21:2

The purpose of this final chapter is to consider the future of the liberal
arts by putting them into an eternal perspective. Here we make the case
for an eschatological dimension to liberal education: the liberal arts are
not for this life only but also for the life to come, when God has promised to make a new heaven and a new earth.

In her prize-winning novel *Gilead*, Marilynne Robinson draws an
analogy that offers a compelling vision of life and art in the eternal city
of God. According to Robinson's lead character, "In eternity this world
will be Troy, and all that has passed here will be the epic of the universe,
the ballad they sing in the streets."[1]

By referring to Troy, these words evoke the memory of *The Iliad* and
The Odyssey—Homer's epic poems based on the Trojan Wars. The novelist is using core texts from the liberal arts tradition to cast our daily experience as an epic struggle or adventure. She is also suggesting that, in the life
to come, the heroic deeds of this life will be remembered and celebrated.

---

[1]Marilynne Robinson, *Gilead* (New York: Farrar, Straus, Giroux, 2004), 57.

Explicit in Robinson's vision is the assumption that heaven is a place for writing and singing, where public art is a daily part of community life. What happens in this life ultimately becomes the subject of the next life's art—"the ballad they sing in the streets." In other words, the liberal arts are for eternity.

FROM HERE TO ETERNITY

From the outset we need to acknowledge that giving liberal education an eschatological orientation may be somewhat controversial. In saying that the liberal arts will flourish in the "new Jerusalem," as the Bible calls it (Rev. 21:2), we are saying that there is substantial continuity between what we think and do in this world and what we will create in the eternal kingdom of God. This may seem to stand against a long Christian tradition of distinguishing between nature and grace, between the life of the human mind and the work of the Holy Spirit.

For some philosophers and theologians—such as John Henry Newman in his seminal book *The Idea of the University*—the liberal arts belong to the earthly order of nature (where even a secular university can cultivate the intellect), not to the heavenly order of grace (which pertains to religion and the church).[2] On this interpretation, the liberal arts would seem to have value only for our earthly existence. But the argument in this chapter is that they also participate in the everlasting kingdom of God.

We need to acknowledge as well that some of our thoughts on this subject will be partly speculative and therefore provisional. We find ourselves living somewhere between the "already" of God's salvation in Jesus Christ and the "not yet" of the new Jerusalem. Although Scripture addresses some realities of the coming kingdom, there are many questions that it (wisely) leaves unanswered. Furthermore, the realities of the coming age go far beyond our present experience. If it is true that "no eye has seen, no ear has heard, no mind has conceived what God has prepared for those who love him" (1 Cor. 2:9 NIV), then until the second coming of Jesus Christ, the liberal arts of the new Jerusalem will remain among the mysteries of our faith.

---

[2]See John Henry Newman, *The Idea of a University*, ed. Martin J. Svaglic (Notre Dame, IN: University of Notre Dame Press, 1982), 91–93.

Despite these difficulties, it seems helpful and even necessary to end this book by putting forward some tentative thoughts about liberal arts and eternal life. Our subject has been liberal arts for the Christian life. But if the life that we have in Christ is everlasting, then it is appropriate to explore the implications of liberal education for eternity. In conducting this exploration we will exercise our theological imagination. But we will also make deductions that are grounded in the prophecies of Scripture, governed by the principles of sound doctrine, and guided by the wisdom of the Holy Spirit as we gather together the strands of revelation that lead toward engagement in the liberal arts as an eternal enterprise.

ART IN HEAVEN

To begin with, the biblical descriptions of heaven—especially in the book of Revelation—portray the people of God living in a dynamic atmosphere of corporate worship that is suffused with artistic beauty and truth.

The beauty of heaven includes lyric poetry that is written in the form of hymns or choruses. These famous songs (such as "Holy, holy, holy" and "Worthy is the Lamb") are chanted or set to music. Furthermore, some of them are described as "new" songs (Rev. 5:9), which presumably requires the work of a composer. There are also harps (Rev. 5:8; 15:2) and trumpets (Revelation 8, 9), proving that there will be musical instruments in heaven. Poetry, composition, instrumentation—these liberal arts are not left behind at the gates of heaven but brought in and elevated to their highest form. They are part of the good life that God has promised for his people.

In addition to lyric poetry, heaven contains other works of literature. Revelation as a whole is presented in the genre of apocalypse, and within the book there are other literary forms that unfold the purposes of God. As author, the apostle John is given scrolls to read and digest (Rev. 10:8–10). Then there is the volume known simply as "the book of life" (Rev. 3:5) or "the Lamb's book of life" (Rev. 21:27).

The presence of a wide variety of artistic forms implies that the full enjoyment of heaven requires the use of skills that are heightened by liberal education. In order to offer musical praise to God, the company of heaven must be able to write and sing and make music. To participate in the eternal dialogue of worship, in which God speaks and his people respond, we must also communicate well by first listening and then speaking. Christian education is not the only way to develop these skills, of course, but engagement with the liberal arts can help prepare us for the glorious business of heaven by growing capacities that we can use to their fullest in the eternal worship of God.

There may even be a place in heaven for the highest achievements of human culture. The gold that paves its streets is "like clear glass" (Rev. 21:18); the gemstones adorning its gates are fashioned into jewels (Rev. 21:19–21). In other words, the city's architectural details are works of art.[3] Furthermore, the Bible makes the provocative promise that the kings of the earth will bring "the glory and the honor of the nations" into the new Jerusalem (Rev. 21:26; cf. Isaiah 60). What will this glory be? Perhaps it will include the earthly works of music, art, and literature that are most in keeping with the eternal glory of Jesus Christ but sanctified in some way that makes them suitable for his glorious presence.[4]

The possibility that the best products of human culture will ascend to glory is portrayed in a dramatic mural by the Swiss artist Paul Robert:

> In the background of this mural he pictured Neuchatel, the lake on which it is situated and even the art museum which contains the mural. In the foreground near the bottom is a great dragon wounded to the death. Underneath the dragon is the vile and the ugly—the pornographic and the rebellious. Near the top Jesus is seen coming in the sky with his endless hosts. On the left side is a beautiful stairway, and on the stairway are young and beautiful men and women carrying the symbols of the various forms of art—architecture, music and so forth. And as they are carrying them up and away from the dragon to present them to Christ, Christ is coming down to accept them.[5]

What we read in Revelation strongly suggests that Robert is right: there is a place in heaven for the liberal arts.

---

[3] Andy Crouch makes this point in *Culture Making: Recovering Our Creative Calling* (Downers Grove, IL: InterVarsity, 2008), 165.

[4] See Richard Mouw, *When the Kings Come Marching In: Isaiah and the New Jerusalem* (Grand Rapids, MI: Eerdmans, 2002).

[5] Francis A. Schaeffer, *Art and the Bible* (Downers Grove, IL: InterVarsity, 1973), 30.

THE NEW CREATION

To be more precise, there is a place for the liberal arts in the new heaven *and the new earth*. The promise of God is not that he will take us away to heaven, but that he will create for us "new heavens and a new earth" (Isa. 65:17; 2 Pet. 3:13).

This way of speaking highlights the continuity between the present and the coming age, between the first and the final creation. When God says, "Behold, I am making all things new" (Rev. 21:5), he means precisely what he says. He is not planning to make "all new things," as if everything needs to be discarded or destroyed.[6] On the contrary, God is planning to take what he has made and transform it. This explains why so much of the imagery in the last chapter of the Bible hearkens back to the garden of Eden, with its living waters and tree of life (Rev. 22:1–2; cf. Gen. 2:9–14). Everything will be renewed. Humanity's final home will be humanity's first home, brought to its full perfection. This has been God's intention all along: not simply paradise regained but creation consummated.

For believers in Christ, the transformation of the new creation will include our physical bodies, which will be refashioned by the Spirit according to the image of Jesus (Rom. 8:29). Many Christians continue to think of heaven only as a resting place for the soul; they envision the dead floating somewhere in the clouds. Yet the hope of eternal life is not disembodied immortality, in which the soul is liberated from the body. Rather, the Bible promises the resurrection of whole persons—body and soul—in a renewed humanity that is conformed to the resurrection life of the risen Christ (1 Corinthians 15). We really do believe what the creeds confess: the resurrection of the body.

The doctrines of new creation and bodily resurrection have immense implications for the future of the liberal arts and sciences. To begin with, in eternity we will retain the creative impulse inherent to our humanity as people made in God's image. Christian thinkers have long maintained that creativity is part of what constitutes the *imago Dei*, the image of

---

[6]As G. K. Beale has demonstrated in his masterful exegesis, the word "new" in Revelation "refers predominantly to a change in quality or essence rather than something new that has never previously been in existence." *The Book of Revelation: A Commentary on the Greek Text* (Grand Rapids, MI: Eerdmans, 1999), 1040.

God.[7] The God who created people in his own image is nothing if not creative (Gen. 1:27). Part of our proper response to his creative work, therefore, is to become cocreators with him, working with the stuff of creation to produce good art that glorifies God.

None of this will be lost in the new Jerusalem. The new humanity will still be made in the image of God (only perfected, because we will be raised in the image of Christ). We will still have the unique personality that makes us who we are, including the gifts that God has given each one of us (only heightened, because we will be uncorrupted by sin). We will still enjoy an embodied existence in a physical universe (only transformed, because God will fill the new heavens and the new earth with his presence). How then will we live, when we make our home in the atmosphere of glory?

The continuity between creation and re-creation teaches us to expect that we will continue to participate in many of the same activities that we enjoy on earth. What is true of the new creation must be in keeping with the first creation, including the creativity that our very humanity demands. The new heavens and the new earth are not static but dynamic—a place to grow deeper in the life of God. We may hope, therefore, that creative work will flourish as the new creation inspires new artists to create new poems, new paintings, and new works of music and dance in the new Jerusalem. We will worship Christ with our creativity, using the work of our hands to display the unity of his beauty and truth.

As we explore the material universe of the new heavens and the new earth, we may also hope to make new discoveries in science. This claim will surprise anyone who believes that the promise of heaven includes the instantaneous and exhaustive comprehension of everything there is to know. This is more than the Bible claims about eternal epistemology, however. To be sure, Paul says, "Now I know in part; then I shall know fully, even as I have been fully known" (1 Cor. 13:12). Yet from the context it is clear that the knowledge the apostle has in mind is not scientific but personal—the face-to-face knowledge of God.

The Bible leaves open the question of scientific knowledge. But

---

[7]For a notable example, see Dorothy L. Sayers, *The Mind of the Maker* (London: Methuen, 1941).

when we consider the continuity between creation and re-creation—including everything we know about human nature and its capacity to grow and develop—it seems likely that the sciences will flourish in the new Jerusalem. Our curiosity runs as deep as our creativity. Whenever we encounter a new environment, our first impulse is to explore it. Will we not seek, therefore, to discover the deep structure of the new heavens and the new earth? This too will be part of our eternal worship: to comprehend what Christ has re-created and then return our praise to him.

KINGDOM COME

Creation is not the only biblical doctrine with eschatological implications for the liberal arts and sciences. Also basic to the story of our salvation is the doctrine of redemption, our release from slavery through the payment of a price. Having fallen from our created innocence, we find freedom from sin through Jesus Christ, "in whom we have redemption, the forgiveness of sins" (Col. 1:14).

Here we need to remember that one of the historic purposes of a liberal education is to develop the intellect in ways that promote human freedom. The liberal arts are the liberating arts. In the famous words of the Greek philosopher Epictetus—who himself was born a slave—"Rulers may say that only free men should be educated, but we believe that only educated men are free."[8] From the biblical point of view, of course, the only lasting freedom comes in Jesus Christ: "If the Son sets you free, you will be free indeed" (John 8:36). But to the extent that the liberal arts promote authentic freedom, they find their highest fulfillment within God's wider plan of redemption.

God's redemptive purposes are eternal. Although in one sense Jesus finished redeeming us the moment he made the purchase for sin, the Bible promises the consummation of redemption in the coming kingdom of God: "We wait eagerly for adoption as sons, the redemption of our bodies" (Rom. 8:23). Indeed, the creation itself—the entire sphere of the arts and sciences—is waiting eagerly for "the freedom of the glory of the children of God" (Rom. 8:19, 21).

In view of these promises of human freedom, would we not expect

---

[8]Epictetus, quoted by Bruce A. Kimball in *Orators and Philosophers: A History of the Idea of Liberal Education* (New York: College Entrance Examination Board, 1995), 214.

to enjoy the liberal arts in the new Jerusalem? When the day of our liberation comes—with full and final freedom from sin—will we not celebrate our release through some of the same pursuits that have brought us the greatest sense of freedom on earth?

The case for viewing the liberal arts from an eschatological perspective is strengthened when we place redemption in the context of the kingdom of God, as the Bible does (Col. 1:13–14). Our ultimate liberation is to belong to the coming kingdom of Jesus Christ. Although the concept of a kingdom may well seem foreign to people who have never lived under such a dominion, the New Testament consistently presents the kingdom as a governing metaphor for God's rule. The Scottish theologian Thomas Boston argued that the Bible does this because kingdoms gather in one place "the greatest number of earthly good things."[9] Thus the kingdom of God is an image for "the good life"—indeed, the best life of all.

Like the doctrine of redemption, the promise of an everlasting kingdom resonates deeply with the best traditions of the liberal arts. If liberal education promotes "the good life," then it will find its apotheosis in the eternal kingdom of God, which truly is "the best of all possible worlds." Recall that one of the original purposes for such an education was to produce democratic citizens capable of pursuing the public good by participating wisely and effectively in civil government. This is also one of the highest purposes of the Christian liberal arts: to help produce good citizens for the kingdom of God—both in this life and in the life to come.

The kingdom of Christ is not a democracy; it is a benevolent monarchy. Yet the well-being of God's eternal dominion invites the active involvement of its citizenry. The Bible describes God's people not merely as subjects, but also as co-regents who share in the work of judging the world and ruling the new heavens and the new earth with Jesus Christ (1 Cor. 6:2; 2 Tim. 2:12). When the day of Christ's redemption comes, the free children of God will share in governing his kingdom—a capacity that is deliberately (though not exclusively) developed through Christian liberal arts education.

---

[9]Thomas Boston, *The Complete Works of The Late Rev. Thomas Boston of Ettrick*, 12 vols., ed. Samuel M'Millan (London, 1853; repr., Wheaton, IL: Richard Owen Roberts, 1980), 8:318.

THE END OF THE MATTER

Biblical truth and theological reason encourage us to hope that the liberal arts are for eternity. Admittedly, some questions will remain unanswered until the second coming. But when we consider the promises of God, the scope of his kingdom, and the enduring nature of the people he has made in his image, we find ample reason to take an eschatological view of art and science.

If it is true that the liberal arts have a place in the new Jerusalem, then this helps to explain the glimpses of transcendence we sometimes catch when we are reading Wordsworth's *Prelude*, playing Mozart's *Piano Concerto Number 20*, or examining the communication networks of DNA. Within the transient we experience moments of the transcendent. These intimations of eternity give us clues that we are destined for a better world in which truth and beauty are not merely momentary but eternally constant. As the Dutch theologian Abraham Kuyper once said, the beauty of art has "the mystical task" of prefiguring the "perfect coming luster" of the kingdom of God.[10] Thus our earthly experience with the liberal arts enables us to anticipate the new creation, when the cosmos will be transfigured with the glory of God.[11]

It follows that Christian liberal arts education is great preparation for life in our eternal home. Of course, God has other ways to prepare his children for eternity, and even the least-prepared believer will find the fullness of joy in the kingdom of God. But if we are destined to live in the new Jerusalem, then as we have the opportunity it is wise for us to nurture the intellectual virtues, cultivate the habits of mind, develop the scientific skills, and strengthen the artistic sensibilities that will enable us to serve as good citizens of that fair city. The highest end of liberal education is everlasting life in the kingdom of Jesus Christ.

---

[10]Abraham Kuyper, *Calvinism: Six Stone Foundation Lectures* (Grand Rapids, MI: Eerdmans, 1943), 165–66.
[11]This idea is developed in the final chapter of Anthony Monti's *A Natural Theology of the Arts: Imprint of the Spirit* (Aldershot, UK: Ashgate, 2003).

CONTRIBUTORS

Henry Allen is professor and chair of the Department of Sociology and Anthropology at Wheaton College. Before his appointment in 1988, he taught at Bethel College (MN), Calvin College (MI), the University of Rochester (NY), and Rochester Institute of Technology (NY). Since his doctoral studies at the University of Chicago, his research has focused on the sociology of global science and the mathematics of academic systems and societies. He is a member of the Oxford Roundtable.

John H. Augustine is a managing director with Barclays Capital, New York and London, where he leads the Higher Education and Academic Medical Center Finance Group. He studied under Professor Ryken at Wheaton College, and then he went on to receive a PhD in English literature from the University of Minnesota and an MBA in finance from Yale.

Jill Peláez Baumgaertner is professor of English and dean of humanities and theological studies at Wheaton College. She is the author of a poetry textbook, a monograph on Flannery O'Connor, and four books of poems: *Leaving Eden*; *Namings*; *Finding Cuba*; and *My Father's Bones*. She is also past president of the Conference on Christianity and Literature and currently serves as poetry editor of the *Christian Century.*

Edith Blumhofer is professor of history and director of the Institute for the Study of American Evangelicals at Wheaton College. She has authored many dictionaries and encyclopedia articles on religion, Christianity, and evangelicalism; several biographies; and books on the Assemblies of God and Pentecostal experience, including *Her Heart Can See: The Life and Hymns of Fanny J. Crosby.*

Dorothy F. Chappell is dean of natural and social sciences and professor of biology at Wheaton College. She is a recipient of professional awards in the research and teaching of cell biology in plants, has served in administrative roles for a number of schools and professional organizations, including president of the American Scientific Association and consultant for the Higher Learning Commission. She coauthored *Not Just Science: Questions Where Christian Faith and Natural Science Intersect.*

Kenneth R. Chase is associate professor and chair of the Department of Communication at Wheaton College, where he teaches public speaking, rhetorical theory, and communication ethics. He has served as director of Wheaton's Center for Applied Christian Ethics, president of the Religious Communication Association, and chair of the Communication Ethics Division of the National Communication Association. His scholarly publications explore secular and Christian models of ethical rhetorical practice.

303

Sharon Coolidge is professor and chair of the Department of English at Wheaton College, where she began the Writing Center and served as the first director of Writing Across the Curriculum. Since joining the Wheaton faculty in 1977, she has taught writing, British literature surveys, and medieval literature. Her scholarship focuses on symbolism in medieval romances, drama, poetry, and religious texts.

Jeffry C. Davis is associate professor of English at Wheaton College, where he is director of the Writing Center and the interdisciplinary studies program. The 2006–2007 recipient of Wheaton's Leland Ryken Award for Teaching Excellence in the Humanities, he was a student of Professor Ryken, who described him affectionately as "the back-row type." His scholarship explores the connections between rhetoric, writing, and teaching; he also champions the liberal arts as an approach to lifelong learning, especially for students in Christian higher education.

Jeffery P. Greenman is associate dean of biblical and theological studies and professor of Christian ethics at Wheaton College. Before coming to Wheaton, he served in various roles at Tyndale Seminary in Toronto, including five years as academic dean. He is the author of numerous articles and book chapters on biblical interpretation, ethics, and higher education, as well as the editor of seven books, and coauthor of *Unwearied Praises: Exploring Christian Faith through Classic Hymns*.

Stephen B. Ivester is director of student activities at Wheaton College. A 1993 Conservatory of Music graduate at Wheaton, Steve is currently a PhD candidate in educational studies at the Talbot School of Theology, Biola University. His research is directed toward discovering the impact of the leadership of social change on identity development in student activists. He mentors many students, encouraging positive attitudes of learning that come through relationship, leadership, and service.

Alan Jacobs is the Clyde S. Kilby professor of English at Wheaton College. An accomplished essayist, his books include *A Theology of Reading: The Hermeneutics of Love*; *Wayfaring: Essays Pleasant and Unpleasant;* and *The Pleasures of Reading in an Age of Distraction*. He earned his doctorate in 1987 from the University of Virginia and has been teaching at Wheaton College since 1984.

Mark Lewis is associate professor of communication and theater at Wheaton College and is the co-director of Arena Theater. For sixteen years he has led Workout, Wheaton's uniquely structured theater ensemble; he also teaches three levels of acting and has directed twenty-seven plays. Prior to coming to Wheaton in 1995, he was a professional actor in New York City, working on stage and in television for fifteen years.

Duane Litfin served for seventeen years as president of Wheaton College. He is the author of numerous articles and five books, most recently *Word vs. Deed: Resetting the Scales to a Biblical Balance* (2012). His *Conceiving the*

Christian College (2004) addressed the nature and purpose of Christ-centered higher education.

Roger Lundin is the Arthur F. Holmes professor of faith and learning at Wheaton College, where he teaches American and modern European literature. He has written and edited ten books, including *Believing Again: Doubt and Faith in a Secular Age* and *Emily Dickinson and the Art of Belief*. He has received major research fellowships from the Erasmus Institute, the Pew Charitable Trusts, and the Evangelical Scholarship Initiative.

Wayne Martindale is emeritus professor of English at Wheaton College, where he has regularly taught courses on C. S. Lewis and British literature. He is author of *Beyond the Shadowlands: C. S. Lewis on Heaven and Hell*; coauthor of *The Soul of Lewis*; coeditor of *The Quotable Lewis*; and editor of *Journey to the Celestial City: Glimpses of Heaven from Great Literary Classics*. He also maintains an active interest in China.

Marjorie Lamp Mead is associate director of the Marion E. Wade Center at Wheaton College. She has published extensively on both Dorothy L. Sayers and C. S. Lewis, including reader's guides on the first two volumes of *The Chronicles of Narnia*, coauthored with Leland Ryken, her former literature professor. She also serves as managing editor of *SEVEN: An Anglo-American Literary Review*, a journal that focuses on the seven authors of the Wade Center.

Lisa Richmond has served as college librarian at Wheaton College since 2003. Her graduate degrees are in theology and library science. A lover of the Great Books, she has read widely in the classic liberal arts curriculum. Blaise Pascal, the seventeenth-century French Christian polymath, represents one of her particular scholarly interests. She has written several articles, including "The Dark Side of Online Journals," published in *Z Magazine*.

Philip G. Ryken is president of Wheaton College. He preached for fifteen years at Tenth Presbyterian Church in Philadelphia, serving as senior minister from 2001–2010. He received his doctorate in historical theology from the University of Oxford, after studying English literature with Leland Ryken (his father) at Wheaton. President Ryken is the author of more than thirty books, including Bible commentaries, guides to Christianity and culture, and other publications for the church.

Read Mercer Schuchardt is associate professor of communication at Wheaton College. He earned his PhD in media ecology at New York University under the late Neil Postman. The 2011–2012 recipient of Wheaton's Leland Ryken Award for Teaching Excellence in the Humanities, he first heard Dr. Ryken speak at a guest lecture at Gordon-Conwell Theological Seminary.

Tamara Townsend is assistant professor of Spanish at Wheaton College, where she double majored in Spanish and English literature. She studied with Leland Ryken, participating on the Wheaton in England program during the summer of 1999. She received her PhD from Ohio State University in 2007 and focuses her scholarship on memory in contemporary Spanish narrative, especially in the writers of Soledad Puèrtolas. She also serves as vice president of the North American Christian Foreign Language Association.

E. John Walford is emeritus professor of art history at Wheaton College, where he served as department chair from 1981–2002. Born in England, he holds degrees in art history from the University of Cambridge (PhD), where he was the Wolfson College Speelman fellow in Dutch and Flemish art, 1976–1980. He is the author of *Jacob van Ruisdael and the Perception of Landscape* and *Great Themes in Art*. Currently he is exploring photography as an alternative means to reflect on the discipline of art history and its relevance to artistic practice.

Peter Walters is professor in the Applied Health Science Department at Wheaton College. He received his doctorate in kinesiology at Texas A & M University. He teaches wellness, lifestyle management, principles of body composition, and integrative seminars. He is coauthor of *Christian Paths to Health and Wellness* with John Byl from Redeemer University in Ontario, Canada.

Michael Wilder is professor of music, serving as dean of the Conservatory of Music and Arts and Communication Division at Wheaton College. A clarinetist, he has performed and taught in a variety of settings, including the Wichita Symphony Orchestra, Camerata Chicago, and the Masterworks Festivals in England and the United States. He is an accreditation evaluator for the National Association of Schools of Music and an elected member of its Commission on Accreditation. He earned his PhD from the University of Michigan.

James Wilhoit is Scripture Press professor of Christian education at Wheaton College. He and Leland Ryken team-taught a course on teaching the Bible for fifteen years, and they have coauthored three books. His research and teaching focuses on teaching the Bible and community-based spiritual formation. He has authored or edited more than a dozen books on Christian education and spiritual formation, as well as on Bible study and teaching.

Jay Wood is professor of philosophy at Wheaton College, where he has taught since 1982. His scholarly interests center on epistemology, philosophy of religion, and virtue theory. A graduate of the University of Notre Dame, he coauthored *Intellectual Virtues: An Essay in Regulative Epistemology* with Robert C. Roberts, among other books.

COVER ART CREDITS

AKG Images, "Astronomer and His Telescope"

"The Crucifixion," a detail from *The Easter Painting*, 1994 (acrylic on canvas) by Laura James (Contemporary Artist) Private Collection/ The Bridgeman Art Library
Nationality / copyright status: American / in copyright

BigStockPhoto.com, "Papyrus Background with Egyptian Painted Relief"

Portrait of Alexander the Great from a tourmaline stamp, probably 4th century BC (plaster impression) by Greek Ashmolean Museum, University of Oxford, UK/ The Bridgeman Art Library
Nationality / copyright status: Greek / out of copyright

Roman Wall Mosaic with Tragic and Comic Masks, 1st century BC–1st century AD (mosaic) by Roman Musei Capitolini, Rome, Italy/ Ancient Art and Architecture Collection Ltd./ The Bridgeman Art Library
Nationality / copyright status: out of copyright

Apollo Playing the Lute by Briton Riviere (1840–1920)
© Bury Art Gallery and Museum, Lancashire, UK/ The Bridgeman Art Library
Nationality / copyright status: English / out of copyright

"Blind Milton dictating his immortal poem," from *Newnes' Pictorial Book of Knowledge* (color litho) by Arthur A. Dixon (fl. 1890–1927) (after)
Private Collection/ The Bridgeman Art Library
Nationality / copyright status: English / out of copyright

Discobolus (marble) by Myron (fl. c. 450 BC) (after)
Victoria and Albert Museum, London, UK/ Ancient Art and Architecture Collection Ltd./ The Bridgeman Art Library
Nationality / copyright status: Greek / out of copyright

Dolphin, 1999 (w/c on paper) by Vivika Alexander (Contemporary Artist)
Private Collection/ The Bridgeman Art Library
Nationality / copyright status: English / in copyright

St. George Slaying the Dragon, 2006 (acrylic on canvas) by Laura James (Contemporary Artist) Private Collection/ The Bridgeman Art Library
Nationality / copyright status: American / in copyright

Hendrik Goltzius, *The Fall of Man*. Patrons' Permanent Fund Image courtesy of the National Gallery of Art, Washington, 1616. 104.5 x 138.4 cm.

GENERAL INDEX

abolition, 57
accountability, 182
Adams, John, 155
Adeney, Miriam, 285
American Education Society, 55
American Home Missionary Society, 55
Amherst College, 57–58
anthropology, 192
anti-intellectualism, 86
Aquinas, 77
Aristotle, 37, 46, 48, 161
Armerding, Hudson, 265
atonement, 189
Auden, W. H., 124
audiation, 211–12
Augustine, 68, 71, 78, 144–45, 270
authenticity, 136–37

Bach, Johann Sebastian, 214
Bacon, Francis, 123–26
Bakhtin, Mikhail, 127–28
Barnes, Albert, 54, 59
beauty, 143–44, 188
Beecher, Lyman, 54, 58–59
Begbie, Jeremy, 210
Bellah, Robert, 172
Best, Harold, 218
biblical scholarship, 65
Blair, Ann, 123
Blamires, Harry, 82–88
Blanchard, Jonathan, 61
Bloesch, Donald, 253, 258–59
Bloom, Allan, 51
body image, 253–64
Bonhoeffer, Dietrich, 263
Boston, Thomas, 300
Boudreaux, Donald J., 285
Brooks, Gwendolyn, 136

Browning, Elizabeth Barrett, 181
Buechner, Frederick, 207
Burke, Kenneth, 240

calling, 15–17, 21–22, 40, 43, 108,
    168–69, 229
Calvin, John, 18, 22, 72–73, 184–85
Calvinism, 60
Camus, Albert, 137
Carnegie, Andrew, 63
Carnegie Foundation for the
    Advancement of Teaching, 63
Carr, Nicholas, 126
Carvill, Barbara, 286
Chase, Philander, 54
Chesterton, G. K., 113
choosing a major, 33
Christian growth, 16, 41–42, 83–89,
    169–73, 276–77
Christians in the Visual Arts (CIVA),
    223–24
church and state separation, 57
Cicero, 144–45
Civil War, 62, 65
classical education, 37–40, 59, 65,
    116–18
cognitive flexibility, 164–65
common grace, 74–75, 188
common revelation, 198
communication, 134–35, 144–54, 214–17,
    241–52
Congregationalists, 59–60
Constantine, 39
contemporary art, 226–27
conversion, 85
Copernicus, 179, 183
Cornelius, Elias, 54–55